FODOR'S

BAHAMAS
1988

Editor: Gail Chasan

Area Editor: *Dorothy M. Zinzow* has been the editor and publisher of *Bahamas Magazine,* a news periodical for the travel trade, since 1972. She has traveled extensively throughout The Bahamas, frequently writing about the islands for international trade and consumer publications. Following her interest in Bahamian history, she is working on a book, *Nostalgia—The Story of Bahamas Tourism,* which traces the course of Bahamian hospitality from the arrival of Christopher Columbus to the present. She is a member of the American Association of Travel Editors, the Federation of International Travel Journalists, and the Overseas Press Club.

Maps and Plans: Pictograph, Xhardez

Drawings: Michael Kaplan

FODOR'S TRAVEL PUBLICATIONS, INC.
New York & London

ISBN 0-679-01468-3
ISBN 0-340-41785-4 (Hodder & Stoughton)

MANUFACTURED IN THE UNITED STATES OF AMERICA
10 9 8 7 6 5 4 3 2 1

CONTENTS

CONTENTS

FOREWORD

The dazzling emerald islands of the Bahamas—with their turquoise seas and white sand beaches, their secluded seaside cottages and glamorous resort palaces, their easy-going yet elegant vacation lifestyle—are indeed America's South Sea Islands. The Bahamas are also an international shopping paradise and one of the most perfect settings for sportsmen of all kinds—those who want to dive among brilliant living reefs, golf on 18-hole championship courses, or gamble day and night in glittering casinos. All of this, plus their proximity to the United States, make The Bahama Islands the most popular destination in the Caribbean area.

Vacation options in The Bahamas range from the historic charm of Nassau, the glitter and excitement of Paradise Island, or the resort and sporting atmosphere of Grand Bahama Island to any one of the more removed Family Islands—over a dozen Out Islands and countless cays each with few small settlements, empty beaches, and unsurpassed fishing, diving, yachting, and more.

Fodor's Bahamas is designed to help you choose which island or group of islands will best suit your vacation ideal—as well as your time and budget requirements—and to help you plan a visit that will be worthwhile as well as pleasurable. All descriptions are based on personal experiences. Much can change while we are on press and during the succeeding twelve months or so that this edition is on sale. We sincerely welcome letters from our readers on these changes, or from those whose opinions differ from ours, and we are ready to revise our entries for next year's edition when the facts warrant it.

Send your letters to the editors at Fodor's Travel Publications, 201 East 50th Street, New York, NY 10022. Continental or British Commonwealth readers may prefer to write to Fodor's Travel Publications, 9-10 Market Place, London W1N 7AG, England.

INTRODUCTION:

THE BAHAMAS, ISLAND BY ISLAND

There are three distinct vacation worlds to explore among the islands of The Bahamas, each different and appealing. The best known and most popular is Nassau and Paradise Island, which combines the colonial charm and historic landmarks of the centuries-old capital city of Nassau with the excitement and sophistication of world-famous resorts and casinos on Paradise Island and along beautiful Cable Beach, just minutes away.

The second world of Bahamas vacations is Grand Bahama Island, with the newly developed resort centers of Freeport and suburban Lucaya, which offer a country-club vacation lifestyle with half a dozen superb 18-hole championship golf courses; UNEXSO, an internationally famous scuba-diving school; elegant hotels and casinos that rival the best of Nassau and Paradise Island; miles of beautiful beaches; and round-the-world bargains in the colorful International Bazaar.

The third world of vacation pleasures offered in The Bahamas is officially called the Family Islands. They encompass all of the other islands in The Bahamas chain, and have been known to generations of visitors and Bahamians as the Out Islands . . . "out" from the glamour of Nassau and Freeport, but very much "in" with sophisticated travelers. The Family Islands are favorite holiday hideaway-havens for international celebrities, the wealthy, the titled and the famous; and a mecca for serious yachtsmen, fishermen and divers. There are more than twenty lovely Family Islands to choose from, some large and some small, some just fifty to one hundred miles off Florida's shores, others more than 350 miles from the capital city of Nassau. Whichever island you choose, you'll find the Family Island "trademarks"—endless, nearly empty beaches to roam, crystal-clear waters to swim and snorkle, colorful coral reefs to dive, fine fishing and good sailing, with a relaxed, uncomplicated lifestyle ideal for "getting away from it all."

In the following chapters, we present *Facts at Your Fingertips* to help you plan your trip to The Bahamas; a chapter to introduce you to The Bahamas—its history, flavor, plus sporting, entertainment, diving, and shopping options; and an island-by-island guide to The Bahamas, with practical information about each resort destination throughout the island chain. We begin with New Providence Island and the major resort centers of Nassau, Cable Beach, and Paradise Island. The second Bahamas vacation destination we cover is Grand Bahama Island, including Freeport, Lucaya, and West End. In the final section, we offer a guide to more than a dozen of The Bahamas Family Islands, including the Abacos, Andros, Bimini, Cat Island, Chub Cay, Crooked Island, Eleuthera, the Exumas, Inagua, Long Island, Rum Cay and San Salvador, and several of the resort centers of offshore cays which can be reached by ferry or water taxi from the main islands, such as Eleuthera's Harbour Island and Spanish Wells, and Abaco's Elbow Cay, Great Guana Cay, and Green Turtle Cay.

FACTS AT YOUR FINGERTIPS

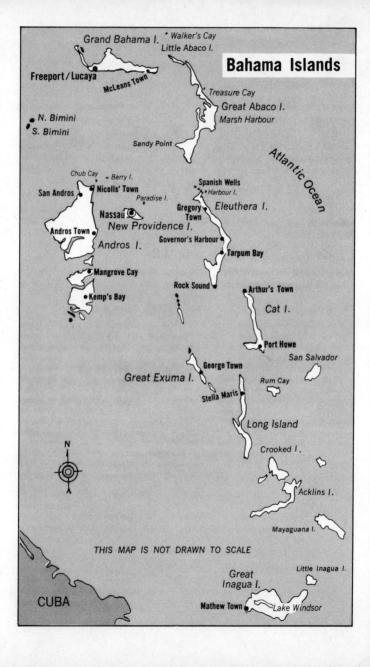

FACTS AT YOUR FINGERTIPS

 FACTS AND FIGURES. The Bahamas is a nation of islands, an archipelago that lies in the warm, western waters of the Atlantic, beginning just 50 miles off the coast of Florida's Palm Beaches and stretching in a great southeasterly arc to the Windward Passage, at the edge of the Caribbean Sea. There are more than 700 emerald islands, scattered over 100,000 square miles of turquoise seas, each edged by broad, white sandy beaches and fringed by living coral reefs.

They are the nearest and most accessible tropical island destinations to all of North America—even Los Angeles is nearer to The Bahamas than to Hawaii. Each year The Bahamas attract over three million visitors from around the world. The "low season," lower-priced summer months, rival in popularity the "high season," higher-priced winter months, making the islands a year-round vacation destination. More than 20 of the Bahamian islands are well-developed resort centers, and offer the broadest variety of vacation lifestyles in the region.

Choose from the historic, colonial charm of Nassau on New Providence Island, with its glittering international resorts and casinos and round-the-world bargain shopping; or the country-club ambience of Grand Bahama Island, offering half-a-dozen championship golf courses, international diving and wind-surfing schools, and equally famous bargain shopping, glamourous resorts, and continental casinos. But if you are looking for a "get away from it all," barefoot, and relaxed tropical island vacation, The Bahamas also have more than a dozen different Family Islands to choose from—the Abacos, Andros, Bimini, Cat Island, Chub Cay, Crooked Island, Eleuthera, the Exumas, Harbour Island, Inagua, Long Island, Rum Cay, Spanish Wells, Treasure Cay, and more. Each has its own charm and out-island ambience, but all offer superb fishing, internationally acclaimed diving, and unmatched cruising for the sail or power yachts that are harbor-hopping among the hundreds of islands and countless cays.

Half of the Bahama Islands are subtropical, the other half tropical: the Tropic of Cancer, stretching through the Exumas and Long Island, bisects the archipelago. This factor, plus the warm waters of the Gulf Stream that sweep the western shores and the gentle tradewinds from the southeast, ensure a nearly perfect year-round climate. Early travelers to The Bahamas called them "The Isles of Perpetual June."

Total land area is just 5,358 square miles, surrounded by 100,000 square miles of ocean. The northernmost island is Walker's Cay in the Abacos, which lies some 100 miles due east of Stuart, Florida; the southernmost island is Inagua, which is less than 50 miles north of the Windward Passage that separates Cuba and Haiti and marks the entrance to the Caribbean Sea. The nearest islands to the U.S. mainland are Bimini, 50 miles off the coast of Miami, and Grand Bahama Island, 60 miles off the coast of Palm Beach. Nassau, the capital city of the Bahamas, on the island of New Providence, is 150 miles from the Florida coast—less than 35 minutes by jet from Miami.

Only 209,505 Bahamians were counted in the last official census taken in May of 1980. Most live in the two major urban/resort centers of Nassau and Freeport on Grand Bahama Island. The population is approximately 85 percent black and 15 percent white. Both races can trace their ancestry back more than 300 years. The English language is spoken throughout the islands.

Tourism is the most important industry in The Bahamas, accounting for some two-thirds of the national income and employing almost three-quarters of

1

the population. Travelers to The Bahamas have come to total more than 3.1 million a year. New Providence Island attracts some 1.7 million visitors; Grand Bahama Island has more than 890,000; and the Family Islands welcome nearly 383,000.

International banking, the second largest industry, has grown steadily in importance to The Bahamas over the past 25 years due to several major factors: the political and economic stability of the country; the excellent communications network linking Nassau to the rest of the world; a favorable investment climate with no sales tax, income tax, or inheritance tax; and strict bank secrecy laws, similar to those of Switzerland. The Bahamas boast more than 350 banks and trust companies, representing most of the world's largest financial institutions. Nassau has become one of the leading international Eurodollar trading centers, on the level of London, Paris, Geneva, and Tokyo.

The Bahamas are among the most politically and economically stable nations in the hemisphere, with one of the highest per capita incomes of any third world nation. A black majority government was elected in 1967, ending 300 years of rule by the white minority. Under the leadership of Sir Lynden O. Pindling, prime minister, The Bahamas became independent of Great Britain on July 10, 1973. However, The Bahamas remain within the British Commonwealth and recognize Queen Elizabeth II as monarch. They retain a British-style government of parliamentary democracy with free elections, a court system based on English law, and still offer much of the colorful pomp and pageantry derived from more than 300 years of British colonial rule and heritage.

 PLANNING YOUR TRIP. Planning a trip to The Bahamas can be as easy as hopping on any one of the dozens of flights that leave daily from Florida cities to Nassau and Freeport. Except during peak travel periods, such as holidays and midwinter, it is not always necessary to have a hotel reservation in advance. Simply call Bahamas Reservation Service, toll free from anywhere in the U.S. or Canada, (800) 327–0787, for information on hotel vacancies and instant reservations. Reservations can even be made when you arrive. The Ministry of Tourism operates information booths at the international airports in Nassau and Freeport, which offer up-to-date listings of hotel vacancies, with telephones available so you can make on-the-spot reservations. However, this technique is for sophisticated travelers only, and you could be stranded.

Thousands of Floridians and Florida vacationers take advantage of The Bahamas proximity and pop over for a long weekend or a week-long holiday whenever the spirit moves them. Day trips are also gaining popularity, with casinos in both Nassau and Freeport offering bargain-rate "casino junkets" daily from several Florida cities. Even New Yorkers and Georgians find that the daily "Bahamas Express" service operated by Bahamasair from Newark and Atlanta makes it easy to set out on an impromptu visit to the islands for a few days in the sun—with round-trip airfare and hotel accommodations included.

If you are traveling from other parts of the U.S., Canada or abroad, it is always best to plan your vacation well in advance, so you can be sure to have your choice of travel dates and resort accommodations. If you prefer to plan your own vacation, you can find a wealth of information about The Bahamas (free of charge) from The Bahamas Tourist Offices located throughout the United States, Canada, and Europe; and from The Bahamas promotion boards, located in Coral Gables, Florida. A complete listing of the BTO's and promotion boards is included in this chapter, under "Tourist Information Services." You can also contact Bahamas resorts and hotels directly, and addresses and telephone numbers are given under each island destination in the following chap-

FACTS AT YOUR FINGERTIPS 3

ters. Most Bahamas hotels and resorts offer their own package programs, with significant savings over standard per day room rates—be sure to ask about them, if you are planning your own vacation. Many airlines serving The Bahamas also offer package programs, with significant savings over separate purchases of airfare and accommodations.

TRAVEL AGENTS AND TOUR OPERATORS. If you prefer to have a professional do your vacation planning, consult your travel agent. Most travel agents in the U.S., Canada, and Europe are very knowledgeable about The Bahamas, and will be able to suggest which island matches your vacation ideal, and offer a whole range of package programs from wholesalers and tour operators worldwide who specialize in Bahamas holidays. Your travel agent will be able to book your airline or cruise trip, arrange transfers to and from the airport, book your hotel accommodations, and even arrange for rental cars and sightseeing tours. In most cases, the services of a travel agent will cost you nothing. They receive commissions from the tour operators, carriers, and hotels, so their services are offered to you free of charge, except for out-of-pocket expenses such as telephone calls or telex messages. You will almost always save a significant amount of money by using a professional travel agent.

 TIPS FOR BRITISH VISITORS. Passports. Citizens of the United Kingdom do not need passports for visits of less than three weeks. A birth certificate or some similar form of identification is acceptable (but don't forget you *will* need a passport to reenter Britain). Citizens of Commonwealth countries do not require visas. All visitors are required to have onward or return tickets and a document that will permit them to enter another country.

Insurance. We heartily recommend that you insure yourself to cover health and motoring mishaps. Contact *Europ Assistance,* 252 High St., Croydon CRO 1NF (01–680–1234).

Bahamas Tourist Office. For any information on The Bahamas, visit, call, or write the London BTO at 10 Chesterfield Street, London W1X 8AH. (629-5238).

Tour Operators. The following offer holidays in the Bahamas:

Albany Travel, (Manchester) Ltd., 190 Deansgate, Manchester M3 3WD (061–833–0202).

Club Mediterranée, 106–108 Brompton Rd., London SW3 1JJ (581–1161).

Dream Islands of the World, 5 Charterhouse Bldgs., Goswell Rd., London EC1M 7AN (253–2662).

Jetsave, Sussex House, London Rd., East Grinstead, West Sussex RH19 1LD (0342–312033).

Kuoni Travel, Kuoni House, Dorking, Surrey RH5 4AZ (0306–885044).

Harlequin Holidays, 146 West St., Sheffield, South Yorkshire S1 4ES (0742–750508).

Speedbird Holidays, Alta House, 152 King St., London W6 0QV (741–8041).

Tradewinds Faraway Holidays, 66-68 Brewer St., London W1R 3PJ (734–1260).

Air Fares. We suggest that you explore the current scene for budget flight possibilities. APEX and other fares are offered by airlines at a considerable saving over the full price. Quite frankly, only business travelers who don't have to watch the price of their tickets fly full price these days—and find themselves sitting right beside APEX passengers!

Cruise Lines. *Carnival Cruise Lines,* 11 Quadrant Arcade, Regent St., London W1R 5PB (734–4404).

Costa Line Cruises, 3-4 Bywell Pl., Wells St., London W1P 3FB (637–9961).
Norwegian Caribbean Lines, 3 Vere St., London W1M 9HQ (493–6041).
Olsen (Fred) Lines, 11 Conduit St., London W1R 0LS.
Royal Caribbean Cruise Line, Bishops Palace House, 2A Riverside Walk, Kingston-upon-Thames, Surrey KT1 1QV (541–5044).
Yacht Charter Agencies. *Camper & Nicholsons (Yacht Agency), Ltd.,* 16 Regency St., London SW1P 4DD (821–1641).
Halsey Marine, Ltd., 22 Boston Place, London NW1 6HZ (724–1303).
Sun Days Charters, Ltd., Weald House, Pluckley, Ashford, Kent TN27 0SN (023384–432).
Worldwide Yachting Holidays, c/o Liz Fenner, 35 Fairfax Pl., London NW6 4EJ (328–1033).

TOURIST INFORMATION SERVICES. Everything you ever wanted to know about The Bahamas—and more—is available with a phone call, visit, or letter to your nearest Bahamas Tourist Office (BTO). The Ministry of Tourism operates a network of information offices in the U.S., Canada, and Europe that are well-stocked with brochures and rate sheets for all hotels and resorts in The Bahamas for both Winter season and Goombay Summer. In addition, they offer special-interest brochures and directories on sports such as golf, tennis, scuba, sailing, fishing, and private flying in The Bahamas. Also available are a year-round Calendar of Events and flyers on Goombay Summer Festival, Student Breakaway months, and the year-round People to People program. The BTO staffs are friendly and anxious to help, so go to your BTO if you plan to visit The Bahamas.

The following are *Bahamas Tourist Offices* in the U.S., Canada, and U.K., with local addresses and telephone numbers:

Atlanta: 1950 Century Blvd., N.E., Suite 26, Atlanta, GA 30345; (404) 633–1793.

Boston: 1027 Statler Office Bldg., Boston, MA 02116; (617) 426–3144.

Chicago: 875 North Michigan Ave., Chicago, IL 60611; (312) 787–8203.

Dallas: World Trade Center, Box 581408, Dallas, TX 75258; (214) 742–1886.

Detroit: 26400 Lahser Rd., Southfield, MI 48034; (313) 357–2940.

Houston: 5177 Richmond Ave., Suite 755, Houston, TX 77056; (713) 626–1566.

Los Angeles: 3450 Wilshire Blvd., Los Angeles, CA 90014; (213) 385–0033.

Miami: 255 Alhambra Circle, Coral Gables, FL 33134; (305) 442–4860.

New York: 150 East 52nd St., New York, NY 10022; (212) 758–2777.

Philadelphia: 437 Chestnut St., Philadelphia, PA 19106; (215) 925–0871.

San Francisco: 44 Montgomery St., Suite 503, San Francisco, CA 94104; (415) 673–0426.

Washington, DC: 1730 Rhode Island Ave., N.W., Washington, DC 20036; (202) 659–9135.

Montreal: 1255 Phillips Square, Montreal, Quebec H3B 3G1; (514) 861–6797.

Toronto: 85 Richmond St., W., Toronto, Ontario M5H 2C9; (416) 363–4441.

Vancouver: 470 Granville St., Vancouver, B.C. V6C 1V5; (604) 688–8334.

London: 10 Chesterfield St., London, England W1X 8AH; 01–629–5238

In addition to the Ministry of Tourism BTO's, The Bahamas promotion boards representing the three destinations, Nassau/Paradise Island, Freeport/Lucaya, and the Family Islands, operate offices abroad that offer helpful information, brochures, and rate sheets.

Nassau/Paradise Island Promotion Board, 255 Alhambra Circle, Coral Gables, FL 33134 (305) 445–3705. In New York, 370 Lexington Ave., Suite 1207, New York, NY 10017 (212) 689–9602. In Chicago, 628 Martin Lane, Deerfield, IL 60015 (312) 541–6250. In London, 79 Dean Street, London W1V 6HY 01–437–8766.

Grand Bahama Island Promotion Board, 255 Alhambra Circle, Coral Gables, FL 33134 (305) 448–3386.

The Family Islands Promotion Board, 255 Alhambra Circle, Coral Gables, FL 33134 (305) 446–4111.

Another excellent source of information about resorts in The Bahamas, seasonal rates, and room availability is *The Bahamas Reservation Service.* Call toll free from anywhere in the U.S. or Canada (800) 327–0787; in Miami, 443–3821. The service is available Monday through Friday from 9 A.M. to 7 P.M. Eastern Standard Time. BRS also operates a reservation service in London at 01–491–4800, and in Frankfurt, West Germany at 069–25–20–27/8. The Bahamas Reservation Service represents over 100 hotels, offering more than 11,000 hotel rooms, and can make instant reservations for you anywhere in The Bahamas at no charge.

 WHEN TO GO. In The Bahamas there are just two seasons. Winter season is the high season, when hotel rates, airfares, and charter packages are at their peak. The winter season begins in mid-December, usually a week before Christmas, and extends through April or the week after Easter. The second season is known as Goombay Summer in The Bahamas, and it lasts all of the rest of the year from the week after Easter to mid-December.

Winter season attracts many wealthy visitors from around the world. It also attracts hundreds of thousands of ordinary Americans and Canadians eager to escape the freezing cold and blizzards of northern climes. The weather in winter months is almost ideal, ranging from 70 to 80 degrees F, with a sea temperature of 70–75 degrees, some seven hours of bright sunshine daily, and almost no rain. However, an occasional "Norther" can move in, usually the last vestiges of a severe winter blizzard in the north, and skies can cloud over for a day or two and temperatures drop into the low 50s.

During the winter season vacation lifestyles tend to be slightly more formal than during the summer. There are gala charity balls, local theater productions, and name entertainers at famous nightclubs. Most of the fine restaurants, lounges, casinos, and nightclubs require a jacket and tie for men, and women usually dress in long skirts, cocktail dresses, or elegant pantsuits. Rarely, however, are evening gowns and black tie appropriate.

In general, during winter season, hotels and resorts enjoy the highest occupancy levels of the year, and prices are somewhat higher across the board for everything from restaurant meals to city tours, from greens fees to shopping bargains. Book well in advance for airline tickets and your first choice of hotel or resort, particularly at the peak periods: the week between Christmas and New Year's, George Washington's Birthday week, and Easter week.

Goombay Summer is the season of low prices and high spirits in The Bahamas. It lasts for eight months, from just after Easter to just before Christmas, and rates for everything are the lowest of the year, usually 20 to 30 percent, sometimes as much as 50 percent, lower. Yet, paradoxically, it may be the most fun and most interesting time of the year to visit The Bahamas. The Goombay Summer calendar is filled with exciting social, cultural, and sporting events such as golf, tennis, and fishing tournaments, and the islands are a riot of color with tropical flowers and magnificent foliage in full bloom.

Drawbacks are, of course, that it tends to be warmer and more humid during Goombay Summer, and it is the rainy season. However, the rain comes in swift tropical showers, rarely lasting more than an hour and almost never causing gray skies—as a matter of fact, the sun usually shines through the rain. Some rain falls nearly every day in the summer months, usually in late afternoon. It clears the air of the sultry humidity, leaving the evenings fresh and cooler. Hurricanes also arrive in Goombay Summer, about once every eight or ten years. (Most likely months are August, September, and October.)

Temperatures average 80 to 90 degrees during midsummer months, lower in the spring and fall. Humidity averages 77 to 82 percent year-round, with 78 to 82 percent common in summer and fall; sea temperature peaks in summer at around 80 degrees. Because of the higher temperatures and humidity during Goombay Summer, both Bahamians and visitors dress more casually and coolly. Restaurants, nightclubs, and casinos are less formal, and dressy sportswear is accepted almost everywhere in the evenings, although many visitors still enjoy dressing up a bit.

YEAR-ROUND WEATHER CHART

	Mean temperature (F)	Mean relative humidity (%)	Mean hours of bright sunshine	Mean rainfall (inches)
Jan.	69.6	79	7.2	1.90
Feb.	70.0	78	7.9	1.57
Mar.	72.0	78	8.4	1.38
Apr.	74.5	77	8.9	1.89
May	77.0	77	8.5	4.83
June	80.1	79	7.5	9.23
July	81.5	78	8.9	6.08
Aug.	81.9	79	8.5	6.30
Sept.	80.7	82	7.1	7.52
Oct.	78.0	81	6.7	8.31
Nov.	74.2	79	7.4	2.29
Dec.	70.9	78	7.1	1.52

 SEASONAL EVENTS. The Bahamas calendar is packed with special events, year-round, and all are open to visitor participation. The official holidays celebrated in The Bahamas, and some of the most popular annual events held month by month, are listed below:

January. The New Year is greeted with the biggest, noisiest, most colorful, and most exciting event on the calendar—the annual *Junkanoo Parade,* a centuries-old masquerade and Goombay music festival, which features exotic sheared crepe-paper costumes and a primitive African beat. The most elaborate parades are held in Nassau and Freeport, with miniparades in the Family Islands. New Year's Day also brings the *Staniel Cay Regatta* in the Exumas. The *Supreme Court Assizes* open with pomp and pageantry on the second Wednesday of the month in Parliament Square; and the *Red Cross* holds its annual charity ball in Nassau. Nassau also hosts the annual *North American Backgammon Championships,* which attract the "class" of world backgammon enthusiasts, held at the Paradise Island Resort and Casino, which also hosts the *PGA-Bahamas Golf Classic.* The annual *International Windsurfing Championships* are held at the

Nassau Beach Hotel and the annual Princess 10K Road Race is held in Freeport.

February. In Nassau, the *Annual Heart Ball* (near Valentine's Day) is held each year, and attracts international socialites as well as "Who's Who in The Bahamas." Late in the month, yachting takes center stage, as the last two races in the prestigious Southern Ocean Racing Conference annual series are sailed in Bahamian waters—the *Miami-Nassau Race* and the *Nassau Cup Race.*

March. *Student Breakaway* programs are offered in both Nassau and Freeport, with a full roster of daily activities and special events for college students on spring break. In Nassau, the *Snipe Winter Championships* have attracted the international Snipe racing set for decades, hosted by the Royal Nassau Sailing Club. Social highlight of the month is the annual *Red Cross Fair,* which is held in the beautiful tropical gardens of Government House, Nassau. In the Family Islands, the annual big game fishing tournament season gets under way on Bimini, with the *Bimini Benefit Tournament,* held at Bimini's Blue Water Resort and the *Bacardi Tournament* at Bimini Big Game Fishing Club. Also at Bimini Blue Water is the *Hemingway* kickoff tournament for the famed *Bahamas Billfish Championship,* a series of six tournaments held annually, which attracts the top anglers on the international big-game fishing circuits.

April. The Family Islands are highlighted with the fun-filled annual Bahamas workboat racing series, *The Family Island Regatta,* held in George Town, Exuma; and major fishing tournaments are scheduled on several islands. In the Abacos, there is the *Abaco Angling Tournament;* Chub Cay Club in the Berry Islands sponsors the *His and Hers Tournament* and annual *Members Tournament;* and Walker's Cay offers the second leg of the *Bahamas Billfish Championship,* followed by third leg of the series held at the Bimini Big Game Fishing Club. In Nassau, the quarterly *Supreme Court Assizes* opening ceremonies are colorful and interesting, with the Royal Bahamas Police Force Band on parade, the first Wednesday of the month. Throughout the islands, *Easter* is celebrated with a long weekend encompassing two official holidays, *Good Friday* and *Easter Monday. Student Breakaway* programs for college students continue through the month.

May. The fishing tournament season is in full swing throughout the Family Islands. On Bimini and Cat Cay, anglers go after the giant bluefin tuna that migrate along the Gulf Stream each spring to their summer feeding grounds off Nova Scotia. Major *Tuna Tournaments* are held at the Cat Cay Club and Bimini's Blue Water. The fourth leg of the *Bahamas Billfish Championship* is hosted by the exclusive Cat Cay Club, their only tournament open to the public. Chub Cay Club holds its *Blue Marlin Tournament,* and in the Abacos, Green Turtle Yacht Club offers a fun-filled week-long *All Fish Tournament.*

June. Two official holidays are celebrated island-wide, *Whit Monday* (seven weeks after Easter, usually falls in June), and *Labour Day,* celebrated the first Friday in June. The Bahamas Billfish Championship series continues with the *Treasure CayBillfish Tournament,* fifth leg of the series; and winds up with the traditional finale at the Chub Cay Club's *Bahamas Championship Tournament.* Treasure Cay Beach Resort also sponsors several big-money prize fishing tournaments in cooperation with the International Billfish League; and the yachting crowd gathers for a racing series with plenty of action afloat and ashore, known as *Regatta Time In Abaco,* which stretches from the last week in June to the 4th of July. In Nassau and Freeport, the four-month-long *Goombay Summer Festival* begins, offering a full calendar of social, cultural, and sporting events scheduled daily (and repeated weekly) for visitors. There are beach parties and boat cruises, art fairs and street dances, Junkanoo parades and Goombay music festivals, guided walking tours and tea parties at Government House, along with golf, tennis, squash, and racquetball tournaments.

July. One of the year's major holidays is celebrated on July 10, *Independence Day,* which occurred July 10, 1973, marking the end of 300 years of British rule, although The Bahamas remain within the British Commonwealth and recognize Queen Elizabeth II as sovereign of The Bahamas. In Nassau and Freeport, the *Goombay Summer Festival* continues; and the quarterly opening of the *Supreme Court Assizes* offer pomp and pageantry in Parliament Square on the first Wednesday of the month. In the Abacos, yacht racing continues as a summer highlight, with the *Green Turtle Cay Independence Regatta* race week beginning on the fourth of July and continuing through the tenth of July. On Bimini, the Bimini Big Game Fishing Club *Blue Marlin Tournament* winds up the big time tournament season; and the Bimini Blue Water Resort sponsors the Jimmy Albury Memorial All-Billfish Tournament.

August. A national holiday is celebrated on the first Monday in August, *Emancipation Day,* marking the freedom of slaves on August 1, 1834. *Fox Hill Day* follows a week later, with residents of an ancient slave village near Nassau putting on an old-fashioned country fair featuring picnics and barbecues, down-home Bahamian cooking, arts and crafts booths, and gospel-singing concerts. In the Family Islands, Emancipation Day is celebrated with picnics, parties, and workboat regattas at Cat Island; Mangrove Cay, Andros; and Black Point, Exuma near Staniel Cay. On Bimini, the most popular fishing tournament of the year takes place during Emancipation Day celebrations—the *Bimini Native Tournament,* which offers a week of rivalry and revelry, attracting hundreds of anglers from The Bahamas and abroad. It is sponsored by the Bimini Blue Water Resort, and has been held annually for more than 30 years. In Nassau and Freeport, *Goombay Summer Festival* events continue weekly, enjoyed by Bahamians and visitors alike.

September. *Goombay Summer Festival* continues to the end of the month in Nassau and Freeport; and there is a trio of golf tournaments held annually on Freeport and Nassau courses that includes the *Freeport City Open,* and the *Bahamas Golf Federation Classic and Open* held at Paradise Island and Cable Beach. In Nassau, the *Bahamas Grand Prix* powerboat races, sponsored by I.P.P.I., are held in the harbor, pitting European and American Formula I in stiff competition for circuit honors and the coveted Champion of Champions Cup. On Bimini, the *B.O.A.T. Tournament* (Bimini Open Angling Tournament) is held, designed for small boats, two-angler teams, and open to most kinds of fishing, sponsored by The Bimini Big Game Fishing Club.

October. A public holiday is celebrated on October 12, *Discovery Day,* marking the anniversary of Christopher Columbus's discovery of The Bahamas in 1492. Of course, he went on to discover much of the Caribbean, as well as a whole new world. But Bahamians never forget that he discovered their island first, when he landed at dawn on October 12, on the island of Guanahani, renamed San Salvador. In Nassau, the final quarterly *Supreme Court Assizes* open, with ceremonial splendor in Parliament Square, on the first Wednesday of the month. In George Town, Exuma, the Hotel Peace 'N Plenty hosts the annual *Bonefish Bonanza,* a boat tournament for afficionados of the feisty fighter of the reefy flats, with fun afloat and parties and prizes ashore. Along with other children around the world, throughout the islands, small Bahamian hobgoblins don masks and costumes to celebrate Halloween.

November. On two consecutive weekends, The Bahamas Humane Society holds its annual fund-raising fetes in Nassau—the *Humane Society Horse Show* at Camperdown Stables, when the local horsey set show off their equestrian skills; and the *Humane Society Dog Show and Mini-Fair,* where everything from mutts to pedigrees show their tricks, held at Nassau Botanic Gardens. Both are delightful, informal, and good fun for a good cause. At the Paradise Island Golf Club, the annual *Paradise Island Celebrity Pro-Am Golf Tournament* attracts a fine international following, usually scheduled for the weekend after the U.S. Thanksgiving holiday. At North Andros, the *Thanksgiving Bonefish Championship Tournament* is held. On Bimini, visiting anglers and native fishermen go after the streamlined Wahoo, known as the fastest fish in Bahamian waters, in the annual *Adam Clayton Powell Memorial Wahoo Tournament,* named for the late New York Congressman, who made Bimini his second home, and in *The Wahoo* at Bimini Big Game Fishing Club.

December. Major sports events attract international athletes and crowds of onlookers in Nassau. *The Bahamas Blue Water Run,* a half marathon sponsored by the Bahamas Striders running club; and the *Marlborough Tennis Tournament,* held at the Ocean Club, which annually attracts a roster of big name tennis stars. In Freeport, the *Grand Bahamas Vintage Grand Prix* features classic racers, such as Ferrari, Aston Martin, Lotus, and Porsche, dating from pre-World War II to the 1970s, an annual attraction for racing buffs and celebrities as well as ordinary visitors. The calendar of events for the year winds up with *Christmas Day* and the day after, *Boxing Day,* both national holidays in The Bahamas. Boxing Day, December 26, is a traditional English holiday, which received its name from the ancient custom of landlords to box up leftover Christmas goodies and present them as gifts to their tenants and serfs. But in The Bahamas, it marks the opening of the traditional *Junkanoo* celebrations. At dawn, hundreds of masked revellers parade through the streets in elaborate crepe-paper costumes to the beat of primitive African drums. The rivalry and revellry is only surpassed by the goings-on on New Year's Day, when a whole new set of costumes are paraded, for even grander prizes and prouder acclaim.

Year-round. In Nassau and Freeport, hundreds of Bahamian volunteers participate in the Ministry of Tourism's *People to People* program which brings visitors and islanders together in informal social and cultural activities. Visitors may be invited home for a party or Bahamian meal; taken on a personally guided tour of the city; invited to participate in a local club meeting, sporting or cultural event, or attend a church service. There is no set format, tourism officials simply introduce visitors to Bahamians who share similar interests or hobbies, professions or clubs; plans and itineraries are left up to the volunteers and their visitors. There is no charge to visitors, the volunteers cover all costs. The program has operated successfully for many years, and visitors who participated have been enthusiastic about the experience and the opportunity to meet Bahamians and to learn something of their lifestyle and culture. It could be the highlight of your Bahamas holiday. To sign up, have your travel agent arrange with the Ministry of Tourism in advance, join through the service desk at your hotel, or contact any Tourist Information Office in Nassau or Freeport. In Nassau, you can contact the People to People division direct, by calling 325–1585 or 325–1656; in Freeport, call 352–8044.

For complete details on sports events in The Bahamas, including entry fees, requirements and regulations, contact the *Bahamas Sports Hot Line,* open weekdays from 9 A.M. to 5 P.M., toll free in the U.S. at (800) 32SPORT. For a *Calendar of Events,* published in December and June each year by the Ministry of Tourism, contact any Bahamas Tourist Office in the U.S., Canada and Europe.

HOW TO GET THERE BY AIR. There are dozens of U.S. flights scheduled daily to both Nassau and Freeport International Airports, offering nonstop or one-stop service from many major U.S. cities. Among the U.S. carriers serving The Bahamas are: *Eastern, Delta, Pan American, TWA,* and United. From Canadian cities, *Air Canada* offers regular service; and from Great Britain and the continent, *British Airways* offers two to four flights weekly.

Bahamasair, national flag carrier of The Bahamas, offers frequent flights to Nassau and Freeport from several U.S. cities—Miami, Fort Lauderdale, Tampa, Atlanta, and Newark; and offers frequent scheduled service to 20 Family Islands from the Nassau hub. In addition, there are several small commuter airlines operating dozens of scheduled flights daily to Nassau, Freeport, and the Family Islands from Florida gateways such as Miami, Fort Lauderdale, Tampa, Orlando, and Palm Beach. For the most convenient carrier, flights, and connections on the major airlines, check with your travel agent or directly with the carrier. For Bahamasair, call (800) 2BAHAMA in the U.S. Telephone numbers for Florida commuter airlines: *Chalk's International,* toll free in the U.S. (800) 327–2521, in Fla. (800) 432–8807. *Florida Express,* in the U.S. (800) FAST JET. *Piedmont Shuttle,* in the U.S. (800) 251–5720. *Aero Coach International,* in the U.S. (800) 327–0010, in Fla. (800) 432–5034. *Gull Air,* (305) 684–1247, in Fla. (800) 222–4855. *Caribbean Express,* in the U.S. (800) 351–0104, in Fla. (800) 223–7652. *Walker's Cay Airlines,* (800) 327–3714 in the U.S.; (800) 432–2092 in Fla.

HOW TO GET THERE BY SEA. There is an entire fleet of sleek, luxury cruiseships that sail twice weekly from Florida ports *only* to The Bahamas. They generally depart each Friday on three-night cruises, calling at Nassau and a Family Island; and each Monday on four-night cruises, calling at Nassau, Freeport, and a Family Island. Each offers a wide range of cabins and price categories with seasonal ups and downs, and most offer greatly discounted airfares from cities across the U.S. on widely advertised "Fly-Cruise" programs.

A cruise is an easy, interesting, and fun-filled introduction to The Bahamas, and many cruise passengers return later to spend longer holidays at their favorite island or resort. Vacation times are the periods when ships are likely to be at their fullest, and highest priced. Cruise bargains are often available during postvacation periods, such as fall to mid-December, the first few weeks after New Year's, and after spring vacations. Christmas–New Year's holidays are almost always sold out in advance, and command a premium rate.

The following is a selected listing of cruiseships sailing from **Florida** to The Bahamas every week on two-, three-, and four-night cruises. Rates quoted are based on minimum and maximum charges per person, double occupancy, were in effect at presstime, and are subject to change.

Carnivale. 950 passengers. Three nights to Nassau, every Friday and four nights to Nassau and Freeport every Monday, $325–$855. Departs from Port of Miami. *Mardi Gras.* Departs from Port Everglades Thursday on 3-day cruises and Sunday on 4-day cruises, $325–$855. Both Carnival Cruise Lines, 5225 N.W. 87th Ave, Miami, FL 33166; (800) 327–7373, U.S.; (800) 325–1214, Fla.

Discovery I. 1300 passengers. Day trips to Freeport/Lucaya from Port Everglades every Monday, Wednesday, Friday and Sunday. From $79 per person includes meals, port and service charges; cabins are extra. Ship 'n Shore vacations from 1–3 nights also available. PCP Vacations, in Miami (305) 386–7590, in Ft. Lauderdale, (305) 476–9999.

Dolphin IV. 566 passengers. Three nights Nassau, Freeport every Friday, four nights to Nassau, Freeport, and a Family Island every Monday, $310–$845. Departs from Port of Miami. Dolphin Cruiseline, 1007 North America Way, Miami, FL 33132; (305) 358–2111, (800) 222–1003 in the U.S.

Emerald Seas. 920 passengers. Three nights Nassau and Little Stirrup Cay every Friday; four nights Nassau, Freeport, and Little Stirrup Cay every Monday, $295–$860. Departs from Port of Miami. Admiral Cruises, Inc., 1220 Biscayne Blvd., Miami, FL 33101; (305) 373–7501, in the U.S. (800) 327–0271.

Galileo. 539 cabins. Two nights to Nassau every Friday from $169. Departs from Port of Miami. Chandris-Fantasy Cruises, 4770 Biscayne Blvd., Miami, FL 33137, (305) 576–9900; (800) 423–2100 U.S.; (800) 432–4132, Fla.

Sunward II. 674 passengers. Three nights to Nassau and a Family Island every Friday; four nights to Nassau, Freeport, and a Family Island every Monday, $325–$820. Departs from Port of Miami. Norwegian Caribbean Line, 1 Biscayne Tower, Biscayne Blvd., Miami, FL 33137; (305) 358–6670, (800) 327–7030 in the U.S.

SeaEscape. The 1100-passenger *Scandinavian Sun* departs daily from Port of Miami to Freeport, returning at midnight, $99, cabins additional. The 900-passenger *Scandinavian Sky* departs Thursdays from Port Everglades, 2 night-one day cruises to Freeport, $89–$209. SeaEscape Ltd., 1080 Port Blvd., Miami, FL 33132. (305) 379–0000; (800) 327–7400 U.S.; (800) 432–0900 in Fla.

S.S. Royale. 772 passengers. Three nights to Nassau and a Family Island every Friday; four nights to Nassau, a Family Island every Monday, $325–885. Premier Cruise Lines, Box 573, Cape Canaveral, FL 32920; (305) 783–5061, (800) 327–7113 in the U.S., (800) 432–2545 in Florida.

Many other cruiseships sailing on 7- and 14- day itineraries from Florida, New York, and other U.S. ports, also call at Nassau and/or a Family Island on their Caribbean cruises. Among these are Carnival Cruiseline's *Festivale Jubilee,* and *Holiday;* Costa Line's *Costa Riviera;* Norwegian Caribbean Line's *S.S. Norway, Skyward, Southward* and *Starward;* Royal Caribbean Line's *Nordic Prince, Song of America, Sun Viking;* Sitmar Cruise's *Fairwind;* Sun Line Cruise's *Stella Solaris;* Home Lines' *Homeric;* and Holland America's *Noordam.*

INTERISLAND TRAVEL. By air: *Bahamasair* offers scheduled and charter service from Nassau to Freeport and 20 Family Islands. Nassau telephone numbers for Bahamasair reservations and information are (809) 327–8511/19; for charters call (809) 327–8316. In addition, several charter operators fly from Nassau and Freeport to the Family Islands, and for families or small groups traveling together, they can often be less expensive than regular fares aboard Bahamasair. From Nassau: *MD Air Service Ltd.,* 327–7335/6; *Pinders Charter Service,* 327–7320; *Trans Island Airways,* 327–8329 or 327–8777. From Freeport: *Helda Charters,* 352–8832 and *Lucaya Air Service,* 352–8885.

By sea: Government-operated *mailboats* depart from Potter's Cay Dock in Nassau, calling at Family Island ports on a weekly schedule. They are an interesting and adventuresome way to travel, recommended only for the intrepid visitor who does not mind limited passenger accommodation and few frills, amid a melange of freight, cargo, vegetables and produce, and perhaps a few chickens and goats, along with the mailbags. Drop by the Potter's Cay Dockmaster's office, located under the Paradise Island Bridge in Nassau, or telephone him at (809) 323–1064 for sailing dates of the Family Island mailboats. Tickets are sold only on sailing day, on a first-come, first-served basis. In the Family Island chapters of this guide, mailboats are listed with their regular, scheduled sailing dates. Rates range from $16 to $45 one-way. However, all data are subject to weekly, daily, and sometimes instantaneous revision—a real adventure!

 YACHTING AND PRIVATE PLANE FLYING. Each year, The Bahamas welcome thousands of yachtsmen and private plane flyers who arrive in their own yachts and aircraft. The Bahamas' proximity to the Florida coast make them ideal for harbor hopping by both yachtsmen and small plane pilots; there are so many islands, and they are so close together, yachts and planes are rarely out of sight of land for very long. Weather is nearly perfect for flying and sailing year-round.

Although there are nearly 50 airstrips and airports throughout The Bahamas, and hundreds of harbors and marinas, private planes and private yachts arriving from foreign ports must clear customs in an official Port of Entry. Once cleared at the first port, flyers and yachtsmen are issued a "Cruising Permit" or a "Flying Permit" that will allow them to sail to any port in The Bahamas or to land at any airport or airstrip in The Bahamas. Official Ports of Entry are as follows:

Abaco: Walker's Cay, Green Turtle Cay, Marsh Harbour, Sandy Point. **Andros:** Nicholl's Town, San Andros, Fresh Creek, Mangrove Cay, Congo Town. **Berry Islands:** Great Harbour Cay, Chub Cay. **Bimini:** Alice Town, North Bimini for yachts, South Bimini airport for planes. **Cat Cay:** Cat Cay Club. **Eleuthera:** Harbour Island, Hatchet Bay, Governor's Harbour, Rock Sound, Cape Eleuthera. **Exuma:** George Town. **Grand Bahama:** West End, Freeport, Lucaya. **Inagua:** Matthew's Town. **New Providence-Nassau:** any yacht basin or Nassau International Airport. **Ragged Island:** Duncan Town. **San Salvador:** Cockburn Town.

Private plane flyers should check with any Fixed Base Operator (FBO) in Florida for aircraft to charter for flights to The Bahamas, and for detailed information on required licenses and necessary equipment needed to fly their own planes to The Bahamas. Most FBOs will have available the excellent *Bahamas Flight Planner Chart,* or it may be obtained from any Bahamas Tourist Office (listed in the "Tourist Information Services" section, above). Private pilots and yachtsmen may also call *The Bahamas Sports Hotline* (800) 32SPORT for information, weekdays during regular office hours. The hotline can also be valuable in suggesting any air rallies or cruise flotillas being planned for yachts and planes from the U.S. to and through The Bahamas.

Yachtsmen in their own vessels can find information about sailing to The Bahamas at most marinas in Florida, and can purchase charts at most marine stores. An invaluable aid in sailing to and through The Bahamas is the annual *Yachtsman's Guide to The Bahamas,* an official publication of the Ministry of Tourism, published by Tropic Isle Publishers, Box 610935, North Miami, FL 33161, (305) 893–4277. For a copy, send $14.95 to the address above, plus $4 postage on overseas orders. It is the "bible" of knowledgeable sailors, and is very valuable for private plane flyers as well, with complete tide tables, VHF and radio facilities, complete charts of every harbor, wind and weather guides, resort and facilities index, and more. An excellent publication specifically for pilots is *Pilot's Bahamas Aviation Guide.* For a copy, write to: Pilot Publications, Box 3190, Ocala, FL 32678. Price is $19.95 ppd.

A limited number of small planes may be chartered in The Bahamas. For a listing of air charter operators in Nassau and Freeport, see "Interisland Travel" above. Yachts with captain or bareboats may be chartered at several marinas in Nassau and on Grand Bahama. See the island chapters for specifics of renting fishing and cruising boats on these and other islands in The Bahamas.

The largest and most diversified bareboat charter fleets in The Bahamas are to be found in the Abacos, at Marsh Harbour and Hope Town, Elbow Cay. The two major operators are: *Abaco Bahamas Charters,* Hope Town, Abaco; call toll free (800) 626–5690 in the U.S. *Bahamas Yachting Services,* in Marsh Harbour, Abaco, in the U.S. call toll free (800) 327–2276. A wide variety of sailing and power yachts is offered, with or without captain, and with or without full provisioning. The sheltered waters of the Abacos are among the finest cruising grounds in the entire Caribbean, perhaps in the world, with dozens of islands and cays to explore, and a different harbor to berth in every night—a sailor's paradise.

PACKING. In choosing your wardrobe for a Bahamas vacation, key words should be cool, comfortable, and casual for day wear, and slightly dressy but not formal for evenings on the town, particularly in the cities of Nassau and Freeport.

Major airlines limit you to checking two bags plus one carry-on, which must fit under your seat. There are charges for extra baggage and sporting equipment such as golf clubs. Local airlines still limit baggage allowances by weight.

Women should pack several changes of shorts, slacks, jeans or casual cotton dresses and skirts with lightweight blouses, tank tops or T-shirts for day wear. Laundry and dry cleaning tends to be expensive, so wash-and-wear choices are ideal. Skimpy bikinis are acceptable on any beach, (no nude bathing, please) but you must have a beach robe or cover-up for walking through lobbies, in shops or restaurants, or walking along the streets. (Bahamians frown on "overexposure.") Men should follow the same general rules—cool, comfortable, and casual for daytime with jeans, slacks, shorts, short-sleeved shirts and T-shirts in cotton or Dacron, a jacket and tie for evenings.

For sailing, fishing, boat cruises, or just an early morning walk along the beach, you will want a light-weight jacket or sweater to protect you from the sun's rays and occasional cool breezes. And if you plan to explore or shop be sure to bring comfortable walking shoes.

Particularly during the winter season, both men and women dress well at the elegant restaurants, nightclubs and casinos. Summers are more casual, but most visitors enjoy dressing up a bit at night. Women may also need an evening sweater, shawl, or dressy jacket for dining out, nightclubbing, or casino hopping. Air conditioners run at full speed practically everywhere.

Pack sun glasses, plenty of film, sun lotion, insect repellant, shampoo, and other personal items, as these tend to be rather expensive in The Bahamas. You might bring along a few paperbacks to read, as these also have a higher price tag. Don't bother bringing a sun hat—dozens of styles are available in the strawmarkets, hand-made, hand-woven, and inexpensive.

PASSPORTS AND VISAS. U.S. citizens do not need a passport or a visa to visit The Bahamas for periods not exceeding eight months. A birth certificate, voter registration card, or the United States Alien Registration Card for noncitizens residing in the U.S. is accepted as proof of citizenship. Bahamas immigration officials sometimes accept a driver's license with photograph as identification for Americans entering The Bahamas. However, visitors should be aware that on occasion, travelers have had difficulty reentering the United States without proof of citizenship.

Canadian citizens and citizens of the United Kingdom do not need passports or visas to enter The Bahamas for periods not exceeding three weeks. Similar identification as required for Americans is accepted as proof of citizenship. (See "Tips for British Visitors," above.) Citizens of all other countries are required to have passports, although there are very few visa requirements.

 CUSTOMS. If you plan to travel with foreign-made articles, such as cameras, binoculars, and expensive timepieces, it is wise to put with your travel documents the receipt from the retailer or some other evidence that the item was bought in your home country. If you bought the article on a previous trip abroad and have already paid duty on it, carry the receipt. Or register such items with customs prior to departure. Otherwise, on returning home, you may be charged duty (for British residents, Value-added Tax as well).

Entry formalities: All visitors to The Bahamas must complete and sign a Bahamas Immigration Form collected upon entry. All carriers provide this form, which has a carbon duplicate that will be returned to you. The duplicate is surrendered upon departure, so be sure not to lose it (tuck it in with your airline or cruise ticket so it will be handy when you leave). All visitors must also have return or onward tickets upon entering The Bahamas.

Customs requires only a verbal baggage declaration, but luggage is subject to customs inspection. There is no restriction on the amount of foreign currency you may bring into the country.

Each adult is allowed 50 cigars, 200 cigarettes or one pound of tobacco, and one quart of spirits free of customs duty, in addition to personal effects.

Cautions: Firearms may not be brought into The Bahamas without an official Bahamian gun license. Animals may not be brought into The Bahamas without an official import permit from the Ministry of Agriculture, Fisheries, and Local Government. The possession of marijuana or other narcotic drugs is a serious offense in The Bahamas, and offenders are subject to heavy fines and/or imprisonment.

Departure formalities: Departure formalities are simple. All visitors departing The Bahamas for U.S. destinations through either Nassau International Airport or Freeport International Airport, actually clear U.S. Customs and Immigration in The Bahamas (thus avoiding long lines and hassles at stateside airports). Customs forms, available at the airports, must be filled out before departure and presented to the U.S. officials, and luggage is subject to inspection. Visitors departing from other destinations in The Bahamas, or travelling to countries other than the United States, clear customs on arrival in the U.S. or the country of debarkation.

Duty-free allowances: U.S. residents may bring home $400 worth of foreign merchandise as gifts or for personal use from The Bahamas without having to pay duty, provided they have been out of the country more than 48 hours and provided they have not claimed a similar exemption within the previous 30 days. Every member of a family is entitled to the same exemption, regardless of age, and the exemptions can be pooled. Included for travelers over the age of 21 are one liter of alcohol, 100 (non-Cuban) cigars, and 200 cigarettes. Only one bottle of perfume trademarked in the U.S. may be brought in. Beyond the first $400, there is a flat tax of 10 percent of the fair retail value on the next $1,000 worth of merchandise. After $1,400, duty is at the discretion of the customs agent, depending on the type of goods you wish to bring in.

Note also that The Bahamas qualify fully for GSP (Generalized System of Preferences), which permits U.S. residents to bring home an unlimited amount of Bahamian-made products without paying duty. Such products include goods that have 35 percent of their value in Bahamian labor, anything manufactured in The Bahamas, and items made from material imported into The Bahamas but significantly altered before sale. Specific items include jewelry made from shells, straw products, clothing and gift items crafted in The Bahamas, local wood carvings and art objects, 100-years-old (or older) antiques, and locally made liqueurs (although U.S. alcohol tax must be paid on the latter). Simply list such items as GSP on your customs form, and ask that GSP rating be applied. *Caution: Turtleshell products, plants, and fruits cannot be taken into the U.S.*

From The Bahamas, gifts valued at less than $50 may be mailed to friends or relatives at home, but not more than one per day (of receipt) to any one addressee. These gifts must not include perfumes costing more than $5, tobacco, or alcohol. Mark package "Unsolicited Gift—Value Under $50."

Canadian residents may bring in 50 cigars, 200 cigarettes, two pounds of tobacco, and 40 ounces of liquor duty free, provided they are declared in writing to customs on arrival and accompany the traveler in hand or checked-through baggage. These are included in the basic exemption of $150 a year. Personal gifts should be mailed as "Unsolicited Gift—Value under $25." Canadian customs regulations are strictly enforced; you are recommended to check what your allowances are and to make sure you have kept receipts for whatever you have bought abroad. For further details, ask for the Canada Customs brochure "I Declare."

British residents, except those under 17 years of age, may import duty free the following: 400 cigarettes or 200 cigarillos or 100 cigars or 500 grams of tobacco; one liter of spirits over 22 percent proof or two liters of other spirits or fortified wine, plus two liters of still table wine; 50 grams of perfume; 9 fluid ounces of toilet water; and £28 worth of other normally dutiable goods (this last to include not more than 50 liters of beer).

AIRPORT TAXES AND OTHER CHARGES. The departure tax from The Bahamas is $5 for adults and children over 12 years; $2.50 for children 2–12 years; children under 2 are exempt. International airline and steamship tickets issued in The Bahamas are subject to a $2 government tax.

A 6 percent government tax/resort levy is collected by all hotels in The Bahamas, based on European-plan room-rate charges. In addition, many hotels add a 10–15 percent service charge to cover gratuities for food and beverages; some add a housekeeping charge (in lieu of a tip to the room maid). Be sure to ask about all charges when you make your reservation or check in to your resort or hotel, so you will not be surprised when presented with your final bill. There is no sales tax on any item purchased in The Bahamas.

MONEY. Currency of The Bahamas is the B$, which is held on an exact par with the U.S. dollar. Both currencies are used interchangeably throughout The Bahamas, and you can expect to receive change in either currency or both. The Bahamian dollar is divided into 1-, 5-, 10-, 25-, and 50-cent coins, and an unusual 15-cent coin. Other coins are $1, $2, and $5, with special issues of larger denominations in gold and silver. Favorite coin souvenirs are the scalloped-edge 10-cent piece, and the square-shaped 15-cent piece. Paper currency is issued in the same denominations as U.S. currency, $1, $5, $10, $20, $50, $100, etc. In addition, there are two unusual paper bills, the 50-cent note and the $3 note—both favorites of collectors. All paper currency is very colorful, and is a favorite souvenir.

Visitors from outside the United States may want to convert their currency into U.S. dollars before arrival. Currency exchange is handled by banks in The Bahamas, although some hotels will convert limited amounts of certain foreign currency at relatively high commission rates. Bank conversion rates are lower, but banking hours are limited throughout The Bahamas. In Nassau and Free-port, banking hours are 9:30–3:00 P.M. Monday to Thursday, 9:30–5:00 P.M. on Friday. All banks, including the airport branches, operate on the same schedule, and are closed on weekends and holidays. In the Family Islands, exchange conversion can be even more difficult, as many islands have very small branch banks open only a few hours or a few days each week; others have no banks at all.

Personal checks are rarely accepted, even with passport identification. However, traveler's checks are accepted by most of the large hotels, fine restaurants, and stores; credit cards are accepted almost everywhere in the major resort centers, including restaurants and stores. It is always wise to check the hotel, store, or restaurant to make sure you can use your traveler's checks or credit card before making a purchase or ordering a meal.

WHAT IT WILL COST. Since we are covering more than a dozen islands and half a dozen offshore cays, we have studied each area individually and given a projected daily estimate (based on winter- or high-season rates), for two persons within each island grouping. This daily rate includes a double room at a beach hotel, and three meals a day with tips, but does *not* include 6 percent room tax/resort levy, service charges, or surcharges. In addition, we have listed separately, the approximate rate for a one-day sight-seeing tour with a taxi driver/tour guide or a 24-hour car rental.

New Providence—Nassau, Cable Beach and Paradise Island	U.S.$
Standard, double room at a beach hotel	$135
Breakfast at your hotel	$ 15
Lunch at an *inexpensive* native restaurant	$ 25
Three-course dinner at an *expensive* restaurant (without liquor)	$ 60
Room, meals, gratuities	$235
One day sight-seeing with taxi driver/tour guide or 24-hour car rental	$ 60
Total:	$295

Grand Bahama—Freeport, Lucaya, West End	
Standard, double room at a beach hotel	$ 95
Breakfast at your hotel	$ 15
Lunch at an *inexpensive* native restaurant	$ 25
Three-course dinner at an *expensive* restaurant (without liquor)	$ 60
Room, meals, gratuities	$195
One day sight-seeing with taxi driver/tour guide or 24-hour car rental	$ 60
Total:	$255

The Family Islands

Standard, double room at a beach hotel	$ 90
Breakfast at your hotel	$ 15
Lunch at an *inexpensive* native restaurant	$ 15
Three-course dinner at an *expensive* restaurant (without liquor)	$ 50
Room, meals, gratuities	$170
One day sight-seeing with taxi driver/tour guide or 24-hour car rental	$ 60
Total:	$230

 HOTELS AND OTHER ACCOMMODATIONS. The Bahamas offer an exceptionally broad range of visitor accommodations to fit almost any vacation lifestyle and budget. There are more than 180 guest houses, hotels, resorts, and apartment or cottage complexes, offering over 13,000 rooms for vacation rentals on some 20 islands throughout the Bahamian archipelago. Most types of vacation accommodations are included in this wide range, with the exception of campgrounds, as camping is illegal anywhere in The Bahamas.

Most of the high-rise, luxury, oceanside resorts, which offer round-the-clock activities, casinos, gourmet dining, elaborate theatre revues and a broad spectrum of sports activities including tennis and golf, are located in the resort centers of Nassau, Cable Beach, and Paradise Island on New Providence, and Freeport/Lucaya on Grand Bahama Island. But both of these islands also offer simple seaside cottages; attractive and modern apartments, townhouses, and villas for self-catering vacations; small, modest hotels with 100 rooms or less offering personalized service and informal atmosphere; charming inns with a dozen rooms or less, some in well-preserved historic homes; and sports enclaves, large and small, that cater to golf, tennis, and diving enthusiasts. On these islands, the range of accommodations is matched by the range of rates. Even the most luxurious international resorts offer a broad range of rates within the hotel complex. Throughout the year, hotel and resort rates on Grand Bahama tend to be significantly lower for comparable accommodations than in Nassau, Cable Beach, and Paradise Island on New Providence.

In the Family Islands, there is almost as broad a range of vacation accommodations as in the resort capitals of Nassau and Freeport, with the exception of large high-rise resorts with casinos and other sophistications. Sports enclaves are particularly popular in the Family Islands. Bimini, Chub Cay, and Walker's Cay are favorites of big game fishermen; scuba divers head for Andros, Harbor Island, Spanish Wells, the Exumas, Rum Cay, and Long Island. For golfers, there are luxurious country club resorts on Eleuthera at Cotton Bay and in the Abacos at Treasure Cay. Rates at Family Island resorts tend to be significantly lower than comparable accommodations in Nassau, with a few famed, world-class exceptions in the deluxe range.

Particularly good rates are offered throughout The Bahamas during the off-season, Goombay Summer, which stretches from just after Easter to right before Christmas, when rates can be anywhere from 20 to more than 40 percent lower than in the high-season winter months.

Most hotels in Nassau and Freeport offer optional EP (European Plan–no meals) or MAP (Modified American Plan–breakfast and dinner). Due to limited outside dining facilities in small villages and island settlements in the Family

Islands, many hotels and resorts offer only MAP or FAP (Full American Plan–all meals). Often, these meal plans can provide significant savings over paying for three meals a day separately.

Hotels and resorts are arranged into five categories: *Super Deluxe, Deluxe, Expensive, Moderate,* and *Inexpensive.* Price is the basic criterion, although other factors, such as comfort, convenience, atmosphere, and facilities, are taken into consideration. As there is such a broad diversity of rates from island to island, the price range for each category varies and is listed in the *Practical Information* section for each island.

Apartment-rental and time-sharing opportunities are also listed in the island-by-island *Practical Information* sections.

 DINING OUT. In Nassau and Freeport, there is a nearly endless variety of dining options, from elegant gourmet dining rooms in the luxury hotels, to fast-food franchises. Most food served in American and Continental-style restaurants tends to be rather expensive, as everything from fresh vegetables to steak is imported. Excellent native restaurants, which are also lower priced, are abundant in Nassau, Freeport, and in nearly every small village and settlement in the Family Islands. (Note: For liquors and liqueurs, wines and beer, the legal drinking age is 18 years.)

The island chapters provide detailed lists of dining options. As with hotels and resorts, restaurants are arranged into five categories, defined in each *Practical Information* section: *Super Deluxe, Deluxe, Expensive, Moderate,* and *Inexpensive.* Price is the basic criterion, although other factors are taken into consideration, such as quality of food, ambience, and service. We have also indicated which restaurants do or do not accept credit cards. For those that do, we have used the following abbreviations: AE, American Express; BA, Bank America; DC, Diners Club; MC, MasterCard; V, Visa.

 TIPPING. Most Bahamas hotels and restaurants have adopted the European custom of automatically adding a service charge to your bill—usually 15 percent but sometimes as little as 10 percent. Use your own discretion when tipping over and above that for exceptional services rendered. Where no fee is added, tip is based on services delivered. In restaurants and nightclubs, and for room, beach, or poolside hotel service, 15 percent is standard. 15 percent is also standard for taxi and surrey drivers, barbers and beauty operators, and even bartenders. Porters and bellmen are tipped 50 cents per bag and something extra for unusually heavy items such as golf clubs.

Many hotels in The Bahamas add on an automatic housekeeping charge or "maid's gratuity" of around $1–1.25 per day to your bill. Be sure to ask about all such automatic charges when you check in, so you won't be surprised when you check out.

 CASINOS. There are currently four casinos in The Bahamas, with a fifth planned to open in late 1988 or early 1989. Visitors must be 21 years of age or over to gamble; Bahamians or Bahamas residents are not permitted to gamble. Dress code is informal during the day, more formal at night. On New Providence, there is the informal Cable Beach Casino, operated by Carnival Leisure Industries; and the more formal and elegant Paradise Island Casino, operated by Resorts International. On Grand Bahama, there is the opulent Princess Casino, operated by Princess Hotels, and the Lucayan Beach Hotel's friendly and attractive Monte Carlo Casino.

All offer virtually round-the-clock gaming action, Continental croupiers with favorite games of chance: roulette, blackjack, baccarat, craps, wheel of fortune, and acres of state-of-the-art slot machines with payoffs up to $100,000 or more. The casinos also offer a choice of bars, restaurants, and entertainment, as well as theaters featuring elaborate floor shows and bare-bosomed stage-girl revues to rival the best of Paris and Las Vegas.

 TELEPHONES, TELEGRAMS, AND TELEX. Direct distance dialing is available from the U.S. and Canada to many Bahamian islands, and service is expanding rapidly. You may dial direct to Nassau; Grand Bahama; Abaco; Andros; Berry Islands; Bimini; Eleuthera; Harbour Island; Spanish Wells; George Town, Exuma; and Stella Maris, Long Island. The area code is 809. To call The Bahamas from Europe and other countries, dial the operator for assistance. From The Bahamas, direct dialing is available to the U.S. and Canada only from the following islands: Nassau, Grand Bahama, Bimini, parts of Andros, George Town in the Exumas, Governor's Harbour and Rock Sound on Eleuthera, and Marsh Harbour, the Abacos. To call abroad from other islands, dial the operator for assistance. Visitors should be aware that many hotels in The Bahamas add a substantial service charge to long-distance telephone calls placed from the hotel. Whenever possible, expensive long-distance calls should be placed through public telephones. There are public telephone centers on most of the islands in The Bahamas.

Telex service is available through most major hotels, and there are public telex services in Nassau and Freeport. Telegraph service is also available. To place a telegram by phone, dial 910.

Emergency numbers are listed in each of the island chapters.

 POSTAGE. Bahamian postage stamps are readily available from post offices throughout the islands and are often sold at hotels and shops. From The Bahamas to the U.S. and Canada, postage rates are as follows: *Air Mail* —first class letters, 31¢ per ½ ounce. Second class letters, 25¢ per ½ ounce. Post cards, 25¢. To the U.K., Europe, South America, and Central America, airmail postage rates are: first class letters, 35¢ per ½ ounce; second class letters, 20¢ per ½ ounce; post cards, 25¢. Air letters to all foreign destinations are 25¢. Package rates vary depending upon size and destination. Post offices are open Mon.–Fri. 8:30 A.M. 5:30 P.M. and until 12:30 P.M. Sat. in Nassau and Freeport. Family Island post offices are sometimes open only a few hours and days each week.

All communications *to* The Bahamas from the U.S. or abroad should be made by airmail, if speed is required. Airmail charge for a letter mailed from the U.S. is 39¢, and it will generally reach Nassau or Freeport within two to four days. However, even airmail letters may take a week or longer to the Family Islands, as they are routed by air to Nassau, but may go by weekly mailboat to the Family Island destination. If the resort or business you wish to contact has a U.S. or Nassau address, use it by preference as it will be much faster.

TIME ZONE. The Bahamas is in the Eastern Standard Time zone, which is exactly the same time as the east coast of the United States, and five hours behind Greenwich Mean Time. From April to October, The Bahamas switch to Daylight Savings Time, on the same dates that the U.S. does.

Whatever time zone you hail from, you'll have to learn to adjust to what the islanders call "Bahamian Time." It's a slow, leisurely pace, more of a ramble than a rush, and it's a way of life in The Bahamas. It affects everything from hotel and restaurant service to telephone calls and business appointments. Relax, slow down, and enjoy it!

 ELECTRIC CURRENT. Electricity is normally 120 volts, 60 cycles throughout The Bahamas, identical to U.S. current, providing compatibility with all American appliances. Occasional brownouts occur in Nassau, more rarely in Freeport/Lucaya. In the Family Islands, many resorts rely on their own generators for electricity, and occasional breakdowns are not uncommon. However, candles are provided in most hotel rooms throughout The Bahamas, guests take the minor inconvenience caused with good-natured patience (usually), and repairs are soon under way.

 TRAVELING WITH PETS. When heading to The Bahamas, we recommend leaving your pets with friends at home or boarding them at an appropriate facility. Bringing pets out of and back into the country—whatever your point of origin—can involve quarantine time and considerable hassles; also, resort hotels rarely have facilities for animals.

If you absolutely must bring your pet, plan well ahead of time—at least a month in advance. Request permission from the Ministry of Agriculture, Fisheries, and Local Government, Box N–3028, Nassau, Bahamas. State the type of pet, and its port of entry into The Bahamas. Then await a reply and an official permit. Upon entering the Bahamas you must present your permit, a Veterinary Health Certificate issued within 24 hours of your departure from home, and proof of a Rabies Vaccination issued not less than ten days nor more than nine months prior to arrival.

TRAVELING WITH CHILDREN. Many Bahamas resorts offer free accommodations for children (usually 12 and under) sharing a room with adults. Those hotels which do not offer free accommodations generally offer reduced rates. Many hotels also offer special facilities for children and baby-sitting services. Check with your travel agent or with the resort at which you intend to stay to learn of special rates or amenities for children.

HINTS TO HANDICAPPED TRAVELERS. The major airlines can usually accommodate wheelchair passengers when notified in advance. An excellent brief guide to airline travel for people confined to a wheelchair or with other handicaps is available free from *TWA*, 605 Third Ave., New York, NY 10016.

"Facilities For The Physically Disabled" is a chart of all resorts and hotels in The Bahamas offering special facilities for the handicapped, compiled by the Bahamas Paraplegic Association. It is published in the annual *Bahamas Travel Agency Guide,* and is available at any Bahamas Tourist Office, and at most travel agencies. In Nassau, contact The Bahamas Paraplegic Association at (809) 324–2980 for a copy or further information.

HEALTH. Few real hazards threaten the health of a visitor to The Bahamas. Poisonous snakes are nonexistent, and the small lizards you seem to encounter everywhere are harmless. The worst problem may well be a tiny predator, the "no see 'um," a small sandfly that tends to appear after a rain, near wet or swampy ground, and around sunset. If you feel particularly vulnerable to insect bites, bring along a good repellent.

Even people who are not normally bothered by strong sun should head into this area with a long-sleeved shirt, a hat, and long pants or a beach wrap. These are essential for a day on a boat, but are also advisable for midday at the beach. Also carry some sun-block lotion for nose, ears, and other sensitive areas such as eyelids, ankles, etc. Be sure to take in enough liquids. Above all, limit your sun time for the first few days until you become used to the heat and the tropical sunshine.

Medical facilities in The Bahamas are considered excellent for an island group so small in population and yet so diverse in distribution. Physicians, dentists, and surgeons in private practice are readily available in both Nassau and Freeport. Nassau has the 455-bed Princess Margaret Hospital, government operated, and the 20-bed Rassin Hospital, privately operated. In Grand Bahama, there is a government-operated hospital and two privately operated clinics. In the Family Islands, there are 13 health centers and 36 clinics. Where intensive or urgent care is required, patients are brought into the nearest major hospital facility by emergency flight service. There are several 24-hour emergency aircraft services operating to The Bahamas from South Florida. Among these are *Air Ambulance Associates* (305) 523–7112, from Ft. Lauderdale; and *Air Ambulance Network* (305) 387–1708, from Miami or Ft. Lauderdale. Medical facilities are listed, along with emergency numbers, under each island grouping in the following chapters.

SECURITY. Don't be fooled by the appearance of paradise when you visit The Bahamas. New Providence Island, especially Nassau and Paradise Island, requires the same precautions you would practice if you visited any other cosmopolitan area. The same goes for Freeport, Grand Bahama Island. Women should not walk unescorted after dusk and all visitors should avoid deserted nighttime streets. Lock your car doors and, no matter where you are staying in The Bahamas, do not leave valuables unattended on the beach or in hotel rooms. Most major resorts and hotels offer safety deposit boxes for your cash and jewelry. Take advantage of this complimentary service. The Family Islands are generally quieter and safer but you'll always be wise to take precautions and secure your valuables no matter where you travel.

THE BAHAMAS: AMERICA'S SOUTH SEA ISLANDS

THE BAHAMAS

AMERICA'S SOUTH SEA ISLANDS

The Bahamas are America's South Sea Islands, a Polynesia that lies just over the horizon, not half a world away. Resort capitals in The Bahamas are only a half hour from Florida's Gold Coast, less than two and a half hours from New York, Chicago, and Toronto, and little more than a breakfast-to-dinner flight from Great Britain and the Continent. The islands have hosted world travelers for more than a century, yet they remain mostly uncrowded, unspoiled, unsophisticated, and many virtually unexplored.

The seven hundred emerald gems in the island chain are bordered by powder-soft, white-sand beaches; lined with whispering casuarinas and swaying palms; and fringed by living coral reefs. They stretch in a long, languid arc from Florida to the Caribbean Sea, surrounded by a palette of blue and green waters of unbelievable clarity and indescribable beauty. An astronaut soaring more than a hundred miles above them said they were "like nothing else on earth . . . a ribbon of turquoise lost in the midnight blue of the world's oceans."

But more than crystal-clear waters and miles of beautiful beaches have attracted visitors to these islands for generations. Their rich history and colonial charm, their foreign flavor and friendly people, and their nearly endless variety of vacation lifestyles today lure more than three million visitors a year, many returning again and again to their favorite island in the sun.

A Colorful History

The *Niña*, the *Pinta*, and the *Santa María*, three small caravels from Spain, were destined to become the most famous ships since Noah's Ark. With Christopher Columbus in command, the small fleet set out on September 8, 1492 to sail the uncharted western seas, searching for a short cut to the fabled wealth of the Indies, the imperial riches of Cipangu (Japan), and the palaces of Kublai Khan in Cathay (China). By October 10, the fleet had been out of sight of land longer than any ships in history, and mutiny was in the air. At two o'clock in the morning, on October 12, 1492, the moment came that would change the course of history. Rodrigo de Triana, the lookout on *Pinta*'s forecastle, shouted "Tierra, tierra!" Land at last. Ahead lay the island of Guanahani, easternmost in the Bahamas chain. At dawn, Columbus went ashore to plant the banners of his sovereigns and claimed the island for Spain. He named it San Salvador, in honor of the Holy Savior.

Gateway to the New World

Columbus had discovered not only The Bahamas but a whole new world. The riches of Cipangu and Cathay still lay a continent away, and beyond another ocean. But Columbus believed he had found the islands of Japan. Perhaps just beyond the next island, or just over the horizon, lay the world of Marco Polo and the splendors of the Great Khan.

On Guanahani, he found a peaceful Arawak Indian village of thatched huts, with friendly natives who had fled to these islands to escape the warlike cannibal tribes of the Caribee. They called themselves Lucayans ("island people"), and welcomed Columbus and his great-winged boats as messengers from heaven. They presented him with fresh water, green parrots, and the handwoven *hamacas* in which they slept. (They would be the Arawaks greatest gift to civilization for, within a decade, hammocks were standard gear on ships around the world—the U.S. Navy phased them out in 1942, 450 years after Columbus discovered them.) But Columbus was much more interested in the bits of gold the natives wore. In sign language he asked where the gold could be found. They pointed to the southwest, to a great island they called Cobla (Cuba). Perhaps he heard "Kublai" in their cries, because

he was more convinced than ever that the land of the great Kublai Khan was nearby.

For the next two weeks, he "harbor hopped" from island to island in the southern Bahamas, discovering and naming Santa Maria de la Concepcion (Rum Cay), Fernandina (Long Island), Isabella (Crooked Island), and Islas de Arena (the Ragged Island chain). He crossed the treacherous shallows and rocks of the Great Bahama Bank and called them Baja Mar, or "shallow sea," which became the name of the entire archipelago, Bahamas. On October 27th, Columbus left Bahamian waters, never to return. He went on to discover Cuba, Hispaniola, and most of the islands of the Caribbean . . . the rest is history.

Although Columbus never returned to the islands of the Lucayans, the Spanish colonists and conquistadores who followed him returned again and again on slaving raids. Between 1500 and 1520, the entire population of The Bahamas was carried off to work the fields of Cuba, the mines of Hispaniola, and the pearl beds of Margarita and Trinidad.

English Colonization

It wasn't until 1629 that Britain's king, Charles I, claimed The Bahamas for the English crown, and granted proprietary rights to his Attorney General, Sir Robert Heath, for "the area of the American mainland he allowed to be called Carolina . . . and also all those our islands of Bahama." Unfortunately, the King lost both his throne and his head, and Heath died in exile. No previous attempt had been made to settle the Carolinas or The Bahamas.

Religious and political dissension rocked England and toppled the King. A growing group of dissenters challenged the burning issue of a state church. They were ridiculed and persecuted, and thousands were driven into exile. The most famous among them were the Pilgrims, who founded Massachusetts Colony in 1620. Others fled to Bermuda, seeking religious freedom, and then had to flee again. Under the leadership of William Sayle, former governor of Bermuda, they set sail for The Bahamas.

They called themselves The Company of Eleutherian Adventurers, named for the Greek word meaning "freedom," and drew up a remarkable document, destined to become the first constitution of The Bahamas. It guaranteed religious freedom, equal justice for all, and a republican form of democracy—the first in the new world. In 1648, they settled on the island of Cigatoo, and renamed it Eleuthera. The small colony of seventy barely managed to survive, making their homes in huts and caves at the northern end of the island and the small cays offshore, Spanish Wells and Harbour Island. Many of their blond, blue-eyed descendants still live there today.

When Charles II was restored to the throne lost by his father, in 1660, religious dissension diminished, but the stream of colonial settlers to America continued. By 1670, there were just eleven hundred settlers in The Bahamas. Some remained on Eleuthera, but most were living on an island where Sayle had once found shelter in a storm, and which he had named New Providence. Life was hard for the handful of settlers. The thin, rocky soil produced few crops, and most earned their living from the sea. Good times came only when Spanish treasure ships were wrecked on their shores and the settlers salvaged the cargoes. Wrecking became a way of life, and while some of the unscrupulous planted false lights to lure the Spanish ships to destruction, others turned to piracy.

Pirates and Buccaneers

The Lord Proprietors, more concerned with the vast plantations they were creating in the Carolinas, paid little attention to The Bahamas, sending out a string of incompetent and unscrupulous governors who encouraged piracy. In 1684, infuriated by the activities of these lawless wreckers, the Spanish governor in Havana sent out ships and troops to attack and burn the settlement at Nassau. The few remaining honest settlers fled to Jamaica and the Carolinas.

For the next forty years, Nassau became the headquarters for countless pirates, buccaneers, and the scum of the seven seas. They ruled the Spanish Main, attacking the treasure galleons bound for Spain, and the merchant ships bound for colonies in America and the Caribbean. Nassau was ideal. It lay astride the trade routes between the old world and the new, and its strategic natural harbor, formed by the barrier of Paradise Island, was shallow and open at both ends, perfect for eluding the cumbersome warships that were brave enough to give chase. There were as many as two thousand pirates operating out of New Providence in those days, and among them were famous names that have survived in history and legend for nearly three hundred years. There was Captain Avery, who had captured the treasure ship of the Great Mogul in the Indian Ocean, and run off with his daughter; the arch pirate Edward Teach, better known as Blackbeard; Charles Vane, Peter Hynd, Stede Bonnet, Benjamin Hornigold, and Calico Jack Rackham and his infamous crew—two buxom young women, Anne Bonney and Mary Read, who reportedly boarded their prize ships stripped to the waist and brandishing cutlasses.

British colonial authorities were besieged with complaints from governors of every maritime colony in America, and threats from France, Holland, and Spain. Proprietary government had failed, and King George I appointed a national hero, Captain Woodes Rogers, to the post of Royal Governor. Rogers was a bit of a rogue himself, and the pirates knew him well. During the War of the Spanish Succession, he had sailed around the world as a privateer. Daniel Defoe told Rogers's story in his immortal classic *Robinson Crusoe* (1719).

When Woodes Rogers arrived in Nassau at daybreak on July 26, 1718, the whole town turned out to greet him, and pirates cheered him. He read the Royal Proclamation of Pardon for pirates who surrendered, and hanged those who refused. Within weeks, he had seized control of Nassau and restored law and order. He even converted pirates to "privateers," and sent them off in their own vessels to repel the French and Spanish warships that continued to threaten the islands. He saved The Bahamas from both the pirates and the Spanish, and the Crown granted him a crest that read "Expulsis Piratis, Restituta Commercia" (Pirates Expelled, Commerce Restored). It would become the motto of The Bahamas for more than 250 years.

Despite the best efforts of Woodes Rogers and the Royal Governors who followed him, the islands remained impoverished and sparsely settled. Privateering flourished briefly during the on-again, off-again wars between England and Spain, but between conflicts the settlers turned once again to wrecking, the perennial standby.

The Bahamas and the American Revolution

While the British colonies in America were seething with revolt, the colony of The Bahamas was quiet, peaceful, calm, and loyal. When the rebellious American colonists declared their independence in 1776, George Washington was named commander in chief of the ragged army of farmers, but he had no navy. His army was desperately short of guns and ammunition, so he commandeered eight small merchant ships, fitted them with cannons, and sent them off to Nassau. The new American Navy captured Nassau without firing a shot, and sailed home two weeks later with most of the arms and ammunition and the Bahamas's governor as hostage.

In retaliation, the British outfitted Nassau as a privateering base to attack rebel ships trading with their French and Spanish allies in the Caribbean. The operations were so successful, and so many American prisoners were captured, that the governor complained that he could not "keep nor victual them," but had to transport them to the nearest American port and set them free.

But on May 6, 1782, a combined fleet of some eighty American, Spanish, and French warships aimed at the fort at Nassau, and the city once more surrendered without a shot being fired. The Spanish occupied The Bahamas for more than a year, until the American Revolutionary War ended with victory for the rebels. When the peace treaty was finally signed in September 1783, the 13 American colonies had gained their independence, Spain had been granted Florida, and, as a consolation prize, The Bahamas were returned to the British crown—a transaction Parliament considered a mixed blessing at best.

Following the revolution, the Americans turned their wrath on the traitors at home, the loyalists. The plantation owners in Virginia and the Carolinas, fled to Florida to begin their lives anew. When they learned that Florida would be ceded to Spain, The Bahamas became their last hope for protection under the British flag . . . but seven hundred Spanish troops still guarded the harbor at Nassau, and a Spanish nobleman occupied the governor's mansion. Undaunted, a group of hearty adventurers, under the leadership of Colonel Andrew

Deveaux of South Carolina, set out to "liberate" Nassau from the
Spanish.

They had less than a hundred men, half of them unarmed, two small
ships, and half a dozen fishing boats filled with volunteers they had
recruited on Eleuthera and Harbour Island to help the cause. By a
series of tricks and ruses, they gained the high ground behind the fort
and Government House, dragging a couple of cannons with them to
the top of the hill. At dawn, they fired a warning shot at the governor's
house and boldly demanded that he surrender, claiming they had more
than a thousand troops surrounding the town. Caught by surprise, the
Spanish capitulated. When the governor returned to Havana, he was
tossed into prison as punishment for his humiliating defeat.

After Deveaux's astonishing success, he was hailed as a hero by the
Bahamians, and became a prominent member of the newly revived
House of Assembly. Loyalists by the thousands followed him to The
Bahamas, from New York and New England, from Virginia, Florida,
and the Carolinas, bringing with them their families and their slaves.
From 1784 to 1789, the population of The Bahamas tripled to 11,300—
nearly eight thousand of them were black slaves.

The aristocratic loyalists thrived in the sunny Bahamas, dominating
the colonial legislature and the trade and commerce, and rebuilding
Nassau into a city of southern charm, with great mansions, schools,
churches, and public buildings, many of which survive today. One of
the most prominent refugees, Lord Dunmore, who had been the last
Royal Governor of Virginia, became governor of The Bahamas. He
erected massive defenses, Fort Charlotte and Fort Fincastle, but nei-
ther would ever fire a shot in anger and no foreign flag would fly over
The Bahamas again. Peace and prosperity seemed assured.

The boom did not last very long, however. By 1800, the thin, rocky
soil was exhausted, and a tiny insect had wiped out most of the crops.
Gradually, the loyalists gave up their plantations and fled back to the
mainland or to richer British colonies to the south. The emancipation
of slaves in 1834 wiped out the last vestiges of a plantation system in
The Bahamas. The remaining settlers once again turned to the sea for
their livelihood, and, wrecking became a thriving industry.

Tourism Roots and the Civil War

A trickle of visitors had been coming to the islands for nearly a
century, invalids looking for a rest cure in the sunny Bahamas. In the
1850s, The Bahamas legislature passed the first "Tourism Encourage-
ment Act," contracted with Samuel Cunard to provide steamship service between New York and Nassau, and authorized the building of a
grand hotel to attract winter visitors from northern climes. The Royal
Victoria Hotel would welcome guests for more than a century—but its
debut in 1861 was a near disaster.

The whole idea of tourism collapsed with the opening guns of the
Civil War on the U.S. mainland. The north launched a blockade against

southern ports, Wilmington, Charleston and Savannah. Nassau was the nearest neutral port to the south, and overnight blockade-running became The Bahamas' biggest industry. The Royal Victoria became its headquarters. Fortunes were made by many Bahamians, and the government treasury benefited hugely from import and export duties imposed upon war supplies arriving from Britain and the Continent and the cotton flowing through the blockade from southern ports. Not since the days of pirates and buccaneers had Nassau seen such a boom. But when the war ended, poverty returned once again to the islands, and even the perennial standby, wrecking, failed when the Imperial Lighthouse Service erected great oil-burning lights throughout the Bahamas chain. Poverty would be a way of life for Bahamians from the Civil War to the end of World War I.

Temperance Folly and Tourism Boom

In 1919, "Prohibition" became the 18th Amendment to the U.S. Constitution, and from 1920 to 1933 bootlegging and rum-running became a rich Bahamian industry, in the swashbuckling tradition of privateers and blockade-runners of earlier days. During the "Roaring Twenties," the islands enjoyed a tourism boom unprecedented in history. Nassau's picturesque harbor was crowded with opulent private yachts, with some of the most powerful names in industry and high finance at their helms: William K. Vanderbilt, Vincent Astor, J.P. Morgan, and E.F. Hutton, as well as Whitneys, Armours, and Mellons. Nassau Harbour was deepened. The grand old Royal Victoria was refurbished; a new Colonial Hotel was built on the ashes of one that had burned in 1921; and the great, sprawling Fort Montagu Beach Hotel made its debut. On January 2, 1929, a fledgling airline named Pan American launched daily air service from Miami to Nassau, operating eight passenger Sikorsky seaplanes—the latest word in comfort and luxury for that early era of commercial flight. Suddenly, the islands were just hours instead of days away from the U.S. mainland, and they became the international playground for wealthy visitors from around the world. The Bahamas had finally found a basic industry that could survive good times and bad.

War and the Windsors

In the early months of World War II, The Bahamas enjoyed another tourism boom as wealthy refugees from the blitzkrieg and the blitz flocked to the islands from Britain and Europe. Most prominent of the new arrivals were the ex-King of England and his American bride, the Duke and Duchess of Windsor. After the abdication the Windsors lived a life of luxury in France, at their Paris mansion and their estate on the Riviera. When the Nazis marched through France the Duke and his Duchess fled to neutral Portugal, a hotbed of Axis intrigue. There they became the victims of a plot hatched by German and Portuguese diplomatic officials to lure the Duke into the German orbit—if necessary, by kidnapping.

The lure would be nothing less than the British throne! The Duke and Duchess would be declared King and Queen in exile and, once Britain was defeated, they would ascend to the throne. If they agreed, unlimited money would be put at their disposal in a Swiss bank account. After the war, cables from German and Portuguese diplomats in Lisbon to Von Ribbentrop and Hitler himself were made public and the plot revealed.

Winston Churchill, Britain's wartime prime minister, learned of the kidnapping plot and determined to send the Duke as far from the war zone as possible. The Duke of Windsor was ordered to the post of governor and commander in chief of The Bahama Islands, a tiny outpost of the empire, five thousand miles away from the war—a post he held from 1940 to 1945. After Pearl Harbor, when the U.S. entered the war, The Bahamas became an important Royal Air Force base. The fighter planes and bombers that poured off American production lines were flown to Nassau, where allied pilots were trained to fly them before delivery to war command posts around the world.

When the war ended in 1945, tourism began to increase once again. The war left The Bahamas a legacy of two modern airports, and a new invention called air-conditioning kept the hotels open year-round. For more than forty years, since the end of World War II, tourism has been the mainstay of The Bahamas' economy, with visitor arrivals increasing each year in a steady upward curve.

The Quiet Revolution

In the 1960s, a "quiet revolution" occurred in The Bahamas. After more than three hundred years of rule by the white minority, a young London-educated black lawyer, Lynden O. Pindling, led his Progressive Liberal Party to victory in the 1967 elections, bringing a black majority government to The Bahamas for the first time in history. He guided his nation to full independence from the British Crown on July 10, 1973. Prince Charles, heir to the English throne, presided over the impressive ceremonies, and The Bahamas chose to remain within the British Commonwealth of Nations, continuing their historic friendship and cultural ties with Great Britain. The Bahamas replaced Woodes Rogers's motto with a proud new crest: "Forward, Upward, Onward Together," but they retained his greatest legacy, a strong parliamentary democracy, which has thrived for more than 250 years.

The Bahamas Today

The 1960s and 1970s brought another revolution in The Bahamas tourism industry. The vintage Royal Victoria Hotel and the Prohibition-era Fort Montagu Beach Hotel quietly closed . . . too dated and too expensive to convert to modern year-round, airconditioned resorts. Of Nassau's original grand hotels, only the 1920s British Colonial stands today under the wing of Sheraton, which maintains the venerable harborside hotel as a moderate-priced, updated resort. New hotels rose along Nassau's famed Cable Beach and in town. Hog Island, across the harbor, which had been an enclave of private mansions for decades, was rechristened Paradise Island with glittering high-rise hotels and a glamorous gaming casino, and linked to Nassau by a soaring bridge. On Grand Bahama Island, the new city of Freeport and its suburb Lucaya were carved from the pine forests, modern hotels and sprawling beach resorts appeared, two Continental casinos made their debut, and thousands of acres of tropical greenery were tamed for half a dozen world-class golf courses. In the Family Islands, small inns, cottage colonies, and country-club resorts sprung up along the beaches on a dozen different islands bringing the benefits of tourism to most Bahamians throughout the island chain.

Bahamians are friendly and gracious hosts, and visitors are warmly welcomed. English is the universal language, but there are many accents, which vary from a southern drawl to a Caribbean lilt, and from a cockney-style dropping of the H as in "Arbour H'Iland" for Harbour Island, to the clipped accents of the British upperclass. Pockets of poverty remain here and there throughout the islands, but most Bahamians manage to earn a decent living, and crime is not a major factor anywhere in the islands. Tourism facilities are among the most modern and luxurious of any sun, sand, and sea destination in the world, and well-educated young Bahamians, both black and white, are becoming increasingly involved on the highest levels of the tourism industry as owners, managers, planners, and decision-makers.

The Sporting Life

From gambling in the casinos to gambolling on the beaches, The Bahamas offer a kaleidoscope of sporting activity guaranteed to satisfy even the most jaded. Year-round, near-perfect weather guarantees something for everyone from anglers to divers, from flyers to windsurfers, from parasailors to water skiers, from golfers to tennis buffs, from horseback riders to beachcombers. Among the biggest drawing cards of The Bahamas for the outdoor sportsman is nearly a dozen world-class, championship 18-hole golf courses found in Nassau and on Paradise Island, Grand Bahama, and on the Family Islands of Abaco and Eleuthera. For those more interested in indoor sports, there's gambling till dawn in Continental casinos, dancing to a merengue or a goombay beat, disco and limbo, fire dances and goatskin drums, and French-style stagegirl revues acclaimed by sophisticates as better than Las Vegas or The Lido.

The Underwater World

The Bahamas are the favorite gathering spot for international divers among any tropical island destination in the world. The more than seven hundred islands and two thousand cays are surrounded by living reefs, with waters so crystal-clear that visibility ranges to two hundred feet or more. Colors vary from pale turquoise to brilliant aquamarine with ever-changing tones of purple, green, and blue and water temperatures are warm year-round. For the sport diver from novice to expert, it is an underwater wonderland waiting to be explored.

There are spectacular drop-offs that begin in twenty feet of water, and plummet vertically thousands of feet, while nearby there are shallow coral gardens abounding in colorful plant life and waving sea fans. There are mysterious ocean blue holes and fascinating historic wrecks dating from the pirate days of the Spanish Main and the blockade-runners of the Civil War. There are reefs with thousands of brilliantly colored tropical fish, giant stingrays and moray eels, and reefs where sharks gather in great schools, lurking for prey; plus giant underwater caverns, labyrinths of winding coral tunnels and steep-walled canyons. The opportunities for underwater adventures are nearly limitless in The Bahamas, and divers from every continent return year after year in quest of new thrills and excitement. Throughout the islands, there are dozens of dive resorts and dive operators offering trips to nearby reefs and underwater attractions; and many of The Bahamas' dive resorts offer full courses of instruction for beginners through experts, including professional training and certification.

Big Game and Light Tackle Fishing

Some of the finest big game fishing in the world can be found in Bahamian waters, and the record books prove it. Anglers fishing in The Bahamas have set more than fifty world records, according to the International Game Fishing Association, and new records are set or broken nearly every year.

Each year from March through July, anglers from all over the world gather in The Bahamas for the annual big game fishing tournament season in quest of world record-setters and the prestigious Bahamas Billfish Championship. They spare no effort or expense in their quest. Half-million dollar fighting machines, Hatteras and Hinckleys, Bertrams and Burgers line the docks, bursting with gleaming tackle and manned by professional crews.

Competitors follow a decades-old tradition, launched in the 1930s when such famed anglers as Ernest Hemingway, Howard Hughes, and Zane Grey "discovered" The Bahamas, and tracked the massive tuna and blue marlin that make their annual migratory runs along the edge of the Gulf Stream and the fathomless depths of the Tongue of The Ocean.

But you needn't be a big-time, big game tournament angler to enjoy the fishing scene in The Bahamas. The fishing season lasts 365 days a year, and virtually every hotel and resort in the islands offers deep-sea, drift or reef fishing charters, either from their own dock or nearby marinas. Rates are moderate to expensive, around $200 to $300 a half day aboard a fully equipped fishing yacht with captain and mate, but if two or three couples share a charter, the costs are well within the average vacationer's budget. Many charter-boat captains are happy to line up other anglers for charter sharing, and hotel managers often arrange fishing groups to spread the costs.

Most awe-inspiring of the big game fish common to The Bahamas are the giant Blue Marlins, ranging in size from 250 pounds to well over 1000 pounds. They roam Bahamian waters throughout the year, but in record numbers in spring and summer months from April to mid-September. Best hunting grounds are along the edge of the Gulf Stream off Bimini, Grand Bahama, and Walker's Cay; at the Tongue of the Ocean off Andros and Chub Cay; and from Eleuthera north to Green Turtle Cay, Abaco. Another monster frequenting these waters is the tackle-busting Bluefin Tuna, weighing up to 1000 pounds. They appear in massive schools each spring from early May to mid-June on their yearly migration northward to the rich herring grounds off Nova Scotia. Their favorite route through The Bahamas is at the edge of the Great Bahamas Bank off Bimini and West End, Grand Bahama.

During the fall and winter seasons, the streamlined, speedy Wahoo is found throughout Bahamian waters. Weighing up to 130 pounds, they are among the world's fastest and most challenging game fish. During the late winter months through early spring, one of the most popular billfish is abundant, the scrappy White Marlin, weighing up to 150 pounds, and found in deep channels from Bimini east to Eleuthera, and from Walker's Cay in the north to the Exuma Cays in the south. Another popular billfish appears during late summer and early autumn, the high-leaping Sailfish, which cruises the depths around Chub Cay, Bimini, Grand Bahama, the Abacos, and the Exumas.

If big game, deep-sea, bluewater fishing is not your style, there are dozens of other possibilities for Bahamas-bound anglers, which include fishing from a dock with a handline, stalking bonefish from a small boat; fly-fishing, plug-casting, spinning in the bays, and trolling or drift fishing over the miles of coral reefs that fringe the island's shores.

Among the favorite light-tackle fighting fish found in these waters are the Allison Tuna, found during the summer months, and the Blackfin Tuna, found during the autumn and winter months. Year-round, Amberjacks roam the reefs and wrecks, the multicolored Dolphin cruises the deeper waters, and Snapper, Grouper, and Snook are found in all reefy areas throughout the island chain—a piscatorial grab bag to satisfy almost any angler.

Around-the-World Shopping

The Bahamas have been known to generations of visitors for bargains on luxury goods imported from around the world. Although there are no duty-free shops on the islands, and no free ports, the savings are substantial over comparable U.S., Canadian, and European prices, because import duties on luxury items are kept low to compete with other Caribbean destinations such as the U.S. Virgin Islands and the Dutch Antilles. In addition, The Bahamas has no sales tax or value-added tax, which results in increased savings, particularly on "big ticket" luxury items.

Best buys on imported goods, and the widest selection in The Bahamas, are found in Nassau's Bay Street shopping district and in the International Bazaar in Freeport. Particularly good bargains are German and Japanese cameras and optics; Swiss and designer watches; English and European bone china, such as Royal Doulton, Wedgwood, Crown Derby, Royal Copenhagen, and Coalport; French, Irish, German, and Scandinavian crystal, such as Baccarat, Lalique, Daum, Waterford, and Orrefors; collectible porcelain figurines such as Hummel, Lladró, and Royal Doulton; French perfumes bottled and packaged in France; Scottish cashmeres and tartans; Irish linens and English woolens.

Native handicrafts are found everywhere in The Bahamas: in the great sprawling Strawmarkets in Nassau and Freeport, along the roadsides, on the grounds of the grand hotels, and beneath the shade of old silk-cotton trees in dozens of tiny villages in the Family Islands. Most famous of the Bahamian handicrafts is strawwork, which is painstakingly woven by hand from palm fronds and shaped into hundreds of different items from straw hats of every shape and size, to purses and totes, placemats and floor mats, picnic baskets and wall hangings, dolls and toy animals. All are gaily decorated with brilliant raffia flowers and figures, seashells, and bits of calico. Other handcrafted items found in the strawmarkets are wood and coconut carvings, polished seashells, and jewelry made from coconut shell, seed pods, berries, seashells, and shark's teeth. There are also delightful island fashions, with men's shirts and ladies' skirts of cool cotton in bold tropical designs and primitive African patterns. Many Bay Street stores and shops in the International Bazaar also feature native handicrafts, such as exquisite jewelry crafted from tortoise-, conch-, and whelk shells, pink and the rare black coral; as well as original island fashions and fabrics such as Androsia, hand-batiked cottons in gay colors from the island of Andros; and Bahama hand prints, silk-screened cotton blends in delightful Bahamian patterns and prints, which are made in Nassau.

Bargaining is a way of life in the strawmarkets of The Bahamas. The straw workers enjoy it nearly as much as the visitors, and they rarely, if ever, expect to receive the first price quoted for their wares. Offer half and then negotiate the rest. Don't try to bargain with the merchants and sales staff of the elegant and sophisticated shops along Bay Street and in the International Bazaar, however, as their prices are fixed.

Gourmet Dining and Conch Cuisine

In Nassau and Freeport, there is a nearly endless variety of dining options, from elegant gourmet dining rooms in the luxury hotels and posh restaurants in historic mansions, to fast-food franchises like Kentucky Fried Chicken, Tony Roma's Ribs, and MacDonald's. The cuisine is just as varied, from Caribbean to Continental, with choices ranging from Japanese Kobe Steak to homemade Italian Pastas; Polynesian delights to English pub food like Steak and Kidney Pie; from French Haute Cuisine to American Rib Roast, and just about everything in between. Most food served in American and Continental-style restaurants tends to be rather expensive as everything from fresh vegetables to steak is imported to this island nation. However, there is a lower-priced alternative, which Bahamians have enjoyed for generations, and visitors have applauded for years—*going native*.

Excellent native restaurants are abundant in Nassau and Freeport, and in nearly every small village and settlement in the Family Islands. They are mostly Bahamian-owned and Bahamian-run family establishments, simple and unpretentious in decor, neat, and serving good down-home Bahamian cooking at reasonable rates. Much of the food served is raised locally and bought fresh daily at the farm markets and fishermen's wharfs, and Bahamian cooks work magic with simple ingredients from the land and the sea.

Here are some favorite island dishes to try; some are served everywhere, even at exclusive restaurants, while others can be found only by "going native."

Conch, pronounced "konk," is the muscular meat of the beautiful pink conch shell found everywhere in The Bahamas. It is a staple of the Bahamian diet, may not be exported, and is served many ways. Most popular are Conch Salad, chopped raw and marinated in lime juice and spices (similar to Seviche); Scorched Conch, fresh and raw, it is scored, sprinkled with lime juice and hot pepper sauce; Conch Chowder, diced with potatoes, vegetables, tomatoes, and spices, and simmered into a thick soup; Conch-Burger, ground up, formed into a patty, fried, and served on a bun like a hamburger; pounded flat, and fried or steamed, called Fractured Conch and Steam Conch; and, perhaps most popular of all, Conch Fritters, diced and combined with flour and eggs, deep-fried into crispy, chewy, bite-sized hors d'oeuvres.

Grouper, is a local fish that abounds in all Bahamian waters. It is firm and mild-tasting, with few bones, and is cooked in many different ways. It is served batter-dipped and deep-fried as grouper fingers; baked, broiled, or fried as grouper steaks or cutlets; and cooked with potatoes and onions in a hearty, spicy stew called Boil Fish, a favorite Bahamian breakfast treat, served with hot johnnycake (delicious), and hominy grits. Another favorite is Stew Fish, grouper steamed in a browned flour gravy with spices.

Peas 'n Rice replaces potatoes in Bahamian cuisine, and is served with everything. It is a tasty blend of white rice and chick-peas or pigeon-peas, with tomatoes, onions, and spices, plus a touch of salt pork or bacon.

Bahamian Lobster is the spiny, clawless lobster or crayfish, with tender, delicious tail meat (similar to South African Rock Lobster Tails). It is served boiled or broiled with drawn butter, in popular recipes such as lobster Newburgh or cream soups, and chilled in lobster salad, which is often stuffed in a melon or avocado half.

Many varieties of *turtle* thrive in Bahamian waters, and the meat is used for turtle soup, patés, stews, and steaks. Occasionally, you can still find a restaurant that will cook Turtle Pie (to order only, as it takes hours), which is a whole turtle baked in the shell with a marvelous, spicy stuffing.

Two varieties of *crab* are native to The Bahamas: the saltwater Stone Crab and the land-dwelling Blue Crab. Stone Crabs have large, succulent claws (when caught, only one claw is removed and the crab returned to the sea where he grows another one!), which are delicious boiled and served hot with drawn butter, or chilled and served with a creamy mustard sauce. Land Crabs are served almost exclusively in native restaurants, usually diced and mixed with a tasty stuffing, returned to the shell, and baked. One of the most famous dishes is Crab 'n Rice, where crab is boiled with rice, tomatoes, and onions.

Desserts. Bahamians have a special way with the fresh fruits which grow abundantly on their islands, using them in cakes, pies, puddings, and ice cream. Look for a few of these delights in native restaurants: Guava Duff, Sweet Potato Pie, Coconut Souffle or Mango Souffle, Banana Fritters, Dilly Bavarois, Pineapple Gumbo, Yam Bread, Carrot Cake, Rum and Raisin or Soursop Ice Cream.

Beverages in The Bahamas cover all popular international brews and vintages, and some have a special Bahamian flair. To begin with, water is potable everywhere in The Bahamas, although it does have a distinctive, slightly salty taste. If you prefer bottled water, it is readily available in most hotels and restaurants on all islands. Although Bahamians prefer tea, the American-style coffee served is good and strong, and European espresso is served in many restaurants. Soft drinks include all international favorites in bottles and cans, plus a Bahamian specialty, "Goombay Punch," a carbonated soda with a pineapple flavor. As virtually all liquor, except rum, is imported with relatively high duty paid, cocktails, beer, and wine tend to be expensive everywhere in the islands in lounges and restaurants. However, excellent buys are available in liquor stores on imported liquors and liqueurs. Rum, which is distilled on Grand Bahama (coconut rum), Eleuthera (pineapple rum), and in Nassau (all Bacardi products), is generally the best buy whether purchased by the bottle in a liquor store or in a drink at a restaurant or lounge. Bahamians do wonders with rum—here are some island specialties: *Bahama Mama,* orange juice, creme de cacao (or coconut rum), and light rum; *Goombay Smash,* pineapple juice, coconut rum, sugar, dash of lemon, and Galliano; *Bahamas Sunrise,* half champagne and half fresh-squeezed orange juice; *Yellow Bird,* banana liqueur, orange juice, Triple Sec, Galliano, and light rum; and *Nassau Royale,* an excellent coconut-rum liqueur, made by Bacardi, and used as an after-dinner drink, as flambé over fruit or ice cream, and mixed with hot black coffee with a dollop of whipped cream for "Bahamian Coffee" (superb!). Other fruity, tropical favorites include Planter's Punch, Banana Daiquiri, Cocoloco, Piña Colada, Rum Punch, and dozens more.

The Bahamas' Beat: Goombay and Junkanoo

Goombay is The Bahamas' beat, primitive, pulsating, and sensuous, almost pure rhythm with virtually no melody. Its cultural roots go deep into an African past, and its origins can be traced to the dance, music, and mask traditions of West Africa and to the ancient harvest festivals celebrated by tribes of the Ivory and Gold Coasts. It was imported to Bermuda, The Bahamas, and the Caribbean with slavery. It is called "Gombey" in Bermuda and "Gombay" in Jamaica, where it is still heard, but it seems to have survived and thrived in its purest and most primitive form in The Bahamas.

The word "goombay" derives from the Bantu language, and means both rhythm and goatskin drum. For centuries, the universal instrument in The Bahamas has been the goatskin drum, which is handcrafted from wooden kegs or steel cans, and covered with taut goatskin or sheepskin hides. Small fires are built inside the drum to shrink the leather to maximum tautness, essential for achieving the basic goombay beat. Today, the goombay drums are still made in the age-old, traditional way throughout The Bahamas.

The goombay beat is heard in its most basic form in the music and dance that accompany the annual Junkanoo masquerades, which are held on the day after Christmas, New Year's Day, and during the Goombay Summer Festival from June through September each year. The Junkanoo parades and the goombay beat of the goatskin drum have been inextricably linked throughout Bahamian history, with written records and descriptions going back nearly two centuries. The costumed Junkanoo paraders dance a slow, rhythmic shuffle, which Bahamians call "rushin," accompanied by the constant, pulsating beat of the goatskin drums, punctuated with the clank of cowbells; the shrill of tin whistles; the blare of brass bugles; the shaking of poinciana pods, which sound like maracas; and the clicking of lignum vitae sticks imitating castanets.

Year-round, the goombay beat is heard wherever Bahamians gather: beach parties, country fairs, street dances, hotel galas, and, especially, native nightclubs, where the goatskin drums are backed up with guitars. Much of The Bahamas' contemporary music, composed by young Bahamian musicians, features the unmistakable goombay beat as well.

Bahamian music and dance have also been deeply influenced by other West Indian rhythms, such as Jamaica's reggae, Martinique's merengue, Trinidad's calypso, and Latin bongo and conga drummers. Favorites are ring dances and jump-in dances, accompanied by Bahamian-calypso folk songs that tell of unrequited love and poke good-natured fun at Bahamian family life. (Ask almost any balladeer to sing "Love, Love Alone," which tells the story of the King of England's romance, his abdication, and his marriage to Wallis Simpson, or the delightful "Shame and Scandal in The Family.") In recent years, the biggest impact on Bahamian music and dance have been American influences, with everything from folk to rock, rhythm and blues, country western, and disco heard everywhere in The Bahamas—but almost always flavored a bit with the goombay beat.

NEW PROVIDENCE ISLAND

Nassau, Cable Beach, and Paradise Island

New Providence Island is best known for the busy, bustling city of Nassau, hub of the island nation, and the crossroads of The Bahamas. Its modern jet-age airport is served daily by a dozen international airlines, and its sheltered deep-water harbor is one of the world's most famous ports of call, hosting more than twenty sleek luxury liners weekly, from Florida, New York, and Europe. Its glittering resorts and casinos along Cable Beach and on Paradise Island attract more than a million and a quarter visitors each year—making Nassau the single most popular destination in all of The Bahamas and the Caribbean.

Although it is one of the smallest islands in the archipelago, some 65 percent of the Bahamian population live on New Providence. Nassau boasts over 135,500 residents, out of an all-Bahamas population of around 225,000.

The 320-year-old capital city was originally named Charles Town, after King Charles I. In 1695, it was renamed Nassau, in honor of King William III, who had been Prince of Orange-Nassau before ascending the English throne. Its colorful history includes Spanish invasions and pirates bold, who used Nassau as their headquarters during raids along the Spanish Main. And it includes old forts seized and occupied by the brave new American navy in 1776, when the Americans won a comic-opera victory without firing a shot. They occupied Nassau for two weeks before sailing home in triumph.

The cultural and ethnic heritage of old Nassau includes southern charm imported by British loyalists from the Carolinas reflected in its architecture, blended with the African tribal traditions of freed slaves, and a bawdy history of blockade-running during the Civil War and rum-running in the Roaring Twenties era of Prohibition. But over it all, there is a subtle layer of civility and sophistication, derived from three centuries of British rule and law.

There are reminders of the British heritage everywhere in Nassau. Court justices still sport scarlet robes and bottom wigs, the police wear colonial garb with starched white jackets, red-striped navy trousers, and tropical pith helmets, traffic is strictly on the left—British-style—and the language is distinctly English, though softened by an easy island-calypso drawl. However, there is much of the Caribbean's charm in old Nassau as well. The colorful harborside market—with out-island

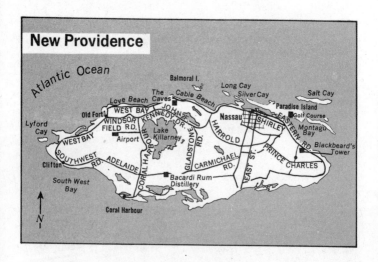

sloops bringing catches of fish and conch, open-air tropical fruit and exotic vegetable stalls, street hawkers vending guava juice and soursop ice cream, and straw ladies weaving their magic on hats and baskets— brings to sophisticated Nassau the flavor of the Caribbean, the essence of the West Indies—side by side with the glamor and glitter of international resorts and Continental casinos.

Exploring Nassau

The centuries-old city of Nassau lies on a sun-splashed hillside overlooking the bustling harbor and busy Bay Street. Its narrow side streets climb the gentle slope and wander along the crest of the hill for less than a mile in either direction, making the most historic sections of the city easy to explore. Along the way, you'll find many old colonial sites reminiscent of prerevolutionary America. There are colonnaded government buildings, reminders of the old South; an unusual octagonal-shaped library that once was Nassau's "gaol" (jail); centuries-old churches; an ancient fort; and many charming historic mansions surrounded by walled tropical gardens. Government House, on the hilltop, is the finest example of Bahamian-British, Colonial-American–influenced architecture. Its graceful columns and broad, circular drive could be in Virginia or the Carolinas, but its pastel pink color and distinctive quoin corners painted white are typically Bahamian. Quoins are a common architectural embellishment, found on many old Bahamian homes and public buildings. For another unique old-Bahamas architectural touch, look for the "Bahama Shutters," wooden louvers that completely enclose large upper and lower verandas on many well-preserved old mansions and are designed to keep out the tropical sun and encourage the tropical breezes.

Old Nassau

If you have two or three hours to spend, and a pair of comfortable shoes, take a walking tour of old Nassau. (*Caution:* Many of the narrow streets have no sidewalks, and traffic may move in both directions. Remember that traffic moves on the left in The Bahamas, and that whenever possible you should walk facing the flow.)

To begin your tour, hop in a taxi, the hotel courtesy bus, or the public jitney service, and head for the Strawmarket on Bay Street. Leave your rental car or scooter behind, because traffic is heavy and parking is very difficult in downtown Nassau.

The Strawmarket, sprawled through the arched, open-air Market Plaza on Bay Street, is lively from early morning till evening, seven days a week. Stroll for a while among the hundreds of stalls and bargain with the straw ladies for a hat and perhaps a woven bag for toting home

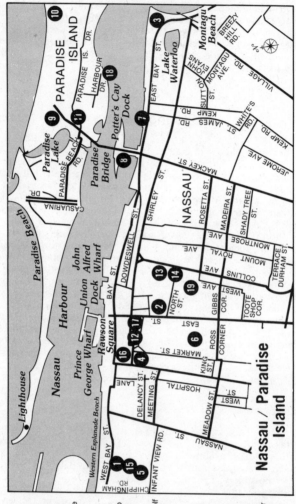

Nassau / Paradise Island

Points of Interest

1) Fort Charlotte
2) Fort Fincastle
3) Fort Montagu
4) Government House
5) Nassau Botanic Gardens
6) Nassau Public Library
7) Nassau Yacht Club
8) Out Island Market
9) Paradise Island Casino
10) Paradise Island Golf Club
11) Paradise Island Shopping Center
12) Parliament Square
13) Princess Margaret Hospital
14) Queen's Staircase
15) Seafloor Aquarium
16) Strawmarket
17) Tourist Information
18) Versailles Gardens and French Cloister
19) Water Tower

other treasures. Exit the Strawmarket on the harborside, and stroll eastward along Woodes Rogers Walk for a fine view of the busy harbor and cruise ship wharf.

At Rawson Square cut across the causeway to Prince George Wharf, where the great white ocean liners tie up. Along the way, you'll see the lively seagoing life of old Nassau, a picturesque mix of small island sloops, interisland freighters crowded with cargo and produce, glass-bottom tour boats, ocean-going yachts and sailing schooners, and the Bahamian "bum boats," which ply back and forth across the harbor to Paradise Island every fifteen or twenty minutes. Here, you will also find a Ministry of Tourism Information Centre well-stocked with booklets, brochures, maps, and expert advice from Bahamahosts, and if it is Goombay Summer time in The Bahamas, you can join a "Goombay Guided Walking tour," conducted by well-trained guides.

To proceed on your own, cross back over the causeway to Rawson Square, the heart of old Nassau. Here you'll find shady benches and a dolphin fountain, a handsome bust of Sir Milo Butler, first Bahamian governor-general of The Bahamas, and a colorful signpost, with dozens of bright signs pointing the direction to every island in The Bahamas. You'll find the straw-hatted surrey horses, their quaint fringe-top carriages, and their friendly drivers eager to carry you off on a ride through the old city and past some of the nearby historic sites. Across from the surrey ranks, you'll find a row of luxurious, air-conditioned limousines, Nassau's fleet of tour cars. If you plan a guided tour of the island, this might be a good time to negotiate the rate and the date with the drivers.

Directly across Bay Street from Rawson Square is Parliament Square, a cluster of pink, colonnaded, and quoined government buildings, dating from the early 1800s and patterned after the southern colonial architecture of New Bern, early capital of North Carolina. In the center of the Square is a statue of the young Queen Victoria on her throne, which was dedicated after her death in 1901. The statue is flanked by a pair of old cannon, and to the right is The Bahamas House of Assembly. Each session of the House is opened with great pomp and pageantry, in the British tradition, then settles down to day-to-day sittings that are sometimes raucous, often lively, and always interesting. Sessions are open to the public, but the chamber is small, and arrangements to attend must be made ahead of time through the Clerk of the House. Behind the statue of Queen Victoria is the Senate Chamber.

To the left of Parliament Square is a narrow street called Bank Lane, but still known by its earlier name, "Gaol Alley," to many Bahamians and antiquarians. Here you'll find the Central Police Station and Rose-lawn, a delightful restaurant. If you're ready for lunch try it or The Terrace Café on Parliament Street, which runs along the right side of Parliament Square. Between Gaol Alley and Parliament Street, there are more interesting and historic government buildings—the old Treasury and the Supreme Court, overlooking the Garden of Remembrance and the Cenotaph, which honors Bahamian war dead from both world wars. At the top of the square, facing Shirley Street, you'll find a unique old octagonal building, once the "gaol" of Gaol Alley and now the Nassau Public Library.

Built in 1799, the structure served as a jail until 1879, when it was converted to the Nassau Public Library. It is open most days, and you can have a quiet look around at the small prison cells, which are now lined with books, and examine its excellent collection of historic prints and old colonial documents. Across the street from the library are the remains of the Royal Victoria Hotel and Gardens. The hotel, the first ever built in The Bahamas, opened in 1860, just at the outbreak of the Civil War in the United States. It became the headquarters for the colorful blockade runners, Confederate officers and English textile tycoons, who traded guns for cotton. The charming old hotel stands abandoned and in disrepair, after welcoming guests for more than a century until 1971. However, the lovely old gardens are still worth a stroll, with a botanical wonderland of more than three-hundred varieties of tropical plants, palms, and a beautiful centuries-old spreading ficus tree.

After leaving the Royal Victoria Gardens, turn east and continue along Shirley Street. As you pass East Street, you might drop down toward the harbor for a look at Cascadilla, at Millar's Court, a lovely house set in a tropical garden. It was the residence of the late Sir Harold Christie, one of The Bahamas' most prominent citizens. Today it houses the H.G. Christie Real Estate firm. Head back to Shirley Street and continue east. Just beyond East Street, you'll see another lovely old Bahamian mansion with broad verandas and Bahama shutters, set in beautiful grounds: Addington House. Built in the 1880s, it is now the home of the Right Reverend Bishop Michael Eldon, the first Bahamian ever to be named the Anglican Bishop of The Bahamas.

Continue along Shirley Street to Elizabeth Avenue and the Queen's Staircase, a famous Nassau landmark. Its 66 steps, hewn from the coral limestone cliff by slaves back in 1793, were designed to provide a direct route from the town to Fort Fincastle at the top of the hill. The staircase was named more than a hundred years later, in honor of the 66 years of Queen Victoria's reign. Climb the staircase to reach Fort Fincastle, another historic Nassau landmark. The fort, shaped like the bow of a ship, was built in the early 1790s by the loyalist Governor of The Bahamas, the Earl of Dunmore. He named the fort for one of his former titles, Viscount Fincastle. The fort never saw a shot fired in anger, but served as a fine lookout and signal tower, guarding Nassau's harbor. The fort is in reasonable repair, and can be explored—there is a fine view over the city and the harbor. But for a really spectacular panoramic view of the whole island of New Providence, climb the nearby Water Tower. (If you are not quite up to the steep, winding stairs, for 50 cents you can take an elevator to the top—there's no charge for the view.) The great white tower rises 126 feet, more than 200 feet above sea level, and is the highest point on the island.

From the grounds of the fort, follow a narrow lane that will take you back to East Street, where you'll find Mortimer's Candy Kitchen and the Best-Ever Candy Company, the oldest candy factory in The Bahamas. They are famous for hot peppermint candies and peppermint balls, Bahamian sesame-seed candy called "benny cakes," coconut creams and coconut chews, home-made fudge, and pink popcorn. Follow East Street south for a short ways to reach East Hill Street, and turn west to Nassau's new Post Office building, a good place to stop if you collect unusual stamps—The Bahamas are known for exceptionally beautiful ones, and the Post Office's Philatelic Bureau has a wide selection, along with first-day covers and other collectibles.

Across from the Post Office, at the top of Parliament Street, there is another notable Bahamian mansion, Jacaranda, built in the 1840s. It is a private home, but you can view it through its graceful wrought-iron entrance gates. Continue down Parliament Street for a block or so towards the harbor to Green Shutters, a very old and charming Bahamian house converted into a famous pub. Dine indoors or out, on anything from "bangers 'n mash" to Bahamian conch chowder. Return to East Hill Street after your pause to refresh, and continue west.

Along East Hill Street, you'll pass two historic mansions on your left. The first is the East Hill Club, a pink-and-white Georgian colonial built in the 1840s. Once the private winter home of Lord Beaverbrook, it is now a small inn. The second is Glenwood, an impressive private home said to have been built in the 1880s. Opposite Glenwood is Bank House, a fine old house built in the mid-1800s by Edwin Charles Moseley, founder and publisher of *The Nassau Guardian*.

Just beyond these mansions, on the north side of the street, you will find a broad flight of stairs, which will bring you down to Prince Street (actually the westward extension of Shirley Street, and sometimes called Duke Street). Here you will find two of Nassau's most historic churches, St. Andrew's Kirk, Presbyterian, built in 1810, and Trinity Methodist, built in 1866. They are open weekdays during the day for a quiet pause and a look around. Nearby is the New Bahamas Central Bank. Its cornerstone was laid by Prince Charles in 1973 during Independence ceremonies and it was officially opened in 1975 by Queen Elizabeth II on one of her visits to Nassau.

Continue west along Prince Street. As you pass Market Street, look up the hill for a good view of Gregory Arch, the graceful, picturesque entrance to Grant's Town. Known as the "over-the-hill" section of Nassau, Grant's Town was laid out in the 1820s by Governor Lewis Grant as a settlement for freed slaves. The arch was named for John Gregory, governor of The Bahamas from 1849 to 1854.

Proceeding west along Prince Street, you will arrive at historic Government House, the gracious mansion which since 1801 has been the official residence of the Royal Governors of The Bahamas. Among the most famous occupants were the ex-King of England, H.R.H. the Duke of Windsor, and his American bride, Wallis Warfield Simpson, who presided over the colony from 1940 to 1945. Today, the mansion is occupied by Governor General Sir Gerald Cash and Lady Cash. Entrance from Prince Street is up a broad staircase with an ancient cannon at its base and an impressive 12-foot-tall statue of Christopher Columbus on the midpoint landing. The statue commemorates Columbus's discovery of The Bahamas in 1492, when he made his first landfall in the New World at the tiny island of Guanahani in the southeastern Bahamas and renamed it San Salvador. As a private residence, Government House is rarely open to the public except during Goombay Summer celebrations, when a monthly "Government House Tea Party" is held on Friday afternoons at 4 P.M. in the tropical gardens. Summer is also the time when various fetes and fairs are held on the grounds of Government House; most are well publicized on local television and radio, in the newspapers, and on posters and flyers in the hotels.

There is pomp and pageantry year-round at the great circular entranceway to Government House, with the colorful Changing of the Guard ceremony scheduled fortnightly on alternate Saturdays at 10 A.M. The famous Royal Bahamas Police Force Band puts on a fine performance, with music and marching in traditional British colonial precision, style, and ceremony. Their uniforms are superb—crisp white tunics, navy trousers with a red stripe, white tropical pith helmets—and the drummers are decked out in leopardskin tabards. And their music—from stirring marches to Bahamian Goombay, from Caribbean Calypso to American pop songs—sounds as good as they look. During Goombay Summer, they bring Bay Street alive with concerts and marching, and each Wednesday from 8 to 9 P.M. they draw great crowds as they perform the traditional "Beat the Retreat."

Back on Prince Street, follow the high Government House wall around the corner to Baillou (pronounced "blue") Road. Here Prince Street becomes West Hill Street and continues westward. Just around the corner on Baillou, you will find the side entrance to Government House. Directly opposite this entrance is another famed landmark, Graycliff, a superb example of Georgian colonial architecture, dating from the mid-1700s. Legend has it that it was built by a Captain Gray, whose privateering vessel was named the *Graywolf,* and its colorful history includes use as an officers' mess by the British West Indian garrison, and a certain notoriety during the rum-running days of Prohibition. Until recently, it was the private winter home of the Earl and Countess of Dudley. Today, the gracious antique-filled mansion is operated as an elegant inn, with a famous gourmet restaurant and well-stocked wine cellar, recognized by the prestigious Relais et Chateaux as the finest in the Caribbean. Its swimming pool was the first built in Nassau, and is still one of the loveliest, surrounded by brilliant tropical flowers and foliage, in a walled garden.

From Graycliff, continue west on West Hill Street. Note the old Bahamian houses on the north side of the street, swathed in wood-louvered Bahama shutters, and more old mansions on the hillside on the south side of the street. Walk along for a block or two until you come to a broad stone staircase on your right, which will lead you down to Queen Street. Queen Street runs for just a block or so, and the large building on your left is the American Embassy. Stop by for information, customs brochures, or just for a look at an interesting painting of *The Landing at New Providence,* which depicts the American navy and marines landing at Nassau in 1776. It usually hangs in the lobby.

At the foot of Queen Street, you'll meet Marlborough Street, and just ahead, stretching along the harbor, you'll see the Sheraton British Colonial, Nassau's oldest resort and one of its most famous. It was built originally in 1899, on the site where Fort Nassau stood from 1696 to 1837. The first wooden structure was destroyed by fire in 1921, and today's huge pink-and-white classical/tropical resort made its debut in winter season 1923. Modernized and up-to-date, it is still one of Nassau's most popular hotels, and is fondly known to Bahamians and generations of visitors as "the B.C."

In front of the British Colonial is a fine statue of Woodes Rogers, who was appointed first Royal Governor of The Bahamas by King George I, in 1718. He routed the pirates who had made Nassau their pillaging headquarters, granting the King's amnesty to all who surrendered and hanging those who refused.

Turn east on Marlborough Street, past Cumberland Street (where Marlborough becomes King Street), to George Street. Here you will find Christ Church Cathedral, built in 1837. The site has been occupied by a church for three-hundred years, according to records dating back to 1684. The simple, lovely old church has been the seat of the Anglican Bishop in The Bahamas since 1861. In that year Queen Victoria issued "Letters of Patent" constituting Christ Church a cathedral and ordained that "The whole town of Nassau henceforth be called The City of Nassau." Stop by for a quiet look around the historic church and lovely churchyard.

Just beyond the cathedral, turn toward the harbor on Market Street. On the west side of the street you will see Balcony House, a small but historic Bahamian home dating from the 1790s. The second-floor balcony of the wooden house hangs over the street, and steps lead directly from the pavement to its front door. Follow Market Street for just a few steps farther, and you'll be back on Bay Street. Just ahead, you will see The Bahamas Electricity Corporation, an unimposing two-story green building. The top floor was added at the turn of this century, but if you look carefully at the ground floor, you can see bricked-over arches that once opened onto a roofed, open-air pavilion. For more than half a century, from 1769 until Emancipation, this was Vendue House, Nassau's notorious slave market, where men, women, and children were put on the auction block along with pigs and cattle, coconuts, and fish. Just a few doors away, you'll find yourself back at the busy, bustling, colorful Strawmarket, where your walking tour began.

Outside Nassau

Outside of the old city of Nassau, to the west and the east of the downtown center, there are several interesting sights to see and areas to explore. These are most easily reached by rental car or motorscooter, taxi tour, or in one of Nassau's luxurious air-conditioned limousine tour cars. If you are on your own, be sure to pick up one or two copies of the *Bahamas Trailblazer Map,* offered free of charge at most hotel front desks or tour desks. You will find two copies helpful, as there are detailed maps of the city environs and of the island of New Providence on opposite sides. Wear comfortable clothes for exploring, and sturdy walking shoes or sneakers. Be sure to bring your camera and pack a tote with suntan lotion, sunglasses, swimsuits, and towels, in case you are tempted to try the warm, crystalline waters lapping the endless beaches that fringe the island. Plan an early start, as the full tour will take most of a day.

Begin at the grounds of old Fort Charlotte, located on West Bay Street at Chippingham Road. The massive fort is located at the top of the hill, commanding a fine view over the water and Arawak Cay, a small man-made island that holds huge storage tanks for fresh water barged in from Andros Island to serve Nassau during periodic water shortages. There is plenty of parking on the grounds of the fort, and you can easily walk to other nearby attractions such as the Ardastra Gardens, Nassau Botanic Gardens, and Seafloor Aquarium.

Fort Charlotte is Nassau's largest and best-preserved fortification, built by Lord Dunmore between 1787 and 1794. He named it in honor of King George III's Queen Charlotte. The fort was dubbed "Dunmore's Folly" because of the staggering costs involved in building it. It cost more than £32,000—eight times more than originally planned. Yet, in all of its nearly two-hundred-year history, the fort has never fired a shot in anger. Wander through the grounds of the fort, see its cannons, cross its waterless moat, and walk along its ramparts. Local guides conduct tours and offer commentary on the history of the fort, and will guide you through the fort and its underground dungeons. There is no charge, but tips are accepted and expected.

The Nassau Botanic Gardens, located directly behind Fort Charlotte, are 18 acres of lovely tropical gardens with beautiful flowering trees, shrubs, and exotic tropical plants. Many trails wander through the gardens, delightful for strolling and identifying the hundreds of species along the way. There are two freshwater ponds with lilies and water plants, along with many varieties of colorful tropical fish. Along the way, you'll also find a small cactus garden with many rare plants, leading to a charming grotto made of local quarry stones and roofed over with conch shells. On the grounds there is an enclosed playground for children, and many shady spots for relaxing.

Ardastra Gardens, located west of the Nassau Botanic Gardens on Chippingham Road, are known to generations of Nassau visitors for the famed "marching flamingos." The lovely gardens also include five acres of tropical greenery and flowering shrubs, a fine aviary of unusual and rare tropical birds, and many species of animals which call the gardens home. Highlight of the garden tour is a unique attraction which has delighted visitors for decades—the parading of a whole flock of brilliant pink flamingos, national bird of The Bahamas. Drillmaster Joseph Lexion barks commands to his colorful long-legged charges; they respond with amazing discipline and seem to enjoy it as much as their trainer, who accompanies the show with a running commentary and amusing if occasionally bizarre lectures.

Seafloor Aquarium is a wonderful showcase of underwater life located just beyond the Nassau Botanic Gardens, where Chippingham Road becomes Columbus Avenue. Here you will find huge tanks that hold a vast variety of tropical sea life, including sharks, manta rays, giant turtles, living coral reefs, and the exotic fish that inhabit them. Every two hours a special show is put on, with delightful performing dolphins and trained sea lions. On the grounds, there is a small factory that makes beautiful conch-shell, coral, and tortoise-shell jewelry, and a gift shop that sells a broad selection of these typical Bahamian souvenirs.

Leaving the area of Fort Charlotte, return along Chippingham Road to West Bay Street and turn right toward the old city of Nassau. On your right you will pass Clifton Park, at the foot of Fort Charlotte. Here there are several sports fields, spectator stands, and a large review field. Running along on your left is the beautiful Western Esplanade Beach, also known as Lighthouse Beach for the stunning view across the harbor to the great Nassau Light at the tip of Paradise Island, and **Coral World,** Nassau's newest attraction at Silver Cay, an exciting marine theme park, offering an underwater observatory where visitors can observe a living coral reef and underwater creatures, without getting wet.

As you approach downtown, at the Sheraton British Colonial Hotel, West Bay Street becomes Bay Street, one-way in the opposite direction. Traffic is routed up Blue Hill Road, on your right, to Shirley Street. This street runs parallel to Bay Street, with one-way traffic traveling eastward through town. (If you have skipped the walking tour of Old Nassau you may want to read that section now as this drive will take you past many of the "not to be missed" sights detailed there, as you travel eastward along Shirley Street.)

Just a block or two before you reach the main traffic intersection at Mackey Street (with a traffic light), look for two small lanes on your left. These are Lover's Lane and Church Street, which run on either side of St. Matthew's Anglican Church, the oldest and most historic church in The Bahamas. Turn down either lane to find a convenient parking spot because you will want to take some time to explore the lovely old church and ancient cemetery.

St. Matthew's Church, built between 1800 and 1804, was designed by a transplanted American loyalist, Joseph Eve. The church is a well-preserved example of the neoclassic forms and gothic proportions popular during the period. Within the same block on Shirley Street are two other sights of interest. There is the small, beautifully maintained Jewish cemetery surrounded by an ornamental iron fence—it is the only Jewish cemetery in The Bahamas. On the opposite side of the street is the Sacred Heart Roman Catholic Church. On the next block, on the right side of Shirley Street, is another of Nassau's landmark churches, surrounded by a cemetery—Ebeneezer Methodist Church, built in 1840 of wood and rebuilt of native stone in 1848.

If your morning of exploring ancient forts, tropical gardens, and old churches has built up your appetite, try a hearty Bahamian lunch at one of the excellent native restaurants nearby. Marietta's and The Fish Net are particularly recommended.

If you would like to do a bit of shopping after lunch, drop into Bahamas Hand Prints at Mackey and Shirley streets. Here you will find an interesting workshop producing delightful handcrafted silkscreened fabrics and fashions in lovely island prints. Another famous Nassau shop in the area, just half a mile south on Mackey Street, is the Nassau Art Gallery, which offers an excellent selection of Bahamian art works, including oils, watercolors, and prints. Also nearby, across the street from St. Matthew's, is Maura's Lumber, an old-fashioned general store that has served Bahamians for generations. Here you will find hardware and lumber, but also a wonderful collection of toys and some surprising bargains in fine European china and crystal. A block or two away, on East Bay Street, there's a marvelous old gingerbread house with an excellent art gallery. It is The Temple Gallery, owned by Brent Malone, one of the most outstanding artists in The Bahamas. Offerings include works by Malone and other Bahamian artists, with frequent art shows and exhibitions. Visitors are welcome.

Follow Mackey Street to Bay Street and the harbor. They meet at the foot of the Paradise Island Bridge. Cross to the foot of the bridge, and turn onto the narrow lane that runs under the bridge to Potter's Cay, one of the most picturesque spots on the island. Here are the open-air fruit-and-vegetable market and the docks for the Family Island sloops that bring their fresh fish and wares to market. Almost any time of day the tiny cay is alive with people and activity. Fishermen hawk their wares from the decks of their colorful out-island sloops—one of the last wind-powered commercial fishing fleets in the world. Women and children set up stalls and sell dozens of varieties of exotic fruits and vegetables. Virtually everyone in Nassau stops by this native marketplace at least once or twice a week to shop, so don't be surprised to see everything from chauffeur-driven limousines to pickup trucks—it's a kaleidoscope of everyday Bahamian life.

Look for the great mounds of conch shells that form artificial islands in the harbor and the out-island freighters and government mailboats with decks loaded with everything from Volkswagens and refrigerators to crates of live chickens, or perhaps a few goats, along with the passengers. If you are considering an adventurous mailboat trip to one of the Family Islands, drop by the Dock Master's Office here on Potter's Cay—he'll be able to give you sailing dates and times.

Potter's Cay is a photographer's delight, but some Bahamians, like other people around the world, may object to being photographed. It's a good idea to ask politely and respect their wishes. Generally you will find the people genial, warmly welcoming, glad to chat for a while, and proud to exhibit their wares. Don't leave without sampling a few—look for Pearline, who makes delicious, crispy conch fritters; pick up a tiny Eleutheran pineapple, delicately flavored and delightful—most vendors will slice it for you, so you can eat it while strolling; or pick out a bagful of exotic fruits like sugar apples, the tiny finger bananas, mangos, and a papaya or two to eat at leisure back at your hotel.

Paradise Island

For a complete change of pace, go "over the bridge" to Paradise, one of the most glittering international resort and casino centers in this part of the world. The toll over the bridge is $2 per car or scooter, 25 cents for walkers. On Paradise Island, the hotels are widely spaced, set amid acres of landscaped gardens, and overlook a half-mile or so of broad ocean beach. Linking the hotels are well-paved roads winding through tropical forests, shady riding trails, biking, hiking, and jogging paths.

As you cross the bridge, you will find yourself on Casino Drive, leading directly to the Paradise Island Resort and Casino, which includes the Britannia Towers and Paradise Towers, and, nearby, the Sheraton Grand Hotel. Turn right at the first intersection, and bear left to Paradise Island Drive, which will take you to the Paradise Island Shopping Village, where there are delightful stores and branches of some exclusive Bay Street shops, all in a compact little shopping mall. Continue along the drive until you reach the parking area for the Versailles Gardens, one of the loveliest spots on the island.

The Versailles Gardens and French Cloister stretch across the island from harborside to oceanside. On a rise overlooking the harbor are the lovely French cloisters, once a monastery in Montrejau, France, built in the fourteenth century. The classic stone cloisters were originally purchased by William Randolph Hearst in the 1920s, dismantled and shipped to California, and stored for decades. Huntington Hartford, heir to the A & P fortune, who first developed Hog Island and renamed it Paradise, purchased the mass of stones in the 1960s and had the cloisters reconstructed as a showcase for his resort island. The views from the rise are lovely across the harbor to old Nassau, and the spot is a favorite for weddings. Wander through the lovely gardens and admire the plants and flowers, as well as a highly eclectic collection of statuary and fountains.

Exit the gardens near the famous Ocean Club on the ocean side of the island. The main clubhouse was once Huntington Hartford's private home. Drop in and make reservations for dinner at the Courtyard Terrace, one of the most romantic settings in the islands. There are many diversions on Paradise Island—the Ocean Club has fine tennis courts and just beyond the Versailles Gardens lies the noted Paradise Island Golf Course. Nearby, you can rent horses for an hour or two for a canter along the beach or through the shady island trails. Or take a quiet stroll along the long lovely beach, which runs for more than a mile in either direction.

If you'd prefer to check out the casino on your tour of Paradise, pick up your car and retrace your route to Casino Drive and the world-famous Paradise Island Casino. In the afternoons the casino is less formal and considerably less crowded, so if you are not too casually dressed (shirtless, barefoot, or otherwise scantily covered sightseers are not welcomed), try your luck at the slot machines, roulette wheels, or blackjack tables. Even if flirting with Lady Luck is not your style, stroll through the shopping arcades and the handsome casino—stop long enough to watch some of the action. If you've planned to attend the lavish casino show, whose stage-girl revue rivals the best of Paris or Las Vegas, now is a good time to make your reservations.

Walk through the nicely landscaped grounds of the resort. Be sure to stop at the narrow wooden bridge across the Paradise Lagoon. Here you'll find a troupe of trained porpoises who love to show off for visitors. Check out the feeding times, when they put on an especially delightful show. Or rent a paddle boat for an hour and pedal your way around the lagoon. If you'd like to sample one of the most beautiful beaches in the world, head back to your car and drive toward the Paradise Island Bridge. At the roundabout (traffic circle) turn to the right, toward the western end of the island, along Paradise Beach Road, which winds through shady pine and palmetto forests.

Along the way, you'll cross the Lagoon and see Club Land 'Or on the right, an attractive apartment resort and time-sharing complex. A little farther along, on your left, is the entrance to Chalk's seaplane base. If you've never seen the classic old seaplanes take off and land in the water, stop in at Chalk's. The airline operates more than a dozen flights a day to Miami, Fort Lauderdale, Palm Beach, and Bimini.

Continuing westward along Paradise Beach Road, turn right at Casuarina Drive to the Paradise Beach Inn. Turn left on the lane that leads to the Paradise Beach Pavillion. This is the entryway to Paradise Beach, one of the most beautiful crescent-shaped strips of white sand in all of the islands—a favorite of visitors to Nassau since the 1890s. There is a $3 entry fee, which includes towels, changing rooms, lockers, and showers, along with a welcoming cocktail for adults. Dotting the beach are "Chickees," palm-thatched umbrellas that provide shelter from the sun between dips in the warm, gin-clear sea. If you've arrived at sunset, the westward view is unforgettable. Enjoy a delicious, informal dining treat at the Paradise Beach Pavillion.

Exploring New Providence

Plan to spend at least five or six hours driving around the island. Although New Providence is just 22 miles long and 7 miles wide, there are several stops you may want to make along the way.

East of Nassau: Fort Montagu and Blackbeard's Tower

From the Paradise Island Bridge, drive eastward along East Bay Street (two-way traffic). On the harbor side, you will see several marinas, gathering spots for international yachtsmen cruising Bahamian waters. The first marina is Nassau Yacht Haven, directly across the street from one of Nassau's oldest and finest small hotels, the Pilot House. A little farther along are the Bayshore Marina, Brown's Boat Basin, and the Nassau Harbour Club, a small hotel and extensive marina catering to the yachting set. On the right is Waterloo Lodge, a palatial mansion once the home of The Bahamas's first Minister of Tourism, Sir Stafford Sands. The house and gardens overlook a small inland lake known as Lake Waterloo, and the mansion now houses a fine Polynesian restaurant, the Mai Tai, and a swinging new nightspot, the Waterloo Discotheque. Just beyond, located on a spit of land overlooking the harbor, you'll see Fort Montagu.

The diminutive fort overlooks the eastern end of Nassau harbor and is the island's oldest fortification. It was built in 1741 of native limestone. Although the smallest of Nassau's forts, it saw more action than the other two combined, and has the dubious distinction of having been occupied by the American rebels for two weeks during 1776. George Washington ordered the new American fleet of eight small merchant ships to "Proceed to Nassau and possess themselves of His Majesty's powder, artillery and other stores in His forts in New Providence." At daybreak on March 3, 1776, Commodore Ezekial Hopkins and his young first lieutenant, John Paul Jones, captured Fort Montagu without ever firing a shot and ran up America's first official flag. The "war" lasted for two weeks, and the Americans claimed a huge success—they sailed off with everything movable from Nassau's forts.

Today, the little fort is well maintained and easy to explore. The broad public beach that stretches for more than a mile beyond the fort is one of Nassau's most popular meeting places, with a good beach bar selling thick, juicy burgers and frosty beers. Sunday afternoons are lively, with a good "rake and scrape" band, and a large local crowd. It overlooks Montagu Bay, where many of the international yacht regattas and colorful Bahamian workboat races are held annually. The Fort Montagu Beach Hotel, the huge, pink 1920s-vintage hotel along the shore was once one of Nassau's grandest, now unused for more than a decade.

At the great curve of the island beyond Fort Montagu, East Bay Street becomes the Eastern Road, and the area is known as the Montagu Foreshore, site of some of the island's loveliest oceanside mansions. One of the most notable is "The Hermitage," built originally by Lord Dunmore in 1787 as his summer residence, and later rebuilt and expanded in the early 1920s. It is built entirely of Bermuda stone and local hardwoods. It serves as the official residence of the Catholic Bishop of The Bahamas.

Near the intersection of Fox Hill Road and the Eastern Road is a winding trail that leads to the ruins of an old tower on the hillside. This is known as Blackbeard's Tower. Legend has it that it was the lookout for Edward Teach, the notorious pirate known as "Blackbeard," who ruled the motley band of buccaneers that operated from the "Pirate's Republic" of Nassau between the 1690s and 1720s. The old stone ruins are much more likely to be a water tower of the 1890s than a pirate's lookout of the 1690s, but the legend persists, and the view from the top is splendid.

Continuing along the Eastern Road, you'll pass more lovely oceanside mansions and a rather eccentric private home, built as an exact replica of a lighthouse. Off to the right a narrow lane leads to Camperdown, gathering spot for the local "horsey set." If there are any major horse shows or dressage or jumping exhibitions scheduled you will see posters or read about them in the newspapers; you should drop by.

Traveling West: Fox Hill Village, St. Augustine's Monastery

As the Eastern Road curves along the eastern end of the island, it links up with Prince Charles Avenue, which cuts off to the right. Follow Prince Charles Avenue to the first traffic light and you will be in the heart of Fox Hill Village, one of the oldest slave settlements on the island. It was once the vast Sandilands Estate, but after emancipation in 1834 the British divided up the land generously among the freed blacks. The second Tuesday of August each year is Fox Hill Day, a highlight on the Bahamian calendar. It is an old-fashioned country fair, alive with Goombay music, gospel singing, arts-and-crafts booths, and fine down-home cooking. Legend has it that Fox Hill celebrates Emancipation Day (a public holiday on the first Monday of August each year) eight days later, because in 1834 it took more than a week for the news of Emancipation to reach the residents of Fox Hill.

From the village, turn right on Fox Hill Road to Bernard Road, and turn left. Here you will find St. Augustine's Monastery, the home of the Benedectine monks in The Bahamas. The great Romanesque monastery, built in 1946, was designed by the famous Monseigneur John Hawes, better known as Fra Jerome, who also designed and built the two great churches on Cat Island.

The impressive buildings of the monastery overlook beautiful grounds and gardens, and the monks of St. Augustine are happy to show visitors around. Be sure to drop into the little bakery—the pastries and bread are excellent, and a favorite souvenir is a jar or two of the homemade guava jam.

Continue along Bernard Road, across the intersection of Village Road, and onto Wulff Road, continuing west. If you are ready for lunch, stop off at the Three Queens' Restaurant along the way for one of their outstanding Bahamian specialties.

Continue west on Wulff Road to Mackey Street, and turn right, heading north. Turn left at the light onto Madeira. This area, known as Palmdale, is a small but thriving middle-class business and residential community. Look for the United Book Shop, which has an excellent selection of books about The Bahamas and books by Bahamians. A good history of the islands is *The Story of the Bahamas* by Dr. Paul Albury, Bahamian dentist, author, and historian. Also look for John S. George, Ltd., the oldest store in The Bahamas, established in 1855.

Continue west on Madeira, passing St. Thomas More's Catholic Church and school, crossing Montrose Avenue, where Madeira becomes Gibbs Corner. Continue west to East Street, and turn left to Young Street. Here you will find the Hardecker Children's Clinic, a very successful American project which helps deprived Bahamian children.

Go west on Young Street to Blue Hill Road, turn left, and continue to the traffic circle, which links up with Harrold Road. You will pass a new and interesting low-income housing development known as Yellow Elder, easily distinguished by the distinctive round African-style architecture of the houses. Still traveling west, you will pass Angelo's Art Centre and Museum, well worth a stop. It is owned and operated by Angelo Roker, a noted Bahamian artist and printer, and offers a good selection of local artworks, along with Angelo's own paintings and prints. There is also an excellent display of old Bahamian and West Indian prints and maps, available as originals and reproductions.

Continue west on Harrold Road, to Prospect Road, and turn left to Prospect Ridge Road. This heavily wooded area is called Prospect Heights, and is one of the most prestigious residential communities on the island, filled with many lovely homes. Follow Prospect Ridge Road to Skyline Drive, where there are several magnificent houses, including the private residences of several high government officials. A famous mansion in the area is "Saffron Hill," private home of the U.S. Ambassador, a graceful yellow house surrounded by tropical gardens and an ornamental fence with a guarded gate.

Cable Beach, The Caves, Love Beach, and Lyford Cay

Retrace your route to Prospect Ridge Road, turn left to Prospect Road, and left once again to the traffic circle that links up with West Bay Street. Here West Bay Street becomes a dual carriageway (the

Bahamian name for a divided highway). Turn left and continue west along the famed Cable Beach hotel strip.

Here you will see some of Nassau's most celebrated hotels, most beautiful oceanside homes, and lovely vistas of turquoise and emerald Bahamian waters. You'll pass the Ambassador Beach Hotel, the Nassau Beach Hotel, and the former Emerald Beach Hotel, now razed, with Carnival's Crystal Palace Hotel under construction. It will consist of five glass towers, offering 750 suites, when completed in 1990. Next is the all-new, $100-million Cable Beach Resort and Casino, The Bahamas' newest and one of its proudest entries into the international resort and convention market. The casino also offers the Bahamas Rhythms Theatre, with "Les Fantastiques," an elaborate French-style stage revue. If you plan to catch the show during your vacation, now is a good time to make reservations. Check out the casino. You'll find it casual, friendly, and informal day or night. In late afternoons, the dealers and croupiers offer free lessons in all of the games, teach you the rules, and tip you off on the odds. Great fun for novices—and some regular players who could use the advice.

After checking out the casino, stroll through the shopping arcade that links the casino to the hotel. An escalator (the only one in The Bahamas) leads to the hotel lobby. Along the corridor, notice particularly the large showcases exhibiting superb examples of Junkanoo Art, a unique Bahamian craft. This is one of the few places in all of the islands where you can get a close-up view of this colorful, creative art form except during the lavish Junkanoo Masquerades held annually at Christmas and New Year's, when hundreds march and cavort in the fantastic handcrafted costumes—some as wide as a street and ten feet tall.

Continue westward along Cable Beach. The dual carriageway ends at Delaporte Point, an attractive condominium apartment complex on a peninsula overlooking the sea. Continuing west, you will pass The Caves on your left, large limestone caverns carved by the wind and the sea, reputedly hiding places for seventeenth-century pirates and their booty. Opposite is a long, winding stretch of sand known as Caves Beach. A short way farther along is a spit of land on the ocean side called "Conference Corner." Here three trees were planted by heads of state attending the Nassau Conference, in December 1962, held at Lyford Cay. Participating were U.S. President John F. Kennedy, Prime Minister John Diefenbaker of Canada, and Prime Minister Harold Macmillan of Britain.

A few miles farther you will pass Traveler's Rest, a famous Bahamian restaurant featuring hearty native fare. Across the street is Gambier Beach, fine for swimming and beachcombing, and nearby is Gambier, a small country village originally settled by freed slaves.

Beyond Gambier the island is less populated, and settlements are few and far between, as the road winds along remote, deserted beaches and through pine and palmetto forests toward the western end of the island. On the right, you will pass Love Beach, with an attractive apartment and condominium colony known as the International Sports Club. At Northwest Point, West Bay curves slowly to the south, and continues southwesterly, a ways inland from the sea. A few miles down the road, you will see the walled and guarded entrance to Lyford Cay, one of the most exclusive private residential clubs anywhere in the world.

Lyford Cay is a posh haven for international socialites, financiers, the titled, and the famous. Britons, Canadians, French, Swiss, Greeks, Brazilians, Spaniards, Germans, and Americans mingle at the yacht club and golf course with old Bahamian families.

Lyford Cay is actually a peninsula; four thousand acres of verdant greenery overlook the sea, intersected by navigable canals and dotted with more than 220 magnificent private homes. The club was founded back in the 1950s by multimillionaire Canadian developer E.P. Taylor. Second and even third generations of the original Lyford Cay members still live on the cay or return each year for holidays at their island hideaway. Unless you are a member or the guest of a member, you won't be permitted beyond the gates, but there is a delightful little shopping center at the entranceway, which is fun to explore. And, if you keep your eye on the daily newspapers, there are frequent charitable events held at Lyford Cay, and some are open to the public.

The South Side

Beyond Lyford Cay, West Bay Street makes a great arc at Clifton Point, the western tip of the island, and continues eastward, where its name changes to Southwest Road. You will pass The Bahamas Electricity Corporation plant and the huge desalinization complex, where much of Nassau's drinking water is converted from sea water. Heading east, you will see the South Ocean Beach Hotel, a completely self-contained country-club resort and time-sharing complex. Guest golfers are welcomed and golf clubs, racquets, and scuba gear can be rented.

The road winds easterly through miles of untamed forest known as the Pine Barrens. Both sides of the road are fringed by thousands of acres of casuarina pines, palmetto and cycads, flowering shrubs, wildflowers, and many varieties of wild orchid. Look for a narrow lane that leads off to the right, toward the sea. This will take you through Adelaide Village, one of the oldest and most picturesque of the early slave settlements on New Providence.

Here time seems to have stood still for 150 years. There are only fifteen or twenty families in the village, many living as their ancestors did in cottages made of stone with thatched roofs woven from palm fronds. They cultivate small gardens, growing pumpkins, sweet potatoes, and melons; raise chickens and a few goats; and fish in homemade boats along the shore. The villagers are friendly and welcoming, although tourists seldom touch their small world. Unlike Fox Hill and Gambier, Adelaide was settled by blacks who had never been slaves. Their ancestors were captured from their African homes and loaded aboard slave ships bound for the New World, but they were rescued on the high seas by the British Royal Navy. In September 1832, the first cargo of rescued slaves reached Nassau. Some were given plots of land at Adelaide; others were settled at Carmichael, a few miles away. Stroll through the village or drive down to Adelaide Beach, one of the loveliest, most remote and unspoiled beaches on the island.

Circle back to the main road, turn right, and continue eastward. Here the road's name changes to Adelaide Road. In a few miles, you will cross an intersection with Coral Harbour Road. A left turn will take you to Nassau International Airport, and a right turn leads to the Coral Harbour development. Back in the 1960s this area was slated for major tourist development and the luxurious Coral Harbour Club and Golf Resort was opened. However, the area did not thrive, and today the hotel is headquarters for the Royal Bahamas Defense Force and its fleet of swift patrol boats. The Coral Harbour beach area has one small resort, Coral Harbour Villas, which offers self-catering cottages for vacation rentals, and the Happy Trail riding stables are nearby. There are renewed development plans for the area, and a new luxury Ramada Renaissance Hotel and Casino is being planned for a beachfront site.

A few miles farther along Adelaide Road, look for another road leading off to the right toward the sea. This leads to the Bacardi Rum Distillery, which produces nearly half a million cases of rum and liqueurs each year, including Nassau Royale, a delightful Bahamian cocoa-rum liqueur (the base for Bahamian coffee, which rivals Irish coffee as an after-dinner treat). Drop by the Visitor's Bar, open each weekday until around 4 P.M., which serves complimentary samples of Bacardi products.

Continuing eastward, Adelaide Road becomes Carmichael Road as it passes through another country village settled by rescued slaves, Carmichael. Beyond, the Pine Barrens are left behind, and the road curves through built-up areas of villages and housing developments, ending at Blue Hill Road. Turn left and travel north along Blue Hill Road.

Blue Hill Road bisects two of Nassau's oldest neighborhoods, Bains Town on the left and Grants Town on the right, both known for generations as "Over the Hill" because of their location just over the ridge from downtown Nassau. These "country villages" within the city were also settled by rescued slaves, along with emancipated blacks who had worked the Bahamian plantations. Both villages today are poor but picturesque, with tiny wooden homes painted in bright tropical colors, often surrounded by bougainvillea and tropical greenery. There are many Baptist and fundamentalist churches in the area, and even more bars, shops, and small grocery stores serving the local population.

At the intersection with Meeting Street (traffic light), turn left to Nassau Street, then right for one block and right on Delancey Street. Here you will pass a lovely old Bahamian home that's now one of Nassau's finest restaurants, Buena Vista. It also operates as a small inn.

Just beyond Buena Vista is the intersection with West Street. On the corner is St. Francis Xavier Cathedral, the oldest Catholic Church in

The Bahamas, constructed in 1885. In 1893, the church purchased the stately mansion next door to use as a priory. The house, known as "Dunmore House," was built by Lord Dunmore in 1787 as his official residence and was used by eighteenth-century governors until today's Government House was completed in 1803. Today, Dunmore House is a beautifully preserved example of early British-colonial architecture.

Turn left on West Street, toward the harbor. West Street ends at Bay Street, between the Sheraton British Colonial Hotel and old Fort Charlotte, where your tour of Nassau and the island began.

PRACTICAL INFORMATION FOR NEW
PROVIDENCE ISLAND

 HOW TO GET THERE. By air. Nassau International Airport is served directly from the U.S. mainland by more than a dozen nonstop international flights daily from American cities such as Miami, Fort Lauderdale, Palm Beach, Tampa, Atlanta, Chicago, Boston, Philadelphia, Newark, and New York. It is linked conveniently to most major cities around the world by a brief 35-minute jet hop from the Miami gateway. Airlines serving Nassau include *Bahamasair, Delta, Eastern, Pan American, TWA, Piedmont, United, Chalk's International, Air Canada,* and *British Airways.* In addition, there are frequent charter flights to Nassau from U.S. cities, Toronto, and Montreal. Telephone numbers for Bahamasair and Florida commuter airlines are listed under "How to Get There by Air" in the *Facts at your Fingertips* section of this book.

By sea. Half a dozen cruise ships sail once or twice weekly to Nassau from Miami, Fort Lauderdale (Port Everglades), or Port Canaveral. The following ships sail each Monday and Friday to Nassau on three- and four-night cruises (four-night cruises also call at Freeport, Grand Bahama): Carnival Cruise Line—*Carnivale;* and *Mardi Gras* (Thursday and Sunday); Admiral Cruiseline—*Emerald Seas;* Norwegian Caribbean Line—*Sunward II;* Dolphin Cruiseline—*Dolphin IV;* and Premier Cruiseline—*Royale* and *Oceanic.* Friday-only sailings to Nassau by Chandris Line—*Galileo* or *Britannis.* For more details on Bahamas cruises, see "How to Get There by Sea" in *Facts at Your Fingertips.*

 TELEPHONES AND EMERGENCY NUMBERS. The area code for Nassau is 809. Dial direct from anywhere in the U.S. or Canada. For local calls, dial only the last five digits of the telephone number. (The first two are 32, if you are calling from outside.) Hotels generally charge 25¢ for local calls, and add a substantial service charge for long-distance calls.

Emergency numbers on New Providence Island: Fire, 919; Police, 2–4444; Ambulance, 2–2221; Bahamas Air Sea Rescue, 2–3877; Hospital, 2–2681.

 HOTELS. Nassau, Cable Beach, and Paradise Island offer the widest range of vacation accommodations on any island in The Bahamas chain, and the broadest price range to match almost any budget. There are small historic inns, clusters of cottages, homey or sophisticated apartment and villa complexes, budget in-town hotels, sprawling country-club resorts, and glittering high-rise beach hotels with nonstop sports and entertainment, gourmet restaurants, casinos, and stage revues—nearly 70 different properties, offering close to 4,000 rooms for rent.

Hotel price categories per room for two people in Winter Season are: $175 and up, *Super Deluxe;* $150 to $174, *Deluxe;* $120 to $149, *Expensive;* $100 to $119, *Moderate;* under $99 *Inexpensive.*

Rates in Goombay Summer Season tend to be 10 to 20 percent lower, and year-round packages can be as much as 20 to 40 percent lower than Winter rates. We have indicated whom to contact for reservations, and you'll note that most may also be booked through Bahamas Reservation Service, tel. 800–327–0787, toll free from anywhere in the U.S. or Canada. It is abbreviated below as BRS.

The **Sheraton British Colonial,** formerly one of downtown Nassau's most elegant hotels, has been purposely omitted from this edition because we cannot recommend it to our readers at this time.

Cable Beach

Cable Beach Hotel and Casino. *Deluxe to Super Deluxe.* Reserve direct: 5775 N.W. 11th St., Suite 400, Miami, FL 33126; tel. in Florida 305–262–1397; in the U.S. 800–822–4200 or through BRS. Nassau's newest and one of its most glittering international resorts. There are 700 large luxury rooms (18 deluxe suites) in twin nine-story wings; each room overlooks the sea. All are fully air-conditioned, with private balconies, telephones, and cable TV. There are six restaurants, from poolside snack bar to gourmet dining rooms; four cocktail lounges; and a nightclub with local entertainment and disco dancing. Adjacent to the hotel and linked to it by an arcade of fine shops is the *Cable Beach Casino* and the 1,000-seat *Casino Theatre,* featuring a French-style showgirl revue; along with a New York–style delicatessen and gourmet Italian restaurant. The sports offerings include an 18-hole championship golf course with pro shop and clubhouse; five clay and five all-weather tennis courts (lighted), plus a stadium for tournament play; three squash and three racquetball courts. The swimming pool is set in an elaborate tropical garden overlooking the beach. All water sports are available at the beach concession stand, including small-boat sailing and fishing expeditions. The resort is owned by The Hotel Corporation of The Bahamas, and operated by Wyndham Hotels Corp.

Carnival's Crystal Palace Hotel. *Deluxe to Super Deluxe.* Reserve Direct: 5225 N.W. 87th Ave., Miami, FL, 33166; tel. 305-599-2600 or through BRS. Expected to be open in 1988, this 225-room, 11-story tower luxury hotel, is located adjacent to the Cable Beach Casino, on the site of the Emerald Beach Hotel.

Nassau Beach Hotel. *Deluxe to Super Deluxe.* Reserve direct: 500 Deer Run, Miami FL 33166, tel. 305–371–1820 or through BRS. This 425-room oceanside resort has recently been completely refurbished and refurnished. There are four fine restaurants with a variety of menus and two lounges offer good local entertainment. All rooms are attractively furnished, air-conditioned, and have private balconies overlooking courtyard gardens or the sea. There is an Olympic-size swimming pool, 3,000 feet of beach, a multitude of water sports, and nine tennis courts (six lighted). The hotel is owned and operated by Trusthouse Forte. Rates include all taxes and charges.

Royal Bahamian. *Deluxe to Super Deluxe.* Reserve direct: 5775 N.W. 11th St., Suite 400, Miami, FL 33126; tel. in Florida 305–262–1397; in the U.S. 800–822–4200; or through BRS. Formerly the Balmoral Beach Hotel. One of Nassau's grand old hotels, with elegant architecture, fountained terraces, two hundred spacious high-ceilinged rooms overlooking the sea, and 16 Georgian villas in the gardens. The hotel has recently reopened after a $7 million top-to-bottom renovation and redecoration. Gracious English country-house decor, afternoon tea in the lounge, elegant dining at *Baccarat,* concierge service, fluffy terry robes, and dozens of other amenities. Fine pool, tennis courts, lovely beach, watersports, and an exclusive health spa complete with masseurs and mud baths. A Hotel Corporation of The Bahamas property, leased by Wyndham Hotels.

Wyndham Ambassador Beach. *Expensive.* Reserve direct: 5775 N.W. 11th St., Miami, FL 33126; tel. 305–262–1397 in Miami; in the U.S. 800–327–3305. A classic Bahamas resort, low-rise and U-shaped, overlooking 1,800 feet of beach. The hotel has recently had a top-to-bottom update. The cramped Playboy Casino has departed, and the spacious lobby has been restored with tropical greenery and an attractive bar/lounge. The 400 newly redecorated rooms each have a balcony, cable TV, and dial telephone. There's an exotic restaurant, *Tsunami,* serving Chinese and Polynesian fare, along with the classic *Rib Room* for gourmet dining, several bars and lounges. Newest attraction is the *B-Beautiful* health and beauty studio. Huge pool and water sports are available at oceanside. There are four all-weather lighted tennis courts and golfing at the Cable Beach Golf course. A Hotel Corporation of The Bahamas property, operated by Wyndham Hotels.

Cable Beach Inn. *Inexpensive.* Box N–4920, Nassau. Tel. 327–7341; or through BRS. (Formerly Bahamas Beach Hotel.) Newly reopened, elegantly refurbished resort with 120 rooms, each air-conditioned with bath or shower. Good dining and entertainment; English-style pub and new state-of-the-art dance club, Inn Spirations. Two tennis courts, two pools, ocean beach, bikes, and water sports. Three popular barbecues weekly, with live entertainment.

Nassau–Downtown

Coral World Hotel. *Deluxe.* Box N344, Nassau; tel. 322–2001/2/3. Expected to open late 1987 or early 1988, at Silver Cay between Cable Beach and downtown Nassau. It is connected with Coral World Marine theme park, Nassau's newest attraction. 20 luxury rooms, each with a private swimming pool, and overlooking the beach.

Graycliff. *Deluxe.* Box N–10246, Nassau; tel. 322–2976/7. A charming and historic inn on a hillside off Bay Street, next to the governor's mansion. The great house is a 230-year-old Georgian Colonial mansion set in a walled tropical garden, once headquarters for Nassau's West Indian Regiment. In more recent years it was the private winter home of the Earl and Countess of Dudley, hosting British royalty and notables. Converted to a small inn and gourmet restaurant half a dozen years ago, Graycliff still has much of the charm of an English country house, with antique-filled rooms and personalized attention from the staff. There are 12 air-conditioned rooms and a poolside cottage that overlooks a magnificent walled swimming pool surrounded by tropical greenery. The hotel is a member of the prestigious Relais et Chateaux.

Buena Vista. *Inexpensive.* Box N–564, Nassau. Tel. 809–322–2811 or 2–4039. Located on Delancey St., on the crest of the hill overlooking old Nassau. A charming 200-year-old estate, with a great rambling house offering just six high-ceilinged, gracious rooms—a fine bargain, but usually booked. There is a superb restaurant of the same name, serving some of the finest Continental cuisine in Nassau. Beautiful gardens, attractive dining terrace, and a friendly country house atmosphere. Walking distance to the Western Esplanade Beach.

Dolphin Hotel. *Inexpensive.* Box N-3236, Nassau; tel. 322–8666; or through BRS. On West Bay Street, a few minutes' walk from downtown, and across the street from Lighthouse Beach (known as the Western Esplanade). Sixty-six modestly furnished, air-conditioned rooms, each with a private balcony and beautiful ocean view. Dining room and dining terrace at poolside offer good hearty Bahamian dishes.

El Greco Hotel. *Inexpensive.* Box N-4187, Nassau; tel. 325-1121/4. West Bay St., very near downtown business and shopping. A small, tastefully decorated and Spanish-flavored 26-room hotel with special appeal for business travelers. Rooms are air-conditioned, spacious, and have private telephones. There is an attractive courtyard pool, and Lighthouse Beach is just across the road. The hotel boasts one of the best gourmet restaurants in Nassau, the *Del Prado,* with Continental decor and cuisine.

Lighthouse Beach Hotel. *Inexpensive.* Box 915, Nassau. Tel. 323-6515, or call BRS. Formerly the Mayfair Hotel. Attractive small hotel, with 94 rooms overlooking the Western Esplanade, also known as Lighthouse Beach. Air-conditioned, friendly, and comfortable atmosphere. Boasts Nassau's only rooftop swimming pool, with a spectacular view of the harbor, the city, and Paradise Island. There is a good dining room serving American, Bahamian, and Continental specialties. Easy walking distance to all Nassau attractions and shopping.

New Olympia Hotel. *Inexpensive.* Box N-984, Nassau; tel. 322-4971/2/3 or through BRS. Small, casual family-run hotel with 53 air-conditioned rooms, some with private balconies and a splendid ocean view. The popular *Pub Lounge* is a gathering spot for guests, locals, and visitors. The dining room offers Greek, Bahamian, and American dishes, and *Sonny's* on the garden patio is a favorite snack spot. Just a few steps away from Lighthouse Beach and an easy stroll to downtown shopping. Small service charge added.

Pilot House Hotel. *Inexpensive.* Box N-4941, Nassau; tel. 322-8431; in the U.S. 800-223-9815; or through BRS. A favorite of cruising yachtsmen, this charmingly nautical hotel overlooks the marina and the harbor, "Across the Bridge from Paradise," on Nassau's East Bay Street. Completely remodeled and updated in 1983, the hotel offers 125 spacious, attractive rooms, each air-conditioned, with private telephone and balcony overlooking a tropical courtyard and sparkling pool. There's island entertainment nightly at the *Windward Mark* or *Captain's Lounge,* and excellent dining in the *Regatta Room* or on the palm-shaded terrace. The resort operates frequent water-taxi service to Paradise Island and downtown Nassau for guests at no charge.

Nassau-Outside of Town

South Ocean Beach Hotel and Golf Club. *Moderate.* Box N-8191, Nassau; tel. 326-4391; or through BRS. A great, sprawling country-club resort located on the southwestern shore of New Providence Island, overlooking miles of beach and the sea. The resort boasts the only USGA-rated 18-hole championship golf course in The Bahamas. There is an elegant clubhouse, pro shop, and a fine restaurant and bar at the golf course. At beachside, the 120-room low-rise hotel offers nightly entertainment, gourmet or casual dining, four tennis courts lighted for night play, a beautiful pool, and 600 feet of private white-sand beach. All rooms are attractively furnished and air-conditioned. Sporting amenities include an excellent scuba program, catamaran sailing, snorkeling, and most other water sports. Bicycles, motor scooters, and automobiles for rent, and frequent complimentary bus service to Nassau.

Paradise Island

Ocean Club. *Deluxe to Super Deluxe.* Box N-4777, Nassau; tel. 326-2501 or in the U.S. 800–321–3000. Elegance and luxury in a sophisticated club-like setting. One of the Caribbean's finest tennis resorts. The main house was once multimillionaire heir Huntington Hartford's mansion. The resort has hosted the celebrated, the noted, and the notorious over the years. It has two low wings with 70 opulent rooms overlooking a lovely garden courtyard, each with balcony or terrace, telephone, and cable TV. There are five 2-bedroom villas with private Jacuzzi pools, and 12 tennis cabanas adjacent to the courts (best buy!). Tennis amenities include resident pro, instruction, nine Har-Tru courts, and free court time for guests. The resort has a long, lovely ocean beach reached by a staircase, and is next door to the beautiful French cloister and Versailles Gardens. There's an attractive pool and patio, with haute cuisine al fresco in the *Courtyard Terrace.* Golf and casino nearby. Owned by Resorts International.

Paradise Island Resort and Casino. *Deluxe to Super Deluxe.* Box N-4777, Nassau; tel. 326–2000/3000; in the U.S. 800–321–3000; or through BRS. Resorts International's two spectacular oceanside hotels offer elegance, luxury, opulence, and glitter with all the accoutrements of an international playground. The 1,200-room resort complex consists of the twin towers of the Britannia Beach Hotel, with 600 rooms, now called the Britannia Towers, and the 500-room Paradise Island Hotel, now called Paradise Towers. They are linked by arcades of shops and restaurants leading to the *Paradise Island Casino* and *Le Cabaret Theatre,* and share several miles of beautiful ocean beach. The landscaped grounds include tropical gardens, palm-lined pathways, blue lagoons, and huge swimming pools. There are a dozen gourmet and specialty restaurants, and half a dozen bars and lounges indoors and at poolside. Rooms are attractively furnished, offer private telephones, cable TV, and balconies with ocean, pool, or lagoon views, including the exclusive "Paradise Club," the four top floors, with VIP pampering and 24-hour concierge service, accessible only by keyed elevator. The resort includes a full water-sports program, 12 tennis courts for day or night play, a Parcourse layout for joggers, health club, and an 18-hole championship golf course.

Sheraton Grand Hotel. *Deluxe to Super Deluxe.* 701 S.W. 27th Ave., Miami, FL 33135; tel. 800–325–3535 or through Sheraton worldwide; or through BRS. An elegant new oceanside resort, member of the worldwide Sheraton Hotel chain, with a super-deluxe penthouse that rents for $11,000 a day! 350 beautiful ocean-view rooms and suites, each air-conditioned, with telephones and cable TV, are set along a broad sandy beach with a terraced pool deck. The atrium lobby features a lovely fountain and lounges overlooking the sea. Top floors are the "Tower" section, reached by keyed elevator, and offer full concierge service, private bar, Continental breakfast, and evening liqueurs, among other amenities —they're very expensive. Sports facilities include scuba, sailing, parasailing, and four tennis courts lighted for night play. Entertainment and dining includes *La Paeon* disco and *Julie's,* a superb gourmet restaurant. Other amenities include a masseur, beauty shop, gift shop, and *Androsia Boutique* (hand-batiked fabrics and fashions from the island of Andros). Located next door to the Paradise Island Casino.

Holiday Inn. *Expensive.* Box SS-6214, Nassau; tel. 326–2101; through Holiday Inn Reservation Service; or through BRS. High-rise Holiday Inn amenities with a tropical, Bahamian flair. There are 535 attractive rooms in a 17-story tower overlooking a splendid crescent ocean beach. Rooms are air-conditioned, have telephones and cable TV. Huge free-form pool with a "floating" bar (stools are in the water), four tennis courts with instructor, all water sports, dining rooms, and lounges with good island entertainment nightly. There's a full activities program with a cheerful, friendly staff who put on their own delightful show every Friday evening.

Loew's Harbour Cove. *Expensive.* Box SS-6249, Nassau; tel. 326–2561: through Loew's worldwide reservation service; or through BRS. Two hundred and fifty newly decorated and attractive rooms, located near the Paradise Island Bridge on the southern shore, overlook the harbor and the island. All are air-conditioned, with telephones, cable TV, and private balconies. There is a small man-made crescent beach with a lovely pool and bar. Very attractive public rooms. Fine dining indoors and on the terrace; lounges with native entertainment and dancing nightly. The resort operates a water-taxi service to Nassau for shopping and sightseeing, complimentary to guests.

Club Med Paradise Island. *Moderate.* Box N-7137, Nassau; tele. 800 CLUB MED. Famous international vacation club for group-fun devotees. The Paradise Club Med offers 300 simply furnished, motel-style rooms set amid tropical gardens, extending across the island from oceanside to harborside. The clubhouse and pool were once part of a lavish private estate. Informality, French flair, and Bahamian flavor mark the nonstop activities, sports, and entertainment, with special emphasis on "Intensive Tennis." There are 20 Har-Tru surface courts, nine lighted for night play, instructors, lessons and ball machines —all free to guests. Other sports include boating and deep-sea fishing expeditions. All-inclusive packages booked direct or through a travel agent.

Paradise Paradise. *Moderate.* Box SS-6259, Nassau; tel. 326–2541; through Resorts International, 800–321–3000 in the U.S.; or through BRS. Casual, cozy, and delightful—just 100 rooms along Paradise Beach, The Bahamas's most famous ocean strand. All rooms are air-conditioned, with telephone and cable TV. A favorite of the younger crowd. Dress code tends to bikinis and jeans, with dress-up time for trips to the casino, cabaret, and nightclubs. A good restaurant, friendly bar/lounge with native show, and an attractive pool. All-inclusive plan with breakfast available, and free sports including sailing, snorkeling, windsurfing, waterskiing, tennis, and biking.

Yoga Retreat. *Inexpensive.* Box N-7550, Nassau; tel. 326–2902. Swami Vishnu Devananda's rustic retreat offers 35 rooms and cottages with spartan furnishings and contemplative lifestyle. Swimming pool, tennis, private beach. Vegetarian dining only. No credit cards.

 APARTMENT HOTELS. Most apartment-rental complexes offering short-term vacation leases operate as apartment hotels, with a clubhouse or dining room, a central pool, and maid service.

Cable Beach

Cable Beach Manor. *Moderate.* Box N-8333, Nassau; tel. 327–7784/5; or through BRS. Thirty-three studio, one- and two-bedroom apartments with kitchens, within walking distance of all Cable Beach attractions and shopping center. All apartments are air-conditioned and have daily maid service. Nicely landscaped grounds, swimming pool, and private beach. Casual atmosphere—a favorite of families for decades.

Casuarinas Apartment Hotel. *Moderate.* Box N-4016, Nassau; tel. 327–7921/2; or through BRS. Family-owned casual resort with personalized Bahamian service. 74 modern studio, two-room and three-room apartments and townhouses for up to six people, all air-conditioned with daily maid service. Excellent native cooking at popular *Round House* and *Albrions.* Pool with whirlpool, minipool for children, small private beach.

Henrea Carlette Apartments. *Moderate.* Box N-4227, Nassau; tel. 327–7801/2/3/4/5; or through BRS. Attractive new apartment hotel complex one block from the beach offering 20 nicely furnished housekeeping units with kitchens. All are air-conditioned, with maid service, and overlook a courtyard and swimming pool. *Androsia* serves Bahamian specialties.

Orange Hill Beach Inn. *Inexpensive.* Box N–8583, Nassau. Tel. 327–7157. Nine nice studio rooms in an old Bahamian house along an ocean beach, near Nassau International Airport. Dining room, bar, lovely grounds. Small boat for the use of guests.

Paradise Island

Villas in Paradise. *Deluxe.* Box SS-6379, Nassau. Tel. 326–2998. Thirty one-, two-, and three-bedroom single or duplex villas, some with private swimming pools. All are attractively furnished, well equipped with full kitchens and air-conditioning. Within easy walking distance of all Paradise Island attractions, including the beach, golf course, casino, and shopping center.

Bay View Village. *Expensive.* Box SS-6308, Nassau; tel. 326–2555/6; or through BRS. A stunning apartment, townhouse, and villa complex located near Loew's Harbour Cove on a hillside overlooking Nassau Harbour and Montagu Bay. There are two solar-heated swimming pools, walled tropical gardens, and a night-lighted tennis court. Eighty-six one-, two-, and three-bedroom units, each with air-conditioning, telephones, maid service, full kitchen, dining and living areas, and a bathroom with each bedroom. Each unit has a terrace or patio and overlooks the gardens, the pool, or the sea. Five-minute walk from the golf course, casino, and beautiful beach. Vacation rentals or purchase.

Club Land 'Or. *Expensive.* Box SS-6429, Nassau; tel. 326–2400; in the U.S. 800–446–3850, or through BRS. A beautiful apartment complex overlooking the Paradise Island Lagoon amid tropical greenery. Seventy-one attractively furnished apartments have full kitchens and two separate sleeping areas for up to four adults, with terrace or patio overlooking the gardens, the pool, or the lagoon. Within easy walking distance of beach, golf, tennis, and casino. *The Blue Lagoon* serves fine seafood specialties, and there is a relaxing lounge with entertainment. Available for vacation rentals or time-share.

Grosvenor Court Apartments. *Moderate.* Box SS-5151, Nassau. Tel. 326–2888. Thirty-five nicely furnished and equipped studios, one- and two-bedroom apartments for up to six people. All are air-conditioned, with telephones and private balconies. There's a swimming pool in a central courtyard, nicely landscaped grounds, a bar, and small restaurant. Located just 150 yards from lovely Cabbage Beach, and within easy walking distance of the shopping center, casino, tennis, and golf. Service charge added. No credit cards.

Outside of Nassau

Coral Harbour Beach Villas. *Inexpensive.* Box N-1674, Nassau. Tel. 326–1144. Located on the beach at the southwestern end of New Providence. 14 studio apartments with pool, bar/lounge, and restaurant, nearby golf club.

Orchard Garden Apartments. *Inexpensive* Box N-1514, Nassau; tel. 323–1297 or 5–9250; or through BRS. Twenty-two rooms in cottages and apartments clustered around a central swimming pool and set in two acres of trees and gardens. Located off East Bay Street on Village Road, near old Fort Montagu and Fort Montagu Beach. Rooms are spacious, clean, and nicely decorated, all with complete kitchens, air-conditioning, and telephone. ($60–75).

TIME SHARING. Studios, one-, two-, and three-bedroom units available by the week, month, or longer for time-share purchase or vacation rental.

Colony Club Resort. Box SS-5420, Nassau. Tel. 325–7405/5–4824. Located on St. Albans Drive off West Bay Street. Twenty studio apartments with kitchen facilities. Bar, pool, beach nearby. Vacation rental or time-share.

Guanahani Village. Guanahani Development Ltd., Box N-3223, Nassau; tel. 323–1331/1031 or 7–8469. Luxury three-bedroom, 2½-bath apartment units oceanside on Cable Beach. Time share or vacation rental. RCI affiliate.

Sandpiper Resort. New Providence Development Co., Box N-4820, Nassau. Tel. 327–4177/4402. Located in the South Ocean Beach Hotel complex at the southwestern end of New Providence Island. One- and two-bedroom apartments, pool, tennis, golf, private beach.

SeaGrape Villas. Box N-1337, Nassau. Tel. 325–4229. Located on St. Albans Drive off West Bay Street. Nine one- and two-bedroom apartments. (N.A.).

Sunrise Beach Village. Foremost Property Sales, Box 55–6519, Nassau. Tel. 326–2234/2–4187 or 4/1044. Studios, one-, two-, and three-bedroom apartments located on Paradise Island at oceanside. Swimming pool. Network I affiliate. Time share or vacation rental. ($175).

Westwind II Club. Box 10481, Nassau. Attractive oceanside, two-bedroom townhouse units located on Cable Beach near the Cable Beach Hotel and Casino. Tel. in Nassau 7–7529; in the U.S. 800–253–7772.

For further information on apartment rentals, purchases, or time-sharing opportunities, contact the *Bahamas Real Estate Association,* located in the Chamber of Commerce building on Shirley Street in downtown Nassau; Box N-8860, Nassau; tel. 325–4942.

 HOW TO GET AROUND. Metered taxis meet all incoming flights at Nassau International Airport and at the cruise-ship port. There is no bus service to or from the airport. However, visitors booked on package tours that specifically include airport transfers are picked up at the airport by tour-operator buses and transported to their hotel free of charge. Approximate metered taxi rates to hotels are as follows: Cable Beach hotels, $8; downtown Nassau hotels, $10; Paradise Island hotels, $16. On New Providence Island, jitney service is available between residential areas, hotels, and downtown Nassau. These are inexpensive (50¢–$1), run on a semiregular basis, and can be anything from modern nine-passenger vans to air-conditioned 40-passenger buses or a converted school bus lettered by hand, "Rapit Transid."

Transportation to Paradise Island is by metered taxi, with an additional $2 charge for the bridge toll (no charge exiting Paradise Island) or via water taxis (small motor launches seating up to 20 passengers) called "bum boats," which criss-cross the harbor every 10 or 15 minutes during daylight hours for about $1 each way. On Paradise Island there is a round-the-island bus service operating every 20 or 30 minutes, making stops at all hotels and attractions such as the casino, beaches, shopping center, golf course, and Chalk's seaplane ramp; and travels to Nassau for shopping. Complimentary to hotel guests.

In addition to the public transportation listed above, many hotels offer regularly scheduled, complimentary bus service (or water-taxi service) to downtown Nassau and Bay Street shopping. Car rentals are available through most hotel desks or at the following locations: *Avis Rent-A-Car,* at the airport, tel. 7–7121; Cable Beach and Nassau, tel. 2–2889, in Paradise Island, 6–2061. *Budget Rent-A-Car,* at the airport, 7–7405/6. *Hertz,* at the airport, tel. 7–8684, Cable Beach, tel. 7–6866. *National Car Rental,* at the airport, tel. 7–7301 or at Sheraton British Colonial, tel. 5–3716, at Cable Beach, tel. 7–6000. Car-rental rates average $45–$85 per day, $279–545 per week, plus gas, depending on type of car, equipment, and season. A deposit of $150 is required with the rental of each car. Insurance is available at all rental locations, and is strongly recommended.

Motorbikes, motorcycles, and motor scooters are available at the following locations: *B & S Scooters,* Union Dock at Bay Street, tel. 2–2580. *Holiday Scooter Rental,* tel. 5–3949. *Summit Scooter Rentals,* tel. 2–3781. Average rental for motor scooters is approximately $28 per day and $18 per half-day, including insurance. Crash helmets are mandatory and included in rental. Scooters are also available at many hotels—check with your front desk.

TOURIST INFORMATION SERVICES. The Bahamas Ministry of Tourism operates information booths in the arrivals section (tel. 7–6833) and the departure section (tel. 7–6782) of Nassau International Airport; at Prince George Wharf cruise-ship port, tel. 5–9155; and at Rawson Square on Bay Street, tel. 5–9171. Ministry of Tourism headquarters is located at the Market Plaza (Strawmarket) on Bay Street, tel. 2–7500/01/02/03/04. The Nassau/Paradise Island Promotion Board has its headquarters in Hotel House on West Bay Street, tel. 2–8381/2/3/4. All locations offer a wide range of colorful brochures, maps, rate sheets covering all hotels for summer and winter seasons, and information on what to do and sights to see, including participation in the popular "People to People" program. For sources of information closer to home, see the "Tourist Information Services" section in the *Facts at Your Fingertips* chapter.

SPECIAL EVENTS. *Bahamas Blue Water Run.* Annual half-marathon event with both men's and women's divisions, attracting a large field of international runners. Sponsored by the Bahamas Striders Road Running Club and usually held in early December.

Bahamas Gran Prix. International powerboat race pitting European and U.S. racing drivers in Formula One competition, held annually in Nassau Harbour on New Providence Island. Spectator viewing is excellent along the lake shores, and competition is keen for top prizes in this National Powerboat Association–sanctioned series, usually held in mid-December.

Fox Hill Day. An old-fashioned country fair held in one of the oldest settlements on New Providence Island, about six miles from downtown Nassau. Look for down-home Bahamian cooking, arts-and-crafts stalls, and marvelous gospel singing, as this early slave settlement celebrates Emancipation Day a week later than the rest of the Bahamas. Held annually on the second Tuesday in August. Emancipation Day is a public holiday in The Bahamas, celebrated on the first Monday of August each year.

Goombay Summer Festival. The Bahamas annual summer festival, featuring special social, cultural, and sporting events scheduled every day of the week June 1–Sept. 30. In Nassau, special events include: beach parties, boat cruises, and Bahamian cookouts; golf and tennis tournaments; racquetball, squash, and volleyball competitions; sailing, windsurfing, and diving; native fashion shows; street theater, dance troupes, and art fairs; guided walking tours, Government House tea parties, miniature Junkanoo parades, and Goombay music festivals; along with discount coupons for many Nassau attractions including shopping, restaurants, nightclub shows, tours, and sightseeing attractions. Events are held all around the island and all visitors are invited to attend.

International Windsurfing Regatta. Held annually along Cable Beach, with headquarters at the Nassau Beach Hotel. The regatta attracts professional and amateur windsurfers from around the world, competing for cash prizes, and awards. Held in early January.

Junkanoo. A 200-year-old festival based on the dance, music, and mask traditions of African slaves in the New World, Junkanoo was once celebrated throughout the West Indies but survives only in The Bahamas. Two separate Junkanoo Parades are held annually, the first on Dec. 26 (Boxing Day) and the second on New Year's Day. Bay St. in Nassau is the scene of the most colorful and extravagant masquerades, although smaller versions are held on many Bahamian islands at holiday time each year. Tens of thousands of Bahamians and delighted visitors turn out to watch the Junkanoos parade in wildly imaginative and utterly unique fringed-paper costumes, accompanied by the primitive, pulsating beat of goatskin drums, lignum vitae sticks, shak-shak gourds, tin whistles, brass bugles, and clanging cowbells. Hundreds of men, women, and childen don costumes and "rush" to the age-old rhythm, and organized groups vie for top prizes awarded to the most ingenious, elaborate, and unusual costumes. Parades begin just before dawn, and prizes are awarded by 9:00 in the morning, although the revelry lasts most of the day.

Southern Ocean Racing Conference. For half a century the last two races of the prestigious international yacht racing annual series have been held in Bahamian waters off Nassau. Held in late February, the Miami-Nassau Race and the Nassau Cup Race are sponsored by the Nassau Yacht Club. Some of the world's most famous yachts and skippers participate, and viewing is excellent along the shoreline of Nassau Harbour and Montagu Bay.

Supreme Court Assizes. Pomp and pageantry in the British Colonial tradition mark the formal opening of the quarterly Supreme Court sessions. Ceremonies are held in Parliament Square on the second Wednesday in January and the first Wednesdays in April, July, and October.

Student Breakaway Program. Every spring from March through April, Nassau and Paradise Island attract thousands of students on spring break with a series of fun-filled free (or inexpensive) events scheduled daily, such as beach picnics, boat cruises, sports tournaments, fishing and diving trips, and more. To participate students must have an official student I.D. card.

TOURS. A variety of interesting tours is available on the island, with a wide range of activities included. Some of the many possibilities are sightseeing tours of the city and the island; tours to the gardens and nature centers; glass-bottom boat tours to the sea gardens, via motor launch or a Hollywood-style submarine; sailing expeditions to offshore cays for beach-party barbecues; sunset and moonlight cruises with dinner and drinks; and nightlife tours to casino cabaret shows or local nightclubs. Tours may be booked at all hotel desks in Nassau, Cable Beach, and Paradise Island, or directly through the following ground-tour operators and taxi/tour guide organization: *B & B Tours,* Box N-8246, Nassau, tel. 5–8849; *Bahamas Taxi Union,* Box N-3227, Nassau, tel. 3–4555; *Good Time Tours,* Box G.T. 2090, Nassau, tel. 5–5561; *Howard Johnson Tours,* Box N-406, Nassau, tel. 2–8181; *Happy Tours Ltd.,* Box N-1077, Nassau, tel. 3–5818; *Island Sun Tours Ltd.,* Box N-4516, Nassau, tel. 5–6959; *Majestic Tours,* Box N-1401, Nassau, tel. 2–2606; *Playtours Ltd.,* Box N-7762, Nassau, tel. 2–2931; *Richard Moss Tours,* Box N-4442, Nassau, tel. 4–2123; *Royal Palm Tours,* Box N-4498, Nassau, tel. 3–2177; *Sunnyland Travel Agency,* Box S.S. 5650, Nassau, tel. 2–8287; *Sunshine Travel Agency,* Box 14359, Nassau, tel. 3–4350; *Tropical Travel Tours,* Box N-448, Nassau, tel. 2–3802; and *United Shipping Ltd.,* Box N-4005, Nassau, tel. 2–1340.

72   NEW PROVIDENCE ISLAND

Airplanes may be chartered in Nassau for sightseeing tours and visits to the Family Islands. The following carriers offer charter flights from Nassau International Airport: *Kwin Aircraft,* Box N-4691, Nassau, tel. 7–8481/2; *MD Air Service,* Box N-25, Nassau, tel. 7–7335/6; *Pinders Charter Service,* Box N-10456, Nassau, tel. 7–7320; *Norman Nixon Charter Service,* Box SS-5980, Nassau, tel. 7–7184 or 7–8573; and *Trans Island Airways,* Box N-291, Nassau, tel. 7–8329/8777/7172.

Other sightseeing options include: *Guided Walking Tour.* Offered only during Goombay Summer (June through September). Tours leave from Prince George Wharf and Parliament Square every day except Friday, at 9:30 and 11 A.M., 1:30 and 3 P.M.

Horse-Drawn Surrey. Nassau's quaint "carriages" and friendly drivers take you on a tour of the sights along Bay Street and some of the byways in the old city. Cost for two persons is around $8–10 a half-hour. For an additional person or longer ride, negotiate the charge with the driver ahead of time. Surreys may be hired at Rawson Square or on Frederick Street just off Bay Street.

Bacardi Distillery. Located off Adelaide Road on the southern shore of New Providence. Guests are welcomed to the "Visitors Bar," where complimentary Bacardi Rum and liqueurs, such as The Bahamas' own Nassau Royale, are served. Open weekdays from 10 A.M. to 4 P.M.

 HISTORIC SITES AND BUILDINGS. *Blackbeard's Tower.* The ruins of an old stone tower, located on East Bay St. near Fox Hill Rd. The ruins command a fine view over Montagu Harbour, Paradise Island, and the offshore cays. The tower is reputed to have been a lookout for the notorious pirate Edward Teach, better known as Blackbeard.

Nassau Public Library. At the south end of Parliament Square, facing Shirley Street, there is an interesting octagonal building which was built as the Nassau Gaol (prison) in 1799. In 1879 it was converted to a library, and since then has served as the main branch of The Bahamas' public library system. The library offers a fine collection of historic documents, prints, and early newspapers. It is open at varying hours during the week, with the times posted on the main door.

Water Tower. The highest point on the island of New Providence, located adjacent to Fort Fincastle, at the top of the Queen's Staircase (Elizabeth Ave.). The 126-foot tower arises 216 feet above sea level, and offers a superb panoramic view of the city and the harbor. Observation platform reached by stairs or elevator. Admission charge is 50 cents per person.

Christ Church Cathedral. Located at King and George streets in downtown Nassau. Built in 1837, and since 1861 the seat of the Anglican Bishop.

St. Andrew's. Located at Duke and Frederick streets in downtown Nassau. The Presbyterian *kirk* was built in 1810.

St. Matthew's. Nassau's oldest church, built by Loyalists in 1800. This Anglican church is surrounded by an interesting old cemetery, dating back to the Loyalist era. Located off of East Bay Street, near the Paradise Island Bridge.

St. Francis Xavier. Nassau's oldest Roman Catholic church, built in 1885. The priory (priest's residence) next door is known as Dunmore House, and was built by the royal governor of The Bahamas in 1787. It served as the residence of governors until Government House was completed in 1803, and from 1829 to 1893 it was the officer's quarters for the West Indian Regiment stationed in Nassau, until it was purchased by the church for use as a priory. Located on Delancey at West Street near downtown Nassau.

St. Augustine's Monastery. Built in 1946 by Fra Jerome, famed in Bahamian history as "The Hermit of Cat Island." It is the home of the Benedictine monks in The Bahamas, an imposing Romanesque structure surrounded by lovely gardens. Located near Fox Hill Road and Bernard Road, off East Bay Street.

Fort Charlotte. Largest of Nassau's forts, built by Lord Dunmore in 1788. The fort, located at Chippingham Road off West Bay Street, overlooks the western end of Nassau Harbour. It offers a moat, ramparts, battlements, ancient cannon, and an intricate system of underground passages and dungeons.

Fort Fincastle. Located high on a hill overlooking Nassau Harbour, the fort was built by Lord Dunmore in 1793. The fort is partially in ruins but offers interesting old guns, a splendid view, and whimsical architecture—it was built in the shape of a ship's prow. It is reached via Elizabeth Avenue or the Queen's Staircase, and is adjacent to the Water Tower.

Fort Montagu. Nassau's oldest and smallest fortification. It was built in 1741 to guard the eastern approach to Nassau Harbour, and in 1776 it was occupied for two weeks by the new American Navy, sent by George Washington to seize His Majesty's cannon and powder in the forts at New Providence.

Government House. The official residence of the governor general. Begun in 1801 and completed in 1803, the mansion is a fine example of British colonial architecture, with strong influence from the southern colonies in America imported to The Bahamas by Loyalists who fled the American Revolution. Splendid tropical gardens, an imposing 12-foot statue of Christopher Columbus, and the fortnightly "Changing of the Guard" ceremony that takes place at 10 A.M. every other Saturday make Government House a top tourist attraction. As a private residence, it is closed to the public; however, it is the site of a monthly "Tea Party" during Goombay Summer celebrations from June through September each year, hosted by Lady Cash, wife of the governor-general. It is also the site of summer fetes and fairs held in the beautiful tropical gardens.

Gregory Arch. The picturesque arch marking the entrance to Grant's Town, an early slave settlement known as "Over the Hill." It is located on the ridge overlooking Nassau at the top of Market Street.

Parliament Square. A cluster of pink, colonnaded government buildings dating from 1803, built by nostalgic Loyalists in the southern colonial style of the Carolinas. For more than 180 years, these buildings have served as the home of The Bahamas House of Assembly, Law Courts, and Legislative Council. At the center of the square is a famous statue of a young Queen Victoria on her throne, dedicated after her death in 1901. Located in the heart of old Nassau, on Bay Street.

Queen's Staircase. An historic flight of 66 steps carved from the limestone cliff by slaves in 1793, leading to Fort Fincastle at the top of the rise. The brick-paved steps rise 102 feet. The landmark received its current name at the turn of the century upon the death of Queen Victoria—there's one step for each year of her reign. Located off Shirley Street at Elizabeth Avenue, near downtown Nassau.

Historic Homes. Many of Nassau's 18th- and 19th-century historic homes have been well preserved as private residences, such as *Addington House,* the home of the Anglican bishop; *The Hermitage,* home of the Catholic bishop; *Dunmore House,* the priory for St. Xavier's Roman Catholic Church; and such other landmarks as *Jacaranda* and *Cascadilla,* both privately owned. Two notable Bahamian mansions have been converted to small inns and gourmet restaurants and are open to the public. *Graycliff,* located on West Hill Street, dates back to the mid-1700s and is an exceptionally well-preserved example of Georgian colonial architecture. *Buena Vista,* a 200-year-old colonial estate, is set amid five acres of tropical gardens and ancient trees. Located on Delancey Street near St. Xavier's.

PARKS AND GARDENS. *Ardastra Gardens.* Beautiful tropical gardens on Chippingham Road, off West Bay Street, near Fort Charlotte. There is also an unique parade of a whole flock of brilliant pink flamingos, who march and strut to the commands of a drill master and have amused Nassau visitors for decades. Show times are 11 A.M. and 4 P.M., Mon.–Sat. Admission is $3 for adults, $1.50 for children 3–12 years old.

Botanic Gardens. A showcase of tropical and semitropical flora located off West Bay Street, near Fort Charlotte. There are 18 acres of flowers, shrubs, and flowering trees and a playground for children. Visiting hours 10 A.M.–4 P.M. daily. Admission is 50 cents for adults and 25 cents for children.

Coral World Bahamas Marine Park. Tel. (809) 322-2001/2/3. A new $10 million attraction, featuring an underwater observatory, 20' beneath the sea, where you can see a living coral reef and reef life without getting wet. Viewing decks, restaurant, and bar. Located off Bay Street, between Cable Beach and downtown Nassau, at Silver Cay. Rates are approximately $10 adults, $7 children.

Royal Victoria Hotel and Gardens. Nassau's oldest hotel, built in 1861. The hotel welcomed guests for more than a century, until it was closed in the early 1970s. The grounds and gardens are well maintained, and offer over 300 species of tropical and subtropical plants. Located on Shirley Street, opposite the Nassau Public Library.

Sea Gardens. Beautiful underwater gardens and living reefs with a great variety of tropical fish life, located in Nassau Harbour. Access is via a fleet of small glass-bottom boats, which depart at frequent intervals all day long from the docks between Rawson Square and Prince George Wharf. The waters are crystal-clear and visibility is excellent, making tours to these unique gardens a favorite of visitors for more than a century. Charge is about $7 per person.

Versailles Gardens and French Cloister. Located on Paradise Island. Lovely terraced gardens, full of tropical plants and flowering shrubs, stretching across the island from harborside to oceanside. Dotted here and there throughout the gardens are museum-quality statues garnered from the William Randolph Hearst collection. On a rise overlooking the harbor is a beautiful fourteenth-century French cloister, once an Augustinian monastery in Montrejau, France.

Seafloor Aquarium. Located near Fort Charlotte on West Bay Street and Chippingham Rd. The aquarium is a showcase of Bahamian underwater reef and fish life, with huge tanks offering fine viewing of exotic species. Open 9 A.M.–5:30 P.M. Mon.–Sat. Aquatic shows featuring trained sea lions and porpoises are offered at 10:30, 12:30, 2:30, and 4:30. Admission charge is $4 for adults, $2 for children under 12. On the grounds, there is an interesting little workshop that produces handcrafted jewelry made from the tortoise-shell, conch, and whelk shells.

 BEACHES. Most of the great hotels on the island are spread along private beaches, but there are several excellent public beaches around the island, all without admittance charge except the famed Paradise Beach on Paradise Island. Among the best beaches are: *Adelaide Beach,* on the southern shore of the island, near Adelaide Village. *Caves Beach,* on West Bay Street, beyond the Cable Beach hotels and near Blake Road, which leads to Nassau International Airport. Nearby are large cave formations reputed to have been pirates' hideaways. *Fort Montagu Beach,* on East Bay Street near Fort Montagu, a popular gathering spot for Bahamians, especially on Sunday afternoons, when there's a good "rake and scrape" band. There's a good beach bar serving juicy burgers and frosty beers. *Goodman's Bay,* on West Bay Street, just before the Cable Beach hotel strip, popular with Bahamians for picnics and cookouts on weekends and public holidays. *Paradise Beach,* The Bahamas' most famous beach, which stretches for more than a mile on the western end of Paradise Island. Admittance charge is $3, which includes a welcome drink, towels, use of changing rooms and lockers. *Western Esplanade,* also known as Lighthouse Beach, it sweeps for several miles along the shore from the Sheraton British Colonial Hotel westward along West Bay Street. There are changing rooms and concession stands.

 PARTICIPANT SPORTS. For the resort vacationer in Nassau, Cable Beach, and Paradise Island, there is an almost unlimited selection of sporting activity for beginners through experts. Rates are subject to change.

Water Sports. *Boating and Fishing:* The following marinas offer deep-sea fishing charters by the day or half-day, and sailboat charters by the day, week, or longer: *East Bay Yacht Basin.* Bareboat charter sailboats offered at an average charter rate of $150–200 per day. The marina offers 25 slips. SS-6394, Nassau. Tel. 2–3754. *Nassau Harbour Club.* Deep-sea fishing charters arranged, ranging from $175 per half day to $300 per day, with bait, tackle, and crew provided; 66 slips. Box SS-6379, Nassau. Tel. 3–1771. *Nassau Yacht Haven.* Deep-sea charter fishing boats available, complete with bait, tackle, and crew. Rates average $250 per half day and $400 per full day. Dock facilities include 120 slips. Box SS-5693, Nassau. Tel. 2–8173. *Hurricane Hole Marina* on Paradise Island. Deep-sea fishing charters available at varied rates depending on size of boat and length of charter; 46 slips. Box N-1216, Nassau. Tel. 6–3000.

Diving. There are many excellent dive sites offshore on the reefs surrounding the island of New Providence, easily reached on dive excursions for beginners and experts offered by several operators who serve resorts on Cable Beach, in Nassau, and on Paradise Island. The following offer one or more dive trips daily, with rates ranging from approximately $30 per trip for experienced divers to $40 per trip for novice divers. Many also offer certification and instruction. *Bahama Divers Ltd.* Two dive trips daily, from 9 A.M. to noon and 2 P.M. to 5 P.M. Sites include drop-offs, wrecks, coral reefs, coral gardens, ocean blue hole. Located on East Bay Street, Box N-5004, Nassau. Tel. 6–5644 or 2–8431. *Nassau Dive Supply.* Daily dive trips visit a variety of dive sites. Located on East Bay Street, Box N-1658, Nassau. Tel. 2–4869. *South Ocean Beach Divers.* Headquartered at the South Ocean Beach Hotel. Two dive boats. Dive sites include drop-offs, coral gardens, shallow reefs. Three dive trips scheduled daily at 9 A.M., 1 P.M., and 7 P.M. Box N-8191, Nassau. Tel. 7–4391/2/3/4/5/6. *Sun Divers.* Daily dive trips scheduled to shallow reefs, deep reefs, and drop-offs. Two dive boats. Headquartered at the Sheraton British Colonial Hotel. Box N-10728, Nassau. Tel. 2–3301. *Underwater Tours Ltd.* Daily reef diving trips aboard four dive boats. Also offers private charters for the following dives: drop-offs, wreck, coral reef, ocean blue hole, and hole drift. Located on East Bay Street Box N-1658, Nassau. Tel. 2–3285. *Underwater Wonderland.* Unique underwater adventure for nonswimmers and nondivers. Walk on the ocean floor amid coral reefs and sea gardens without getting your hair wet! Using sealed diving helmets, linked to an air supply from a boat, Captain Chris Hartley personally conducts twice-daily cruises and "undersea walks" (except Sun.). Tour includes ½-day cruise aboard the 57-foot yacht *Pied Piper.* Rates are $28 per person, departures at 9:30 A.M. and 1:30 P.M. Tel. 2–8234.

Golf. There are four excellent 18-hole championship golf courses on the island, and a nine-hole course near downtown Nassau. All are open for play by the general public. A fifth 18-hole championship course, the Lyford Cay Gulf Club, is private and available only to members and their guests. Greens fees average $10–20 for 18 holes, under $10 for 9 holes. Some hotel courses are free to guests. Carts, clubs, and lessons are extra. *Cable Beach Golf Club.* Located opposite the new Cable Beach Hotel and Casino. Par 72, 18 holes, with a restaurant, pro shop, and clubhouse. Box N-3026, Nassau. Tel. 7–8231. *Atlantis Hotel Golf Course.* Located near downtown Nassau. Nine-hole par 3 course with a pro shop. Box N-8347, Nassau. Tel. 3–4481. *Coral Harbour Golf Club.* Located in the Coral Harbour area on the southwestern shore of New Providence. Par 72, 18-hole course with pro shop, bar, and snack bar. Practice and putting green available. Box N-4826, Nassau. Tel. 7–7146. *Paradise Island Golf Club.* Par 72, 18-hole championship, oceanside course at the eastern end of Paradise Island. Restaurant and pro shop. Box N-4777, Nassau. Tel. 6–3925. *South Ocean Beach Golf Club.* Located adjacent to the South Ocean Beach Hotel, on the southwestern end of New Providence. A USGA-rated, 18-hole, par 72 course. Facilities include a lounge, bars, restaurant, and pro shop. Box N-8191, Nassau. Tel. 6–4391 to 6–4399.

Horseback Riding. Horses may be rented by the hour, with a choice of saddles, at the Harbourside Riding Stables on Paradise Island. There are excellent wooded trails across the island and along the ocean shore $10 per hour. Box 4171, Nassau. Tel. 6–3733. Horseback riding may also be arranged on New Providence Island, on the southwestern shore near Coral Harbour, at *Happy Trails Stable.* Rate for 1½-hour trail rides is $18 including transportation to and from your hotel. Experienced guide accompanies riders. Tel. 6–1820.

Parasailing. Exciting flights over the ocean waters along the shore of Cable Beach and Paradise Island. Parasailors are harnessed to a parachute, then take off from a special raft, towed by a speedboat. The following hotels offer parasailing: *Ambassador Beach Hotel* on Cable Beach. $20 for 5–6 minutes; $30 for 8–10 minutes. Tel. 7–8231. *Nassau Beach Hotel* on Cable Beach. $20 for 5 minutes; $30 for 8 minutes. Tel. 7–7711. *Cable Beach Hotel,* $25 for 15 minutes. Tel. 7–7070. *The Grand Hotel* on Paradise Island. $20 for 7–10 minutes. Tel. 6–2011. *Paradise Island Resort & Casino,* $20 for 5–6 minutes. Tel. 6–3000.

Tennis. The following hotels and resorts have tennis courts open to hotel guests and visitors. Rates run $2–8 per hour; court use may be free to guests.

Cable Beach: *Ambassador Beach Hotel.* Eight asphalt courts, four lighted for night play. Lessons available. Tel. 7–8231. *Cable Beach Hotel and Casino.* Five clay and five all-weather courts lighted for night play; three indoor squash courts; three racquetball courts and pro shop. Tel. 7–6000. *Cable Beach Inn.* Two hard-surface courts. Lessons available, including group tennis clinics. Tel. 7–7341. *Nassau Beach Hotel.* Nine Flexipave surface courts, six lighted for night play. Lessons available. Tel. 7–7711.

Nassau: *Nassau Squash and Racquet Club.* Located on Independence Drive. Three Har-Tru surface courts, plus squash and racquetball courts. Open seven days a week. Tel. 2–3882. *Royal Bahamian.* 2 flexipave courts, lighted. Lessons available. Tel. 7–7481. *Sheraton British Colonial Hotel.* Three hard-surface courts, lighted for night play. Lessons available. Tel. 2–3301. *Atlantis Hotel.* Two asphalt-surface courts. Tel. 3–4481. *South Ocean Beach Hotel.* Four asphalt-surface courts, two lighted; ball machine. Tel. 6–4391.

Paradise Island: *Britannia Towers.* Nine hard-surface courts. Tel. 6–3000. (Paradise Island Resort and Casino.) *Club Mediterranée.* 20 Har-Tru courts, nine lighted for night play; ball machines, video replay machine; lessons available. 6–2640. Tel. *Holiday Inn.* Four asphalt-surface courts, two lighted for night play (reservations only). Lessons available. Tel. 6–2101. *Loew's Harbour Cove.* Two asphalt-surface courts lighted for night play, lessons available. Tel.

6–2561. *Ocean Club.* Nine Har-Tru courts, four lighted for night play; lessons available. Tel. 6–2501. *Paradise Towers.* Three asphalt-surface courts, lighted for night play. (Paradise Island Resort and Casino.) Tel. 6–2000. *The Grand Hotel.* Four asphalt-surface courts, lighted for night play. Tel. 6–2011.

Windsurfing. The following hotels offer windsurfing: *Ambassador Beach,* $11 per hour. Tel. 7–8231. *Cable Beach Hotel,* $12 first hour, $8 additional hours; lessons $35 per hour. Tel. 7–6000; Paradise Island Resort & Casino, $15 per hour, $25 for 2 hours; lessons free, Tel. 6–3000.

Boat Cruises. One of the highlights of most Nassau vacations is a boat cruise through the harbor and to some of the lovely offshore cays. Many small, glass-bottom boats are available at oceanfront hotels and from the docks and marinas, usually offering one- to two-hour tours of the sea gardens and reefs that fringe Nassau's shores. Rates average $5–7 per person. Other longer and more elaborate cruises of the surrounding waters and cays are also available, many including beach parties, picnics, and entertainment. They may be booked through the tour desk at your hotel or directly through the operator. Several examples follow, with approximate rates. All rates quoted are subject to change.

M/V Calypso. New 80-foot catamaran offers full-day excursions from Nassau Harbour to beautiful Blue Lagoon Island, a private secluded cay off Paradise Island. The *Calypso* has three decks, native bands for dancing, and snack bars on board. Day excursions are $35 per person. Dinner cruises offered Mon., Wed., and Sat. at $30 per person; moonlight cruises offered on Fri., 8 P.M. to midnight. Tel. 6–3577/3578.

J&M Sports Fishing & Cruises. Fishing and sightseeing cruises by the day or week. Choice of 3 boats: 50' Hatteras sleeps 6, with captain, mate, and cook; 33' Bertram, sleeps 2, with captain and mate; and 27' Sport Fisherman, accommodates 6, with captain. Rates vary by length of cruises and boat chosen. Deveaux and Bay Street. Tel. 5–2871 or 4–2178.

Keewatin Sailing Cruise. Daily cruises aboard a 56-foot Alden schooner, which departs from the British Colonial and Loew's Harbour Cove docks around 9:30 A.M., returns around 4 P.M. Cruise includes sailing and a two-hour beach party with picnic lunch at lovely Rose Island off Paradise Island. $30 per person. Tel. 5–1821.

Nautilus Cruise. A unique 97-foot glass-bottom submarine, built originally for the James Bond movie *Thunderball,* cruises Nassau Harbour and nearby sea gardens, reefs, and wrecks. Viewing is superb through individual underwater glass portholes, although the ship does not submerge. Departs John Alfred Wharf at Deveaux St. (next to Captain Nemo's Restaurant) at 9:30 and 11:30 A.M. and 1:30 and 3:30 P.M. Rate is $15 per person. Dinner cruises depart at 6 P.M., cost $25 per person. Moonlight cruises, priced at $20 per person, offer excellent viewing with underwater lights. Tel. 5–2871/6.

Tropic Bird. One of the largest catamarans on the Atlantic offers daily cruises from Prince George Wharf to a lovely Paradise Island beach. Goombay music and beach picnic. Cost for the three-hour cruise is $15 per person. Departure at 10:15 A.M. Tel. 2–2931.

MUSIC, DANCE, AND STAGE. Nassau has a sophisticated international population, and many Bahamians and foreign residents are involved in local musical and theatrical societies that put on amateur and semiprofessional productions. Other organizations promote performances by guest artists from abroad, often as fund-raising events for charitable organizations. Among the active groups on the island are the *Nassau Music Society* and the *Bahamas Music Society,* both of which sponsor guest artists. Amateur theatrical groups include the *Bahamas Drama Circle, Nassau Players,* and the *Bahamas School of Theatre;* amateur dance groups include the *Children of Atlantis Dance Troupe, National School of Dance,* and the *Nassau Civic Ballet.* Choral groups are also popular in the capital city, as well as gospel singers and choirs. Among these are the *Diocesan Chorale, Lucayan Chorale, Chamber Singers, Nassau Operatic Society,* and the *Renaissance Singers.* In addition, Bahamian dialect comedy has had a successful revival in recent years, with *James Catalyn and Friends,* an excellent professional troupe, offering regularly scheduled performances. All locally produced and guest performances are well publicized on the island through newspapers, flyers, and placards placed at hotel desks. Many performances are held at the 50-year-old, newly renovated *Dundas Centre for the Performing Arts* on Mackey Street in Nassau, tel. 2–2728.

SHOPPING. The prestigious international business magazine *Forbes* recently published an article which claimed that the two cities in the world with the best buys on watches were Hong Kong and Nassau. The article could have mentioned several other items available in Nassau that belong on any world-class "best buys" list—German and Japanese cameras and optics, French perfumes bottled and packaged in France, all the great names and patterns of European china and crystal, Scotch cashmeres, Irish linens, and Colombian emeralds (which, if uncut, unpolished, or unmounted enjoy an unusual duty-free entrance status to the U.S.). There are hundreds of shops throughout New Providence which offer a broad selection of all these items, but most are clustered along an eight-block stretch of Bay Street in old Nassau or spill over onto a few side streets downtown. Some of the most elegant jewelry and clothing stores have branches in the shopping arcades or the large oceanside hotels on Cable Beach and Paradise Island. The shops that follow are all located on Bay Street or within a block or two on the side streets in downtown. Savings on many big-ticket items average 20 to 50 percent over identical purchases in the U.S. and Canada. However, if you plan to make a major purchase, it is always wise to check out the prices back home before you begin your vacation. Store hours are 9 A.M. to 5 P.M. Monday through Saturday, although some shops close at noon one day a week, usually Thursday or Friday. Only the Strawmarket is open seven days a week. Most shops accept major credit cards.

Bay Street

Bernards. An extensive collection of china and crystal. Agents for such lines as Wedgwood in china; Lalique in crystal. Also carries Ernest Borel and Seiko watches and gift items. Tel. 2–2841.

John Bull. The longest established and largest camera store in The Bahamas, noted for excellent buys on watches. In cameras, Konica, Nikon, Olympus, Hasselblad, Minolta, and Vivitar. In watches, included are Rolex, Concord, Corum, Omega, Pulsar, Longines, and Seiko. There's also an extensive selection of gold and silver jewelry and very good buys on saltwater or freshwater pearls under the name Adeana Creations (manufactured in The Bahamas, and duty-free to the U.S.). Three shops on Bay Street and in Paradise. Tel. 2–4252.

Carib Jewelers. Fine china, crystal, and watches. Tel. 2–1239.

Colombian Emeralds. Fine investment-quality gems unmounted or mounted in original settings, an excellent selection of gold and silver jewelry, plus Girard-Perregeaux and Seiko watches. Certified appraisals and a U.S. service office. The shop also has a Royal Doulton boutique. Tel. 2–2201/1484.

Discount Warehouse. Good buys in jewelry set with precious and semi-precious stones, gold and silver jewelry. Best buys are on coral and conch-shell costume jewelry made on the premises. Watches. A money-back guarantee if you can buy identical items in Nassau for less. Tel. 5–1522.

Francis Peek. Fine antiques and collectibles. Outstanding collection of Vista Alegre hand-painted birds and Herend china from Hungary. Tel. 2–2332.

Gold. Direct importers of fine gold jewelry sold by weight. Prices vary daily with the London gold fixings. Tel. 2–1851.

Gold Mine. Imports gold and silver jewelry items which are sold by weight based on daily quotations. Additional items include gemstones of investment quality and gift items. Tel. 2–4957.

Gold and Silversmiths Ltd. A fine line of handcrafted Caribbean jewelry in gold and silver by Y de Lima of Trinidad. Tel. 2–8651/2067.

Greenfire Emeralds Ltd. Specializes in cut, uncut, polished, and unpolished emeralds, and exquisite handcrafted jewelry designs and settings. Branch stores in the Paradise Towers and Grand Hotel on Paradise Island. Tel. 6–6564.

Island Shop. "Everything Under the Sun," one of Nassau's oldest and best-known shops. Men's, women's and children's fashions, swimwear, and sportswear, including cashmeres, lambswool, and Shetland sweaters. Also carries a line of cameras and watches. The shop offers the largest selection of books by Bahamians and about The Bahamas found anywhere in the islands. Tel. 2–4183.

Johnson Brothers Ltd. The Bahamas' oldest and finest designers and manufacturers of conch, whelk, tortoise-shell, and coral jewelry. Superb handcrafted items in all price ranges. Sold at their Bay Street shop and in other fine stores throughout The Bahamas. Tel. 2–4098.

Lightbourns Pharmacy. Serving Nassau shoppers since 1889, with the largest selection of imported designer French perfumes in Nassau. Beauty products by Dior, Orlane, and Stendahl; Badedas and Roger & Gallet soaps. Tel. 2–2095.

Lords Limited. Fine jewelry and gift items, exclusive agents for Patek-Philippe watches, a good selection of Cartier watches, lighters. Tel. 2–1449.

Mademoiselle. Another Nassau "landmark," offering a fine selection of men's, women's, and children's fashions including an Androsia boutique (handcrafted batiks from the island of Andros). A wide selection of moderate to expensive gift items, jewelry, and watches. Branches on Cable Beach and Paradise Island. Tel. 2–1404/5/6/7/8.

Nassau Shop. One of Nassau's oldest and largest department stores, with an excellent collection of clothing for men, women, and children. Watch brands include the Piaget Polo, Baume & Mercier, Lanvin, and Concord. Broad range of Irish linens, European leather belts and bags, gold and silver jewelry, plus hundreds of souvenir items in all price ranges. Tel. 2–8405.

Perfume Bar. All the great names in designer and imported perfumes. One-stop perfume shopping, as prices vary little from store to store. Several branches. 2–8400.

Pipe of Peace. "World's most complete tobacconist" and one of Nassau's best-known shops for half a century. Also offers a good line of watches, cameras, and stereos. Branches at Paradise Village, Loew's Harbour Cove. Tel. 5–2022.

Relax-Sir. For the best-dressed men around town, European designer fashions in shirts, slacks, leisure, swimwear, and shoes. Tel. 2–2422.

Strawmarket. One of the world's largest strawmarkets, and the action spot of old Nassau. Hundreds of straw ladies hawk their wares, amid tens of thousands of brilliantly decorated and magically woven hats and bags, baskets and totes, mats and slippers, wall hangings and dolls, and more. You'll also find Queen Conch shells, King Helmet shells, sea fans, and corals of every shape from the Bahamian sea. Look for necklaces and bracelets strung with pea shells, sharks' teeth, and bright beans, berries or pods; primitive African print dashikis and shirts, skirts, and the marvelous "Seven-Way Calypso Dress" in matching fabric and prints, all fashioned and sewn by the island women. Or seek out original oils and prints by local artists and fearsome wood carvings, reminders of the Bahamian-African heritage. Bargain with the vendors—all prices are negotiable, and the straw ladies love to bargain. The Strawmarket is open from early morning to early evening, seven days a week, and it is located in Nassau's new Market Plaza on Bay Street.

Solomon's Mines. Another classic Nassau shop known for decades to Bay Street shoppers, offering the largest assortment of china, crystal, jewelry, and French perfumes in The Bahamas. Tel. 2–8324.

Treasure Box. A jewelry boutique famous for an exclusive line of exotic elephant-hair and 18-karat rolled-gold rings, bracelets, and earrings. They also offer a beautiful collection of Chinese cloisonné accessories, cultured pearls, coral, jade, and conch jewelry. Tel. 2–1662.

Treasure Traders. A wonderful collection of crystal, Lladró figurines from Spain, the Studio-Line by Rosenthal, as well as Austrian Swarovski pieces. Tel. 2–8521.

T-Shirts Unlimited. That says it all. Two shops on Bay Street and a third shop on Marlborough Street. Tel. 2–1336.

Vanité. Original Hummel figurines and dolls. Anri Toriart, Schatz clocks, music boxes, children's gifts. Tel. 2–2594.

British Colonial Arcade
(At the west end of Bay Street)

Black Coral and. . . . One of Nassau's finest art studios, featuring stunning black-coral sculptures and gold and diamond jewelry by renowned international sculptor Bernard K. Passman. Tel. 5–3364, 5–4538.

Optique Shoppe. Designer eyeglasses and sunglasses. Eye examinations, one-day service on prescription glasses and repairs. Tel. 5–2386.

Charbay Plaza
(Near Rawson Square, on harbor side of Bay Street)

Galaxy Shoes. Men's and women's imported European footwear and leather accessories. Tel. 5–2443.

Jade Dolphin. Nassau's newest department store, with an extensive collection of Scotch cashmeres, clan plaids, Irish linen, jewelry, and cameras. A broad selection of watches. Tel. 5–7554, 5–8750.

International Bazaar
(Arcade linking Bay Street and the harbor)

Candy Bar. Finest candies and chocolates from around the world, homemade Bahamian candies and Scottish shortbreads featured. Tel. 2–4466.

Maison Pierre. Men's designer fashions and gift items. Tel. 5–7523.

Patrick's Camera Specialists. 24-hour film processing, camera repairs, and a wide range of cameras and accessories. A branch in the Britannia Beach Hotel. Tel. 5–0851.

Pied Piper. Large selection of gifts and souvenirs, from European chocolates to imported backgammon and chess sets and Citizen watches. Tel. 5–3515.

Off Bay Street

Leather Masters, Bank Ln. Exclusive line of Gucci handbags and leather accessories, plus other fine leather products from Europe. Tel. 2–7697.

Balmain Antiques, Charlotte St. One of the world's largest and finest collection of antique prints, maps, and charts of The Bahamas and West Indies. Many of investment quality, and there is no U.S. duty on antiques. Same-day framing by expert craftsmen. Upstairs location, next to Cellar Restaurant. Tel. 3–7421.

Bahamas Fragrances & Cosmetic Factory, Charlotte St. Made-in-The Bahamas, aloe suntan, after-tan, body lotions, and cosmetics. Tel. 3–8030.

Brass and Leather Shop, Charlotte St. Exclusive agents for prestigious Land luggage, along with other fine leather ware. An extensive collection of English brassware. Two shops on Charlotte Street. Tel. 2–3806.

Coin of the Realm, Charlotte St. The Bahamas' finest collection of investment-grade coins and stamps. They offer mountings for both gold and silver coins, and chains. Exclusive jewelry items. Tel. 2–4862.

Harbour View Gifts, Charlotte St. North on the harbor. Offers a broad range of leather and eelskin goods, tropical resort fashions, porcelain floral arrangements, and many other gift items, including Ravisa watches. Tel. 2–8351.

Scottish Shop, Charlotte St. Nassau's most complete line of Scotch products including: tartans, clan jewelry, cashmere sweaters, Edinburgh crystal, kilts and skirts, mohair rugs, heraldic plaques, Perthshire paperweights, Peggy Nisbet dolls. Thistle pottery and Kangol hats. Tel. 2–4720.

Ambrosine, Marlborough St. One of the most exclusive women's fashion shops in Nassau, with an extensive collection of Italian resort wear. Also on hand are Thai cottons and silks, Bleyle of West Germany pants and jackets, and dozens of gift items. Tel. 2–4205.

Amanda's, Marlborough St. The right place for fine cashmeres by Pringle of Scotland, Ballantyne, and other fine European sweaters, blouses, gloves, stoles, and scarves. In addition, there is a full line of Mary Chess designs. Tel. 2–2707.

Chez Mizpah, Marlborough St. Lovely designer boutique featuring women's fashions, sportswear, swimwear, imported lingerie, footwear, makeup, and accessories. Custom fitting and designs available. Tel. 2–8653.

Francise, Marlborough St. A fine fashion center for evening wear and cocktail dresses by leading Canadian designers, Alpinit Swiss fashions, English and German swimsuits and poolside wear. Tel. 2–8800.

Cole's of Nassau, Parliament St. A favorite fashion shop for Bahamians and visitors alike, with a colorful collection of designer dresses, beachwear, sundresses, and accessories. The shop also offers the famous rattan-handle "Bermuda Bags." Tel. 2–8393.

The Linen Shop, Parliament St. Wide selection of Irish linens. The shop also carries Bahama Hand Prints, European silk blouses, Belgian tapestries, hand-embroidered infant's wear, and unique gift items. Tel. 2–4266.

Mr. Photo. One-hour mechanized film processing. The shop will print your photos on postcards for a unique message to folks back home. Carries a full line of Fuji film. Near the Strawmarket, on the harbor. Tel. 3–7070.

Off East Bay Street, Near Paradise Island Bridge

Bahama Hand Prints, Mackey St. Workshop and showroom for one of The Bahamas' oldest and most famous cottage industries, original silk-screen designs on fine cotton blends in fabrics or fashions. Watch the whole process, from design to finished piece, or choose a ready-made item for men, women, or children. There are also many handmade gift items such as tea towels, placemats, tablecloths, pot holders, and more. Located north of Shirley Street, about ¼ mile from the Paradise Island Bridge.

Nassau Glass Art Gallery, Mackey St. Nassau's largest and most complete art gallery, with works of Bahamian artists on exhibit and for sale, as well as Haitian art and other foreign originals and reproductions in a broad price range. Expert framing, packing, and shipping anywhere in the world. Located on Mackey Street, about ½ mile south of the Paradise Island Bridge. Tel. 2–8165/2723.

Temple Gallery. Fine art gallery in an old gingerbread house on East Bay Street. Owned by Brent Malone, outstanding Bahamian artist. Frequent exhibitions, visitors welcome.

 RESTAURANTS. Nassau, Cable Beach, and Paradise Island offer a cornucopia of dining pleasures in all price ranges, from down-home Bahamian cooking to haute cuisine, and ambience ranging from candlelight-and-crystal to plastic-and-chrome. There are world-famous dining legends such as Café Martinique, a must since James Bond made it famous in *Thunderball,* and Graycliff, where everyone who is anyone wines and dines.

We call $36 and up *Deluxe;* $25–35 *Expensive;* $15–24 *Moderate;* and under $15 *Inexpensive* for a three-course meal for one, excluding tip and beverage. Be sure to call ahead for reservations.

Cable Beach

Baccarat. *Deluxe.* Tel. 7–6400. The Royal Bahamian Hotels' superb addition to Nassau's elegant French restaurants. Beautiful room, lovely view, lace cloths, and Wedgwood china. Fine wine list, extensive menu of traditional gourmet French dishes. Dinner only, jackets suggested. All major credit cards.

Le Relais. *Deluxe.* Tel. 7–7711. Nassau Beach Hotel's gourmet dining spot. Rosy pink, mirrored decor, fine service. French cuisine, veal, beef, and creative seafood. Try the stuffed quail with tarragon sauce, flambéed bananas au rhum. Good wine list. Dinner only, jackets required. AE, BA, DC, MC, V.

Regency Room. *Deluxe.* Tel. 7–6000. Elegance at the lavish new Cable Beach Hotel and Casino, at the top of the four-story atrium lobby. Superb selection of continental cuisine. Try the crème de papaya soup, mousse of deep sea scallops in champagne, and entrecote villette (aged prime steak). Classic wine selection. Dinner only, jackets required. All major credit cards.

Sol e Mare. *Deluxe.* Tel. 7–6200. Superb Northern Italian specialties in an elegant setting overlooking the sea. Located in the Cable Beach Casino. Try the veal marsala with fettucine alfredo and Italian pastries. Fine Italian and French wines. Dinner only, jackets required. AE, BA, DC, MC, V.

Lobster Pot. *Expensive.* Tel. 7–7711. Fine seafood at the Nassau Beach Hotel. Nautical decor, relaxed setting, indoor or outdoor dining. Specialties include flying fish pie, bouillabaisse carib, and Nassau Grouper. Good, reasonable wines. Dinner only. AE, BA, DC, MC, V.

Rib Room. *Expensive.* Tel. 7–8231. Ambassador Beach Hotel. English hunt-club setting, polished woods, gracious service. Beef the specialty in many delicious forms. Favored standbys are roast prime ribs, filet mignon, and pepper steak. Top it off with "Bahamian Coffee," flambeed Nassau Royale liqueur and whipped cream. Dinner only, jackets suggested. AE, BA, DC, MC, V.

Tsunami. *Expensive.* Nassau's newest Oriental dining spot, in the Ambassador Beach Hotel. Distinctive Polynesian island setting, Chinese, Cantonese, and South Seas specialties. Try the braised crab with cashews and black bean sauce. Good wine list and tropical drinks. Dinner only, jackets suggested. AE, BA, DC, MC, V.

Albrion's. *Moderate.* Tel. 7–7922/4. At Casuarinas Apartment Hotel, some of the best Bahamian food on Cable Beach. Located across West Bay Street in the new wing, with indoor and outdoor dining, breakfast, lunch, and dinner. Famous dishes include conch creole, pork chops with peas 'n rice, Eleutheran pineapple, and guava duff. AE, DC, MC, V.

Androsia. *Moderate.* Tel. 7–7801. Bahamian and American dishes in a cheerful setting at the Henrea Carlette apartment hotel. Breakfast, lunch, and dinner served daily. Chicken 'n rice or grouper fingers are good choices, plus home-made pies and cakes. AE, MC, V.

The Back Stage Deli. *Moderate.* Tel. 7–6200. A New Yorker's delight at the Cable Beach Casino. Thick deli sandwiches of pastrami and corned beef; smoked fish, chopped liver, and other favorites. AE, BA, DC, MC, V.

Traveller's Rest. *Moderate.* Tel. 7–7633. West of Cable Beach, near Gambier Village. Legendary Bahamian cookery, informal indoor-outdoor-oceanside dining. Try the fine turtle steak or conch fritters, and Courage on tap. Open for lunch and dinner daily, and a favorite spot for Bahamian musicians—don't miss one of their "anything goes" Sunday-afternoon jam sessions. AE.

Swank Pizza. *Moderate.* Tel. 7–7495. At Cable Beach shopping center; on Woodes Rogers Walk, downtown Nassau; Paradise Island Village; and Oakes Field. Casual atmosphere, friendly service featuring sizzling steaks, seafood, and delicious pizza till the wee hours. (Ever tried conch pizza?) AE, MC.

Nassau

Buena Vista. *Deluxe.* Tel. 2–2811 or 2–4039. Superb nouvelle cuisine in historic old Bahamian house up the hill from Bay Street on Delancey. Creative cookery, attention to detail, and personalized service are hallmarks, rack of lamb, stuffed shrimp, Bahamian lobster, and soft island music are trademarks. Excellent California and European wines. Dine indoors or on the tropical garden terrace. Lunch and dinner daily; jackets suggested. DC, MC, V.

Graycliff. *Deluxe.* Tel. 2–2796 or 5–4832. Magnificent 200-year-old colonial mansion, filled with antiques and English country-house charm. Outstanding Continental and Bahamian menu includes Beluga caviar, French escargots, and foie gras with truffles for starters. Delights are grouper au poivre vert, chateaubriand, and tournedos Rossini, with elegant pastries and flaming coffees for dessert. Wine cellars recognized as the finest in the Caribbean by Relais et Chateaux. Located on the hilltop off Bay Street across from Government House. Open for lunch and dinner. Jackets suggested. AE, BA, DC, MC, V.

Ristorante Da Vinci. *Deluxe.* Tel. 2–2748. Impeccable service with notable Italian and French cuisine. Homemade pastas highlight house specialties of beef, veal, and fresh seafood. Try the veal scallopine or scampi meuniere, topped off with a flambéed dessert and brandied coffee. Soft piano and strings provide background music; candlelight and crystal make for romantic decor. One of the finest wine selections in The Bahamas, priced at $14–250. Dinner only, jacket required. Located near downtown on West Bay Street. AE, MC, V.

Del Prado. *Expensive.* Tel. 5–0324/5. Old-world Spanish decor with international fare prepared to order at the El Greco Hotel on West Bay Street. Gracious service and friendly atmosphere, marked by excellent French and Italian specialties. House favorite is steak Diane flambéed at your table; a variety of Bahamian grouper dishes such as le filet de grouper Normandy, sauteed in a tempting wine sauce. Excellent *carte de vin* with vintage champagnes and French wines. Dinner only, jackets required. MC, V, DC, AE.

Liz's. *Expensive.* Tel. 2–4780. In the heart of downtown Nassau, just off Bay Street on Elizabeth Avenue. Delightful island decor, casual and friendly atmosphere. Features thick, juicy steaks and a potpourri of Bahamian seafood, plus tall tropical drinks. Dinner only, jackets suggested. AE, MC, V.

Sun And. . . . *Expensive.* Tel. 3–1205. Located in the Fort Montagu Beach area, at Lakeview Road off Shirley Street. A fine old Bahamian home amid tropical gardens and a blue lagoon. Known for more than a decade of fine dining. Now owned and operated by Chef Ronny, who formerly presided over the cuisine at Graycliff and at the posh millionaire's hideaway of Cat Cay. Al fresco dining under the palms or amid candlelit elegance indoors, from an international menu which includes such unusual delicacies as veal sweetbreads and duckling paté, along with hearty entrees of roast beef, rack of lamb, and grilled steaks. Dinner only, jackets suggested. All major credit cards.

La Regata Room. *Expensive.* Tel. 2–8431. Nautical and nice, located at Nassau's charming Pilot House Hotel at the foot of the Paradise Island Bridge. Traditional gathering spot for yachtsmen and the sport-fishing set (it is just across the street from Nassau Yacht Haven). The atmosphere is casual and friendly, and the food is excellent. Choose from American or Continental dishes —lobster sautéed in brandy, mushrooms, and shallots is a favorite. Dancing nightly to a Goombay beat or an island balladeer, indoors or outdoors amid tropical greenery on the poolside terrace. Lunch and dinner. AE, BA, DC, M, V.

Bayside. *Moderate.* Tel. 2–3301. 1 Bay St., in the Sheraton British Colonial Hotel, with the best harborside view in all of Nassau. Delightful decor with a nautical flair. Super salad bar, fresh seafood, steaks and ribs, tasty and plentiful. Newly opened is *Blackbeard's Forge,* with lobster, shrimp, and steak grilled at your table, located in the patio bar. Dancing and Disco music nightly. AE, BA, DC, MC, V.

Bridge Inn. *Moderate.* Tel. 3–2077 or 3–1806. Nassau side of the Paradise Bridge. A prized Bahamian eatery with a happy crowd, good dining, and dancing nightly. Island seafoods are a specialty, with American dishes such as beef, steak, and chops, plus a generous salad bar. Early-bird prices from 4–6 P.M.; happy hour with hot hors d'oeuvres AE, MC, V.

Captain Nemo's. *Moderate.* Tel. 5–2876 or 5–2871. Right on the water overlooking busy Nassau Harbour and Paradise Island. Native Bahamian dishes are featured—try the cracked conch or chicken with peas 'n rice. Dining indoors or on the terrace. Easy nautical decor and ambience. About four blocks east of Rawson Square, at John Alfred Wharf, Deveaux Street. No credit cards.

Green Shutters. *Moderate.* Tel. 5–5702. A classic English pub in a classic old Bahamian house just off Rawson Square on Parliament Street. Good hearty pub fare like steak-and-kidney pie, roast beef and Yorkshire pudding, with five imported beers on draught. Casual and friendly atmosphere. Lunch and dinner.

Mai Tai. *Moderate.* Tel. 6–5088 or 3–3106. One of the prettiest settings in old Nassau, at Waterloo Lodge. Located on East Bay Street near Fort Montagu. Excellent Chinese and Polynesian food presented with flair; tall tropical drinks, flaming appetizers, and everything from pork fried rice to sizzling *War Bah* and sweet-and-sour ribs. Lunch and dinner daily to midnight. All major credit cards.

Pronto Ristorante. *Moderate.* Tel. 3–3771. New Italian dining spot overlooking the harbor and marina at Nassau Harbour Club, presided over by Pino Garofanelli, doyen of Nassau's best Italian cookery for more than 20 years. Extensive menu, relaxed atmosphere, and spectacular view from second-floor vantage point—eat indoors or outdoors under a covered terrace. East Bay Street near the Paradise Bridge. Lunch and dinner. MC, AE.

Roselawn Cafe. *Moderate.* Tel. 5–1018. Delightful atmosphere indoors or outdoors in an old Bahamian house just off Parliament Square on Bank Lane downtown. Count on fresh homemade pastas, lasagna, fettucine, spaghetti al dente; or try the Spanish paella—delicious. Lunch and dinner except Sunday, live entertainment. AE, MC, V.

The Terrace. *Moderate.* Tel. 2–2836/7. At the Parliament Hotel just off Bay Street at Rawson Square. Attractive, tropical outdoor setting. Succulent Bahamian dishes such as conch curry and sousse chicken, plus steaks and chops. Superb native buffet Tues. and Fri. Live music nightly. Lunch and dinner.

Tony Roma's. *Moderate.* Tel. 5–2020. "The Place for Ribs." Branch of the Florida/California minichain, which draws crowds everywhere. Succulent barbecued baby back ribs are the house specialty, along with delicious "loaves" of French onion rings. Located on West Bay Street between downtown Nassau and Cable Beach. Live entertainment nightly. Lunch and dinner. AE, MC, V.

Bahamian Kitchen. *Inexpensive.* Tel. 5–0702. One block off Bay Street at Market St. and Trinity Place. Authentic Bahamian cooking, turtle steak, okra soup, stew fish, steamed mutton, and local desserts like guava duff, rum cake, and coconut pie.

Casablanca. *Inexpensive.* Tel. 2–7638 or 5–3403. On Marlborough Street. Outstanding Bahamian specialties cooked and served with an island flair. Lunch and dinner daily plus take-out service. Major credit cards.

Europe. *Inexpensive.* Tel. 2–8032. Near downtown, in the Ocean Spray Hotel opposite Lighthouse Beach. Simple, quiet dining room with hearty German dishes, Bahamian and American specialties. Breakfast, lunch, and dinner, plus late snacks. AE, MC, V.

Fish Net. *Inexpensive.* Tel. 3–2568. Unpretentious decor, friendly atmosphere, personal service—and some of the best Bahamian cooking on the island. Boiled fish or stewed fish with grits and johnnycake (the traditional Bahamian Sunday breakfast) is outstanding; chicken, pork, conch, and fish dishes are great—"all you can eat." Open daily for breakfast, lunch, dinner till 2 A.M. Located on East Bay Street opposite the Paradise Island Bridge. AE, MC, V.

Grand Central. *Inexpensive.* Tel. 2–8356. A landmark for Greek cooking since the 1930s, right downtown on Charlotte Street just off Bay Street. Very simple, counter and booths, but notable Greek salads, shishkebobs, and pastries, plus Bahamian specialties like boiled fish and johnny cake, conch chowder, green turtle steak. Breakfast, lunch, and dinner. AE, DC, MC, V.

Harbour Moon Chinese Restaurant. *Inexpensive.* Tel. 2–1599. At Bay and Devaux sts. Original Chinese dishes. Cantonese and Szechuan. Open to midnight, 7 days. Take-out, too.

Marietta's. *Inexpensive.* Tel. 2–8395 or 5–1809. On Okra Hill off East Bay Street near the Paradise Island Bridge. Neat, little 40-room family-owned hotel with a very popular native restaurant. Great island dishes—try the Andros crab stew. (Many Bahamians say it's the best home cooking in town.) AE, V.

Palm Restaurant. *Inexpensive.* Tel. 3–7444. Bay Street's newest dining option, right downtown opposite the John Bull Shop. Food is plentiful, wholesome, and delicious. Soups, salads, pastas, and hot or cold sandwiches for lunch or late afternoon snacks; 16 flavors of Ho-Jo ice cream and homemade pies at *Scoops* next door. Breakfast and lunch.

Outside Nassau

Larry's Pub II. *Inexpensive to Moderate.* Tel. 2–3800. On the cross-island airport road at Thompson Boulevard and John F. Kennedy Drive, on the way to Nassau International. A friendly, casual pub atmosphere. Steaks and burgers offered, but notable for cracked conch, native steamed turtle, and broiled Bahamian lobster. Open every day, serving till 2 A.M. AE, MC, V.

The Shoal. *Inexpensive to Moderate.* Tel. 3–4400. Also located on the airport road, closer to downtown, at Nassau Street. Fresh seafood and Bahamian dishes are excellent—try the "Fisherman's Special," with steamed conch, fried grouper, and sweet plantains, plus the best johnnycake in Nassau. No credit cards.

Paradise Island

Café Martinique. *Deluxe.* Tel. 6–3000. Fin de siècle decor and elegant Parsienne flair. Continental dining indoors and dancing on a moonlit terrace overlooking the Paradise Lagoon. A full French a la carte menu—try the turtle soup and shrimp de jong or escargots and beef Wellington, topped off with a piping hot Grand Marnier soufflé and flaming coffee. Superb wine list. Dinner daily and elegant Sunday brunch, jackets required. (Next to Britannia Towers.) AE, DC, MC, V.

Julie's. *Deluxe.* Tel. 6–2011. A rising star in Paradise, showcase of The Grand Hotel. Sophisticated continental menu, with a setting to match and impeccable service. For starters, hot loaves of Bahamian bread appear at your table—delicious! Deftly prepared Caesar salad is a good choice, followed by roast duck and peaches in a zesty sauce, or the unusual seafood ragout. Pastries are excellent, or try fresh strawberries marinated in Grand Marnier and topped with whipped cream and toasted almonds. Limited but well-chosen wine list. Dinner only, jackets required. AE, BA, DC, MC, V.

The Courtyard Terrace. *Deluxe.* Tel. 6–2501. Perhaps the most romantic setting in The Bahamas, with some of the finest international cuisine. Al fresco dining under the stars in the Ocean Club's lovely inner courtyard amid tropical greenery, tinkling fountains, and soft music. The chateaubriand is classic and the curried shrimp memorable. Excellent choice of French and European wines. Dinner only, jackets required. AE, BA, DC, MC, V.

Bahamian Club. *Expensive.* Tel. 6–3000. One of The Bahamas' most celebrated restaurants for half a century. A stately setting of brass, leather, and gleaming oak paneling showcases prime beef carved at your table, succulent steaks, and an unmatched Caesar salad. Music and dancing nightly. Located in the Britannia Towers. Dinner only, jackets required. AE, DC, MC, V.

Blue Lagoon. *Expensive.* Tel. 6–2400. The newest fine dining spot on Paradise, at Club Land 'Or (across the water from Café Martinique). A spectacular view from the third-floor vantage point, warm and welcoming service, attractive decor. Seafood stars include crawfish cocktail, and consommé de poisson, followed by broiled grouper amadine or lobster thermidor; for beef lovers, there's steak au poivre vert or chateaubriand. Island combo and dancing on the terrace at poolside. Dinner only, jackets suggested. AE, DC, MC, V.

Boat House. *Expensive.* Tel. 6–3000. Casual dining amid nautical decor. Excellent service, personalized at your table, where your waiter cooks your dinner to order at your own grill. Succulent prime steaks and seafood delicacies are featured; hearty portions. Located on the Paradise Lagoon across from Britannia Towers. Dinner only, jackets suggested. AE, DC, MC, V.

Coyaba Room. *Expensive.* Tel. 6–3000. Authentic Cantonese cuisine in a romantic South Sea island setting. Tall exotic drinks are a specialty, along with rich sweet-and-sour ribs, Polynesian-style chicken, and lobster Cantonese. Located in the Britannia Towers. Dinner only, jackets suggested. AE, DC, MC, V.

Grill Room. *Expensive.* Tel. 6–2000. The Paradise Towers newest restaurant, with a bird-of-paradise motif, classically elegant decor. Steaks and seafood sizzling from the grill; duckling a l'orange or escallope of veal with avocado and crabmeat rate high. The appetizers are succulent—try fresh oysters, salmon paté, or gin-and-tomato soup. Wind up with French pastry or fruit flambé. Rare wines and attentive service. Dinner only, jackets suggested. AE, DC, MC, V.

Gulfstream. *Expensive.* Tel. 6–2000. Fresh Bahamian and imported seafood dominate the menu at Paradise Tower's attractive dining spot, with everything from Alaskan king crab to Bahamian crawfish. Excellent service, relaxed atmosphere, contemporary decor. Dinner only, jackets suggested. AE, DC, MC, V.

Villa d'Este. *Expensive.* Tel. 6–3000. The most notable Italian cuisine in the Bahamas, served with elegance and flair in a tasteful old-world setting at the Britannia Towers. The fettucine is feather-light in a rich creamy cheese sauce, and the veal marsala is memorable. Choose anything from the devastatingly delicious Italian pastries. Dinner only; jackets suggested. AE, BA, DC, MC, V.

Captain's Table. *Moderate.* Tel. 6–2561. Loew's Harbour Cove Hotel offers excellent, informal dining in a nicely nautical atmosphere with a superb view of old Nassau Harbour. American, Bahamian, and continental cuisine served up by "hands" in seamen's kit. Try the sirloin steak with green peppercorns, or turtle steak. Guitar-music background. Dinner only. AE, BA, DC, MC, V.

Neptune's Table. *Moderate.* Tel. 6–2101. At the Holiday Inn on Pirate's Cove. A very attractive room with a ship's motif. Hearty seafood plus thick steaks and prime ribs. Or try the poolside deck, with island barbecues and theme parties nearly every night of the week, accented by calypso entertainment and dancing indoors and outdoors. Dinner only. AE, DC, MC, V.

Café Casino. *Inexpensive.* Tel. 6–3000. New York-style delicatessen in the Paradise Island Casino, serving everything from hot pastrami and corned-beef sandwiches to a complete meal. Open daily from noon till the wee hours. Relaxing and informal. AE, DC, MC, V.

Paradise Beach Pavilion. *Inexpensive.* Tel. 6–2541. The Pavilion offers indoor and outdoor dining for breakfast, lunch, and dinner, with live entertainment in the evenings, a good native buffet and show on Wed. Hearty food from burgers and sandwiches to full meals. Located on Paradise Beach at the Paradise-Paradise resort. AE, DC, MC, V.

Spices. *Inexpensive.* Tel. 6–3000. A tropical lobby restaurant at the Britannia Towers, serving breakfast, lunch, and dinner daily—try the eggs Benedict or chef's salad for lunch while you people watch amid island greenery in the great bustling hotel-and-casino complex. AE, DC, MC, V.

Swank Club Pizzeria. *Inexpensive.* Tel. 7–7495. Twenty different varieties of pizza served in a relaxed, casual setting at the Paradise Island Village shopping center. Also excellent Italian spaghetti or lasagna, spicy Bahamian chowders. Beer and wine. Plus a dozen flavors of Howard Johnson's ice cream. AE, MC.

Note: On both Cable Beach and Paradise Island, vacationers can take advantage of unique "Dine-Around" plans, which permit sampling of many different restaurants and cuisines, all at special package rates or discounts. Listed below are typical programs on both Cable Beach and Paradise Island, though rates and specifics may vary with the season. For complete details check with your travel agent or ask about "Dine-Around" options when making reservations.

Cable Beach: Guests from any of the following hotels may take advantage of the Cable Beach Dine-Around plan: *Cable Beach Hotel and Casino, Ambassador Beach Hotel, Nassau Beach Hotel,* and the *Royal Bahamian.* To participate, guests must be registered under the MAP, or modified American plan, or under a package arrangement that includes breakfast and dinner as part of daily rate. Inform the front desk at your own hotel that you want to dine in one of the other hotels or the casino and you will receive a credit coupon for up to $25 (depending on your hotel). After dining at the restaurant of your choice, present the coupon, and the value will be deducted from your check. You pay only the difference. Dining options include four restaurants in the Cable Beach Hotel, two in the Cable Beach Casino, three at the Ambassador Beach Hotel, four at the Nassau Beach Hotel, one at the Emerald Beach Hotel, and two at the Royal Bahamian.

Paradise Island: The Gourmet Dine-Around Plan offered for guests of the *Paradise Island Resort and Casino* is even simpler. For a flat rate of $45–$50 (depending on the season) per person per day, you may enjoy breakfast and dinner anywhere in the resort complex, plus the dinner and show at the casino's Le Cabaret theater. Unlimited menu selection is included at all of the top gourmet restaurants—Café Martinique, the Ocean Club's Courtyard Terrace, Coyaba, Boat House, Gulfstream, Grill Room, Villa d'Este, Bahamian Club, and more. (Wines, alcoholic beverages, and 15 percent gratuity not included.)

 NIGHTLIFE. There is nonstop entertainment nightly in Nassau, along Cable Beach and on Paradise Island. All of the larger hotels offer lounges with island combos for listening or dancing, restaurants with soft guitar or piano background music, or dancing under the stars. Many offer weekly "theme nights" at poolside, accompanied by a barbecue or native buffet and a Goombay-calypso band. Many private restaurants around the island offer entertainment along with dining or a local combo for dancing after dinner. Both casinos, at Cable Beach and Paradise Island, offer a variety of entertainment. There are half a dozen lights-and-action discos, and another half-dozen native nightclubs with music, singers, and Goombay-calypso-Junkanoo acts. Acts change, combos move from club to club, discos switch to slow dance music, headliners appear from North America or Europe, now and then an old favorite closes and a new one opens. The nightlife and entertainment scene, here as everywhere, changes constantly—but here are some old and new "standbys" that shouldn't be missed when you're vacationing in Nassau:

Casino Theaters. *Bahama Rhythms Theatre,* in the Cable Beach Casino, offers "Les Fantastiques," a fast-paced, French-flavored, Las Vegas-type spectacular. The revue features a corps of long-legged showgirls, spectacular costumes, and a musical tribute to Broadway and Hollywood, as well as a space odyssey complete with spaceship and laser lights. Theater-style seating for 1,000; 12 performances each week, twice-nightly Tues.–Sun. Tickets are priced around $14, for the show. Supper club and disco. Reservation: 7–6200. *Le Cabaret Theatre,* in the Paradise Island Casino, offers an all-new Las Vegas–style revue, "Dazzling Deceptions." The multimillion-dollar showgirl extravaganza features elaborate feathered and jeweled costuming, laser lighting, magicians and acrobats, live jungle animals, and a very funny comedian. Viewers sit at stageside tables where drinks and dinner are served. Thirteen performances weekly; per-person cost is approximately $23 with two drinks and $38 with dinner. Reservations: 6–3000.

Discos. *Waterloo Discotheque.* Located at Waterloo Lodge, an old mansion on East Bay Street next to the Mai Tai restaurant. One of Nassau's newest swinging nightspots, 'til the wee hours. Tel. 6–5088. *Le Paeon.* The Peacock, at the Grand Hotel on Paradise Island, offers four sound zones and an ocean view. Open nightly. Tel. 6–2011. *Pastiche.* Located at the Paradise Island Casino, with dazzling decor, sound, light, and plenty of action. Open nightly. Tel. 6–3000.

Hotels, Restaurants, and Lounges. *Bayside Lounge.* Located in the Sheraton British Colonial arcade at the harbor, on Bay Street in downtown Nassau. Dining and dancing nightly from 9:30 P.M. to 2:30 A.M. to live and disco music. Tel. 2–3301. *Bridge Inn.* Located on East Bay Street on the Nassau side of the Paradise Island Bridge. Dining and a local island trio for dancing from 8 P.M. to 1 A.M. nightly. Tel. 3–2077/1806. *Blue Lagoon.* Located at the Club Land 'Or resort on Paradise Island. Dining with piano music in the background; dancing to an island combo on the terrace overlooking the Paradise Island Lagoon. Open nightly except Sunday. Tel. 6–2400. *Captain's Lounge.* Dancing nightly to the music of a live calypso/Goombay band. Located at the Pilot House Hotel on the Nassau side of the Paradise Island Bridge. Tel. 2–8431. Cover/minimum. *The Palace.* A very popular local island combo, Al Collie and the VIP's, operate a nightclub-style disco with live music and entertainment, two dance floors.

The dazzling Bahamian islands are known for uncrowded white-sand beaches and clear turquoise seas.

Local fishing boats carry loads of conch shells and other goods. The Bahamian waters are a favorite of yachtsmen who often harbor hop from island to island.

The Bahamas offer the best of the sporting life from golf on one of the many excellent courses to superb diving among miles of living reef.

In historic Nassau, the Royal Bahamas Police Force Band performs in Parliament Square. The New Year is celebrated in The Bahamas with the Junkanoo Parade, a masquerade and music festival.

Located in town off Bay Street on Elizabeth Avenue. Tel. 5–7733. Cover/ minimum. *Junkanoo Lounge.* Located at the Cable Beach Hotel and Casino, offering live music and entertainment nightly with calypso rhythms and dancing. Tel. 2–7070. Cover/minimum. *La Marina Restaurant and Bar.* Live music and dancing on the terrace nightly at the Nassau Harbour Club overlooking the marina. Tel. 3–1771. *Out Island Bar.* Located off the lobby in the Nassau Beach Hotel, on Cable Beach. Lively atmosphere, live and loud music from an island combo nightly. Tel. 7–7711. Cover/minimum. *Pirate's Cove.* Located at the Holiday Inn on Paradise Island, live indoor and outdoor entertainment nightly, with "theme nights," native shows, and staff shows weekly. Tel. 5–6451. *The Terrace.* Located at the Parliament Hotel, just off Bay Street on Parliament Street in downtown Nassau. Outdoor dining and dancing in the gardens under a roofed terrace. Live entertainment nightly. Tel. 2–2836/7. *Rendezvous Lounge.* Top island entertainment, nonstop dancing till the early hours nightly. Located in the Britannia Towers on Paradise Island, at the Paradise Island Resort and Casino. Local and international groups. Tel. 6–3000. Cover/minimum. *Trade Winds Lounge.* More top island entertainment and nonstop dancing till the early hours nightly. Located in the Paradise Towers on Paradise Island at the Paradise Island Resort and Casino. Tel. 6–2000. Cover/minimum.

Native Nightclubs. *Peanuts Taylor's Drumbeat Club.* The Bahamas' most famous entertainer for 25 years, Peanuts Taylor, master bongo drummer, stars in his own all-star native review nightly. Adding to the fun is Bahamian songstress Portia Butterfield, a Goombay/calypso band, a group of fire dancers, and a true limbo artist. Nightly at 10:30 P.M. Located in downtown Nassau, on West Bay Street, just west of the Sheraton British Colonial Hotel. Tel. 2–4233. Admission charge. *Valentine's Love Club.* Located on West Bay Street near downtown Nassau, adjacent to the Atlantis Hotel. Limbo dancing, a dazzling fire dancer, calypso "revival singers," and a Goombay band with steel drums. Showtime is 10:30 P.M. Sun., Tue., Sat., 8:30 P.M. Wed. Closed Thur. Sun. Jazz Jam 4–9 P.M. Admission charge. The Grand Hotel on Paradise Island offers a good native show, *Junkanoo Revue,* Wed. nights, featuring Sabu the Great, with voodoo dancing, fire dances, glass eating, limbo, and steel band. Admission charge. Tel. 6–2011.

 CASINOS. There are two casinos on New Providence Island. Both open early in the day and remain active into the wee hours of the morning and offer Continental gambling. Visitors must be 18 to enter casino, and 21 years of age or over to gamble; Bahamians or Bahamas residents are not permitted to gamble. Dress code is informal during the day, more formal at night.

Cable Beach Casino. Casual, informal casino atmosphere, with male and female, international and Bahamian croupiers and dealers, all friendly and helpful. A favorite of high rollers and low rollers alike. State-of-the-art slot machines go from 5¢ to $1 and blackjack tables start at a $2 minimum. The casino occupies 20,000 square feet and offers 57 gaming tables: 44 blackjack, 6 craps, 4 roulette, 1 baccarat, 2 wheels of fortune, and 526 slot machines. Hours are from 10 A.M. to 6 A.M. daily and complimentary gaming lessons are offered every afternoon. Other amenities include a casino bar with big-screen satellite TV and a stage for island entertainment; a New York-style delicatessen; and a gourmet restaurant, Sol e Mare, offering elegant dining from 6 P.M. to midnight nightly. The casino complex includes the 1,000-seat Bahama Rhythms Theatre. Tel. 7–6200.

Paradise Island Casino. More formal, elegant atmosphere, with English and Continental dealers and croupiers. Long known as one of the most glittering gaming palaces in the Caribbean, it has recently undergone a $1.5-million remodeling and is now more glamorous than ever, and has recently been expanded to 30,000 square feet. Linked to the Britannia Towers and the Paradise Towers, the casino features 41 tables of blackjack with a $5 minimum bet, 7 crap tables, 8 roulette tables, 2 Big Six tables, and 1 table of baccarat. There are also 500 slot machines, from 25¢ to $1 and multiples. Slot machines are open 24 hours, gaming tables open 10 A.M. until dawn, and gaming lessons are offered free in the afternoon, with a complimentary cocktail. Other amenities include several casino bars; a New York-style delicatessan; several gourmet restaurants adjacent; Pastiche, a sound-and-lights disco; and Le Cabaret Theatre, with table seating for about eight hundred, fine dining, and an elaborate revue. Tel. 6–3000.

GRAND BAHAMA ISLAND

Freeport, Lucaya, and West End

The second world of vacation pleasures to be discovered in The Bahamas is Grand Bahama Island, which has emerged just in the past two decades as a major international resort destination. Grand Bahama attracts more than 800,000 visitors each year—rivaling the most popular destinations in all of the Caribbean.

One of the largest islands in the Bahamian archipelago, Grand Bahama forms the northern border of The Bahamas, with its western tip lying less than sixty miles off Florida's Palm Beach coast. Its 530-square-mile interior is heavily forested with palmetto and casuarina pines. The 96 mile southern coastline is pocketed by sheltered harbors, bordered by miles of unspoiled white-sand beaches, and fringed with a nearly unbroken line of spectacular reefs. Virtually unknown and largely unpopulated a generation ago, Grand Bahama was developed in the early 1960s by a visionary group of American, European, and Bahamian entrepreneurs. Today, Grand Bahama boasts 35,000 residents (the second-largest population in The Bahamas), a major industrial complex, a deep-water cruise-ship port, a modern international airport, and one of the most glittering residential/resort/country-club centers of any island in The Bahamas.

Centerpiece of Grand Bahama's development is the attractive, well-planned "garden city" of Freeport, where broad boulevards and sophisticated shops are linked by a palm-lined road to the lovely suburb of Lucaya, set among thousands of acres of lush tropical greenery and sprawling along miles of canals and ocean beach. Scattered here and there around and between Freeport/Lucaya are large and small hotels, a world-famous shopping center known as "The International Bazaar," six superb golf courses, a pair of enormous casinos, and more.

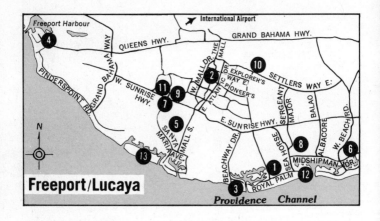

Points of Interest

1) Bahama Reef Golf Course
2) Churchill Square
3) Coral Beach
4) Cruise Ship Port
5) Emerald Golf Course
6) The Garden of the Groves
7) International Bazaar
8) Lucayan Golf & Country Club
9) Princess Casino
10) Rand Memorial Nature Center
11) Ruby Golf Course
12) UNEXSO
13) Xanadu Beach

Exploring Freeport/Lucaya

There are no historic sites or crumbling forts to explore around Freeport/Lucaya, but there are several interesting sights which should not be missed, and many sporting adventures well worth trying. Best bet for an overview of the city and suburban attractions is a two-hour bus tour that stops by most hotels. The tour moves through downtown Freeport and the lovely residential areas and exclusive suburbs with celebrity homes, through parks and gardens, along oceanside beaches and seaside resorts, and around the cruise-ship harbor and industrial park, with stops at the colorful International Bazaar and the picturesque quayside fish market at Hawksbill Creek. A bus tour of Grand Bahama Island, from Freeport to West End, lasting most of a day, is also available. Or you can rent a car or scooter and explore the island on your own.

The best place to begin your tour is at the Ministry of Tourism Information Center at the International Bazaar on West Sunrise Highway. Pick up maps and brochures on local attractions. While there you may want to sign up for the unusual "People to People" program. Available only in Nassau and Freeport, this volunteer program matches up visitors with Bahamians of similar interests and hobbies for a genuine personal and cultural exchange. All expenses are taken care of by the Bahamian volunteers—and there are more than two hundred of them in Freeport/Lucaya. It can be a vacation experience you'll treasure for years. To join, call the Ministry of Tourism, Tel. 352–8044.

If you have rented a car, you'll love driving or riding around Freeport/Lucaya. Broad, landscaped dual carriageways (the Grand Bahamian name for a divided highway) and tree-lined streets wind through parks, past lovely homes, and along lush green fairways. All are complete with well-marked lanes, traffic lights and traffic circles. Always keep in mind that all traffic is on the left, British style, even bikes and scooters.

International Bazaar and Strawmarket

The colorful International Bazaar is located on West Sunrise Highway next door to the Princess Casino—within easy walking distance of downtown Freeport hotels, and adjacent to the Princess resort complex. If you are staying at one of the oceanside resorts, hop on the bus or take a taxi to this unique attraction. Save your rental transport for another day, as you won't be able to ride or bike through its narrow lanes. But bring along your walking shoes, because you'll probably want to spend hours sampling its delights.

You'll enter the International Bazaar through the great 35-foot-high, red-lacquered Torii Gate, traditional symbol of welcome in Japan. Within the Bazaar, you'll find a kaleidoscope of street markets and exotic shops, with bargain wares from around the world (most at prices 20 to 40 percent lower than in the United States and Canada). Along the narrow winding lanes and byways, there's a bit of London, Paris, and Rome; something of Istanbul and Tangiers, Acapulco and Hong Kong; with Latin American touches from Colombia and Brazil, and Asian style from Japan, India, and Thailand. There are English pubs and French cafés, a Japanese steakhouse and a Chinese tearoom, as well as Polynesian, Italian, and health-food dining spots to suit any taste or budget. Nearly a dozen different countries are authentically represented in the sprawling 12-acre Bazaar, and there are nearly a hundred different shops. If the whole thing reminds you of a vast Hollywood movie set, that's all right—it was created more than a dozen years ago by one of the film world's leading stage designers.

Before beginning your shopping and sightseeing tour of the labyrinthine bazaar, drop by the picturesque native Strawmarket located just to the right of the entrance. Bargain with the straw ladies for a colorful woven hat and a roomy handcrafted tote bag in which to carry home your bargains. Here you'll find thousands of delightful souvenirs and practical gift items woven by hand from straw, raffia, and palm fronds. The straw ladies will even personalize your souvenir with your own name or most anything else you choose. You'll also find handcrafted jewelry made from conch and tortoise-shell, coconut husks and native berries or pods, along with wood carvings and sculptures of native pine, lignum vitae, or mahogany. Prices on everything are negotiable, and the straw ladies love to bargain—but don't expect to bargain with the shopkeepers in the elegant stores and jewelry salons in the Bazaar. The savings in these stores are substantial on imported watches and cameras, gold and silver, cashmere and linens, crystal and china, colognes and perfumes—but the prices are fixed.

The Rand Memorial Nature Center

Travel eastward by car to the first traffic circle and turn left onto The Mall, which will take you to Churchill Square in downtown Freeport. There's plenty of parking, and you might want to spend an hour or two wandering through some of the attractive shops around the square, along the side streets, or in the West Mall Shopping Center, a block or two away. If you haven't had breakfast, or it's time for lunch, stop in at Mum's Coffee Shop & Bakery for delicious home-made bread and pastries, hot soups, and thick sandwiches. You might want to take a few sandwiches along for a picnic lunch in a park or on the beach.

Continue north on The Mall to link up with Settler's Way East, turn right, and follow the tree-lined highway to The Rand Memorial Nature Center. The beautiful hundred-acre park encompasses natural, unspoiled Grand Bahama woodland, and is a preserve for more than four hundred varieties of subtropical plants, trees, flowers, and foliage indigenous to The Bahamas. It is also a sanctuary for thousands of native and migratory birds. Look carefully for two rare and lovely native hummingbirds. One is the Cuban Emerald, independent, fearless, and bright emerald green, usually found sipping the nectar of a bright hibiscus blossom. The other is the tiny Bahama Woodstar, shy and easily missed (it is little bigger than a flying insect) but brilliantly hued, with a bright reddish-violet forehead and throat. It is found only in The Bahamas.

Within the park, a mile of well-marked nature trails leads to a sparkling thirty-foot waterfall tumbling to lovely blue lagoon. Here you can photograph the brilliant pink flamingos (national bird of The Bahamas) that live and nest along its shores. Those who want to learn all about the flora and avian life in the park may take one of the walks conducted by resident naturalists. They'll tell you all about where the "straw" comes from that is woven into hats and bags at the Bahamian markets, and even show you how bubble gum "grows." They'll point out hundreds of varieties of plants, including wild vanilla orchids, devil's potato, straw lily, five fingers, and love vine. They may even introduce you to the native racoons and "curly-tailed" lizards, or the world's smallest snake.

The Garden of the Groves and UNEXSO

After leaving the nature center, continue east on Settler's Way to Balao Road or West Beach Road, then turn south to Midshipman Road, which fringes Lucayan Harbour on the north. If it's time for lunch, and pub fare with an English flair appeals to you, make your way to the Britannia Pub on King's Road overlooking Bell Channel. After lunch, head back to Midshipman Road and continue east to another wondrous natureland, the Garden of the Groves.

These prize-winning botanical gardens were named for Wallace and Georgette Groves, the founders of Freeport/Lucaya. The park, which covers more than a dozen acres features some five thousand varieties of rare and familiar subtropical and tropical trees, shrubs, plants, and flowers. Entrance is through a lovely "hanging garden," a canopied arbor of lush, green tropical vines. Centerpiece of the gardens is a series of cool waterfalls, fountains, winding streams, and tranquil lagoons. Well-marked pathways lead past clearly identified plant species, the verdant fern gully and grotto, and a tiny native-stone interdenominational chapel (a replica of the earliest church on Grand Bahama). There is also an interesting small museum called Discovery House, where you can learn about the history of Grand Bahama Island over the last four centuries, and the modern development of Freeport/Lucaya in the last two decades. There are many quiet shady benches throughout the gardens for resting and relaxing, or sharing a picnic lunch, and there's a children's playground.

After leaving the Garden of the Groves, head for the sea—some of Grand Bahama's most beautiful beaches and interesting harbors are in the Lucayan area, off Midshipman Road. Travel west, then turn south on West Beach Road to Jolly Roger Drive, which runs along the ocean. Drop by Taino Beach, the island's prettiest public beach, and plan drinks or dinner at The Stoned Crab, a rustic, romantic seaside restaurant with a dining terrace overlooking the water.

If you'd like to learn to dive on your vacation, or if you are a trained diver interested in reef, wreck, cave, or blue-hole dives, you should check out UNEXSO (the Underwater Explorer's Society).

To reach the UNEXSO after leaving the Garden of the Groves, continue west along Midshipman Road, beyond Lucayan Harbour to Sea Horse Lane. There, turn south to Royal Palm Way and the sea. Here you'll find the Lucayan Beach Hotel, and nearby, the clubhouse of UNEXSO. You can pick up brochures and rate sheets, talk to the instructors, and mingle with the divers. The après-dive crowd is casual, relaxed, and full of wondrous tales of The Bahamas' underwater world, and there's a nearly nonstop showing of underwater films and slides to pique your interest in exploring beneath the sea. Check out the tamed and trained dolphins who put on a good show, and cavort in the sea with swimmers. And drop by the Lucayan Beach Casino for a game or two of chance; it is casual and informal in the afternoons.

East of Freeport/Lucaya

Beyond Freeport/Lucaya the Grand Bahama Highway winds eastward, crossing the Grand Lucayan Waterway. The canal meanders across the island from north to south providing protected passage for yachts cruising the northern Bahamas. Continue through miles of untamed pine forest, and beyond acres of "Top Secret—No Admittance" land, home of one of the U.S. Air Force's newest and most sophisticated guided-missile and satellite-tracking centers. A few miles beyond, the road curves through a picturesque little fishing village called McLean's Town, where nothing has changed very much for more than a hundred years. The residents earn their living from the sea, fishing, crabbing, and lobstering in the ocean depths and the marshy shallows that intersect the island's eastern end. Nothing much happens here most of the year, but on the October 12th Discovery Day holiday the village comes alive with an annual ritual known as "The Conch-Cracking Contest"—don't miss it if you are in the area. (On one of the offshore cays nearby, there is an exclusive little fishing camp known as the Deep Water Cay Club catering to serious anglers.) From McLean's Town, the highway circles back along the island's southern shore to Freeport/Lucaya, passing through other small fishing villages by the sea—Pelican Point, High Rock, and Freetown.

West of Freeport/Lucaya

Traveling westward from Freeport/Lucaya, follow the signs along Queen's Highway to West End. The road takes you through a series of small villages, many over one hundred years old. Some were thriving towns back in the "Roaring Twenties," when rum-runners made Grand Bahama their headquarters and fast speedboats and seaplanes plied the Florida Channel nightly, bringing illicit loads of liquor to Prohibition-weary U.S. mainlanders. Just west of town is Hawksbill Creek, which has a colorful harborside fish market. Continuing westward, the road loops around the busy commercial harbor areas, where you might see huge oil tankers and sleek white cruise ships, great oil refineries and sprawling factories. Back on the main road to West End, you will pass through the village of Eight Mile Rock, a long, narrow hamlet that sprawls for eight miles along both sides of the road. Drive down one or two of the side streets for a look at some of the small, attractive older homes, then drop into St. Stephen's Church, built on the seashore in 1851. Also near the beach is Fragrance of The Bahamas, a small native perfume factory housed in a former Baptist church. Distilled from local flowers and plants such as hibiscus and frangipani, the scents are delightful—try "Island Promises" for a unique Bahamian souvenir. Just down the road is a quaint little village called Seagrape, with a tiny bakery offering some of the best bread on Grand Bahama. The next village is Holmes Rock, worth a stop for the nearby Hydro Flora Gardens, whose dense tropical foliage, native fruit trees and hydroponic gardens illustrate the science of raising plants without soil. Trained naturalists are generally on hand to show you around. Continuing on, you'll pass Bootle Bay and West End Point, where there are fine views of the offshore cays of Indian Cay, Wood Cay, and Memory Rock light.

West End

The road (and the island) ends, appropriately enough, at West End. It's a delightful little seaside village with a couple of churches and a dozen bars. Stop for a cool drink at the Star, a weathered old building that was a hotel back in the 1940s. You'll find hearty native food served all day and night. Nearby Austin's Calypso Bar, with its local music and dancing most nights, is a favorite with locals and visitors from the huge Jack Tar Village resort just down the road.

As you head back for Freeport/Lucaya, stop off at Harry's American Bar in Eight Mile Rock. If your timing is right, you'll enjoy a fantastic view of the sunset from the patio overlooking the sea. Relax and enjoy it, while sipping one of "Harry's Hurricanes." For really good down-home Bahamian cooking, plan dinner at the New Peace & Plenty just down the road.

PRACTICAL INFORMATION FOR GRAND
BAHAMA ISLAND

HOW TO GET THERE. By air: Several major air carriers serve Grand Bahama Island's modern, jet-age Freeport International Airport from U.S. and Canadian gateways: *Eastern, Delta, Pan Am, TWA, United,* and *Air Canada.* From Miami and Nassau, *Bahamasair* offers frequent daily service; and from Ft. Lauderdale, Palm Beach, Orlando, and Tampa several scheduled commuter airlines serve Grand Bahama, such as *Aero-Coach, Gull Air* and *Caribbean Express.*

By sea: There is a unique daily cruise-ship service linking Grand Bahama Island to the Florida mainland. Departing every morning at 8 A.M. from the Port of Miami, the *Scandinavian Sun* sails to Freeport, arriving at 2 P.M. The ship departs Freeport each afternoon at 5 P.M. and arrives in Miami at 11 P.M. Rates vary, but are around $99, round-trip. Tel. 305–379–0000, Miami; 800–432–0900, FL; 800–327–7400, U.S. And the newest way to reach Grand Bahama by sea is *Viking Express,* luxury, high-speed catamaran service daily from Port Everglades (Ft. Lauderdale). Departs 8:30 A.M., arrives 11:00 A.M. Departs Freeport 6:00 P.M. Fast, comfortable, smooth sailing. Airline-style seats, meal service, stewardesses, bar and slot machines. From $69 round trip. Tel. 305–760–4550. Also leaving on day trips to Grand Bahama from Port Everglades is *Discovery I,* 1,100 passenger cruise ship which sails round-trip Mon., Wed., Fri., and Sun. to Freeport. From $79 round trip. Tel. 305–274–9626.

TELEPHONES AND EMERGENCY NUMBERS. Area code for Grand Bahama Island is 809. Ambulance: 352–2689 or 352–6735; fire department: 352–8888; police: 911; Air Sea Rescue: 352–2628.

HOTELS. There is an excellent range of accommodations on Grand Bahama Island, from luxurious full-service resorts in town and along the beaches, to small in-town motel-style hotels and attractive self-catering apartment complexes. The rates for hotel rooms and apartments on Grand Bahama are in most cases significantly lower than comparable accommodations on New Providence Island. All hotels offer MAP (Modified American Plan), which includes breakfast and dinner daily. Packages are available at all Grand Bahama resorts. We have indicated whom to contact for reservations and, in many cases, you'll note that they may be made through the Bahamas Reservation Service, tel. 800–327–0787 in the U.S. and Canada, abbreviated as BRS.

Hotel price categories, based on high-season, double occupancy on Grand Bahama are: $95 and up, *Expensive;* $65–94, *Moderate;* and $64 and below, *Inexpensive.* Low season rates tend to run 10 to 20 percent lower than winter season rates, and package rates run from 20 to 40 percent lower.

Freeport

Bahamas Princess Resort & Casino. *Expensive.* Reservations for either Princess property: Box F-2623, Freeport, Grand Bahama Island. Tel. 352–6721 (Country Club) or 352–9661 (Tower); toll-free in the U.S.: 800–223–1818, in New York 800–442–8418; or Princess Casino Vacations, 800–545–1300. Located 3½ miles from Freeport International Airport. 15 percent service charge added. The international chain operates two fine resorts in Freeport: the Princess Tower and the Princess Country Club, with a total of 965 rooms. Princess also runs the Princess Casino and two championship 18-hole golf courses, the Emerald and Ruby. Both hotels are located on West Sunrise Highway, next to the casino and International Bazaar.

Princess Towers. Dramatic, Moorish-style architecture, a dazzling octagonal lobby and a colonnade of Arabesque arches. There are four hundred rooms in a ten-story tower. All are spacious, attractively decorated, air-conditioned, and have private telephones and cable TV. There are several excellent restaurants, coffee shop and poolside dining; varied entertainment nightly in notable lounges, and the *Sultan's Tent Disco*. A large freshwater pool, six tennis courts for day and night play, and complimentary transportation to Xanadu Beach.

Princess Country Club. A sprawling, low-rise resort with a two-story main building housing the lobby, restaurants, and bars. There are 565 guest rooms in nine two- and three-story wings radiating from a central pool and patio area. Landscaping is lush and tropical, and the pool is an extravaganza of tumbling waterfalls, islands, greenery, and a Jacuzzi. Rooms are large, well furnished, air-conditioned, and equipped with private telephones and cable TV. There are six fine restaurants some offering poolside dining; several bars and lounges provide entertainment almost every night. Six tennis courts for day and night play, and complimentary transportation to Xanadu Beach. Note: Several wings of this resort have been converted to time-share kitchen apartments under the name Princess Vacation Club International.

Xanadu Beach Hotel. *Expensive.* Box F-2438, Freeport, Grand Bahama; tel. 352–6782; in the U.S. 800–222–3788; 804–270–4313 international. Located five miles from International Airport. A luxurious oceanside resort with 184 rooms, two three-bedroom villas and one two-bedroom villa. Located on a mile-long ocean beach, with a full-service marina. Four tennis courts lighted for night play, boats and fishing charters for hire, large freshwater pool, a noted dining room, bar, entertainment, and disco. The resort is now operated by an American firm, Land 'Or International, and has been completely refurbished.

Silver Sands. *Moderate.* Box F-2385, Freeport, Grand Bahama; tel. 373–5700 or through BRS. A comfortable apartment hotel, near lovely ocean beach, with 164 studio and 1-bedroom units, each with balcony, full kitchen, and bar. 2 swimming pools, 2 tennis courts, and watersports. 2 bars with frequent live entertainment, an Italian restaurant, and beachside snack bar. 7 miles from the airport.

Castaways Resort. *Inexpensive.* Box F-2629, Freeport, Grand Bahama; tel. 352–6682, or through BRS. 138 nicely furnished motel-style rooms, including nine suites with kitchenettes. All are air-conditioned and have private telephones. There is a *Howard Johnson's* restaurant, bar, lounge, and the popular *Yellowbird Nightclub*. Amenities include an attractive indoor/outdoor patio, pool, and gardens. 15 percent service charge added. Located three miles from the airport, adjacent to the Princess Casino and International Bazaar.

Freeport Inn. *Inexpensive.* Box F-200, Freeport, Grand Bahama; tel. 352–6648; or through BRS. 150 neatly furnished motel-style rooms (50 with kitchenettes) and 15 suites. All are air-conditioned and have private telephones.

There is a swimming pool, good restaurant, cocktail lounge with live music nightly and a native show weekly. Complimentary scheduled transportation daily to Xanadu Beach. Located near the center of town, about a mile from the Princess Casino and International Bazaar, two miles from airport. 15 percent service charge.

Windward Palms. *Inexpensive.* Box F-2549, Freeport, Grand Bahama; tel. 352-8821. 100 comfortable rooms in town, near the International Bazaar and Princess Casino. Caribe dining room offers good, inexpensive fare, and there's a popular bar and lounge. Attractive pool and patio bar. 3½ miles from airport.

Lucaya

Atlantik Beach Hotel. *Expensive.* Box F-531, Lucaya, Grand Bahama; tel. (305)-592-5757, 800-622-6770 or through BRS. A Swiss International Hotel favored by Europeans with a good mix of Canadians and Americans. 123 rooms, 52 1-2 bedroom apartments with kitchens, all attractively furnished. Corona Classic Club offers concierge amenities and VIP treatment. Set along a beautiful beach, offering a range of watersports, beach club, pool, and windsurfing school. Several attractive dining rooms and a lounge with entertainment. The hotel operates the Lucayan Golf & Country Club, an 18-hole championship course nearby. 6 miles from the airport.

Genting's Lucayan Beach Resort & Casino. *Expensive.* Box F-336, Lucaya, Grand Bahama; tel. 800-772-1227, 800-331-2538, or through BRS. Once Grand Bahama's premiere resort, now fully restored to its former glory. Set along 1½ miles of ocean beach, with 248 well-appointed rooms. 4 restaurants from gourmet to fast foods, 5 bars and lounges. The glittering *Monte Carlo Casino* offers all games of chance and a lavish theater revue. Lanai Wing features Club Lucaya, with concierge service and VIP amenities. Full sports program includes windsurfing, parasailing, UNEXSO scuba, 2 swimming pools, 4 tennis courts, and golf nearby. 6 miles from the airport.

Holiday Inn. *Expensive.* Box F-760, Lucaya, Grand Bahama; tel. 373-1333, Holiday Inn Reservations or through BRS. Typical Holiday Inn comforts, in a tropical resort setting. 500 attractive rooms, set along a mile of ocean beach. Day and night activity, health club, pool, 4 tennis courts, watersports, and a children's playground. 3 dining rooms, 3 lounges with entertainment, and the *Panache* nightclub. 6 miles from the airport.

Discovery Bay. *Moderate.* Box F-3229, Lucaya, Grand Bahama. Tel. 373-7318. Formerly the Arawak Hotel, closed for several years, now re-opened, completely refurbished, and operated as an all-inclusive resort. 104 nicely furnished rooms, 16 one- and two-bedroom suites. Packages include all meals and beverages. Unlimited golf at refurbished 18-hole Shannon course and tennis on 10 courts, 5 lit for night play. Range of watersports. Located on Bell Channel, 6 miles from airport.

Lucayan Marina Hotel. *Moderate.* Box F-336, Lucaya, Grand Bahama; tel. 800-772-1227, 800-331-2538, or through BRS. Formerly Lucayan Harbour Inn, completely refurbished, now operated by Genting's Lucayan Beach Resort. 153 comfortable rooms, delightful new restaurant, *Hemingways*, with indoor-outdoor dining, and a full service 156-slip marina. A favorite with the yachting set. A ferry plies back and forth to the beach and Casino.

West End

Jack Tar Village. *Moderate.* 403 South Akard, Dallas, TX 75202; tel. 800-527-9299. Self-contained all-inclusive resort at western end of Grand Bahama Island, 32 miles from Freeport. Air charters arrive at the resort's international airport at West End. 537 rooms, neatly furnished. Huge swimming pool, 27 holes of golf, full-service marina with charter boats for fishing. Full scuba program and 16 tennis courts. Several dining rooms, bars, and a full schedule of entertainment.

APARTMENT RENTALS. In addition to the apartment hotels and resorts offering housekeeping facilities listed above, the following offer apartment rentals for vacationers:

Coral Beach. Box F-2468, Freeport, Grand Bahama. Tel. 373–2468/9. Ten studio and one-bedroom apartments in a landscaped condo setting along a nice private beach. Amenities include balcony or terrace, attractive furnishings, roof solarium, pool, central dining room, and bar.

Channel House Resort Club. Box F-1337, Freeport, Grand Bahama; tel. 373–5405. 18 studio and one-bedroom apartments located across from the Holiday Inn and Lucaya Beach. Attractive setting with a pool and tennis courts. Club membership plans available.

Sea/Sun Manor. Box F-1255, Freeport, Grand Bahama. Tel. 352–2140. Located on East Mall Drive, Freeport. 64 studio, one- and two-bedroom apartments, with swimming pool and beach privileges.

TIME SHARING. There is a growing number of time-sharing resorts and condominium properties on Grand Bahama Island. A sampling follows:

Bahama Reef. Box F–2695, Freeport, Grand Bahama; tel. 373–5580. Eleven one-bedroom units and one three-bedroom penthouse for time sharing and rental. Located 3½ blocks from the beach.

Dundee Bay Villas. One World Development Ltd., Box F-2690, Freeport, Grand Bahama; tel. 352–4222. One-, two-, and three-bedroom units located on the beach next to the Xanadu Beach Hotel. Time sharing and rentals.

Freeport Resort & Club. Box F-2514, Freeport, Grand Bahama; tel. 352–5371. Located on wooded acreage near Princess Casino, International Bazaar, and golf courses. Choice of apartment sizes and styles.

Lakeview Manor Club. Box F-2699, Freeport, Grand Bahama; tel. 352–2283. Located on the fairway of the fifth hole of the Ruby Golf Course. Time sharing and rental. One- and two-bedroom apartments.

Mayfield Beach & Tennis Club. Box F-458, Freeport, Grand Bahama; tel. 352–9776. Located on Port of Call Drive at Bahama Terrace, on the ocean. Pool, sundeck, tennis court, various sizes of apartments.

North Star Resorts. Box F2997, Freeport, Grand Bahama; tel. 373–4250 or 373–4636. Located along the Grand Lucayan Waterway and beach. Phase I consists of 72 apartments with two bedrooms, two baths.

Ocean Reef Resort & Club. Box F-898, Freeport, Grand Bahama; tel. 373–4661. Three-bedroom, three-bath luxury apartments with docks, swimming pool. Located near the Casino, Bazaar, and golf courses.

Princess Vacation Club. Box F-207, Freeport, Grand Bahama; tel. 352–6721. Part of the Bahamas Princess Resort & Casino complex in Freeport, adjacent to the Casino and Bazaar. Apartments are located in the Princess Country Club Hotel and owners have access to all of the resort's amenities, pools, golf courses, tennis courts, and beach club.

Woodbourne Estates. Box F–1098, Freeport, Grand Bahama; tel. 352–4069. Located on Hawksbill Street, Bahama Terrace, near the International Bazaar and Casino. Two-bedroom apartments, with full kitchen.

For additional rental apartments, homes, condominiums, and time-sharing vacations contact the following realtors: *Timesales (Bahamas) Ltd.,* Box F-2656, Freeport, Grand Bahama; tel. 352-7039. *Caribbean International Realty,*

Box F-2489, Freeport, Grand Bahama; tel. 352–8795/6. *Charlow Realty Ltd.*, Box F-3814, Freeport, Grand Bahama; tel. 373–5443.

HOW TO GET AROUND. Metered taxis meet all incoming flights at Freeport International Airport and at the cruise-ship port. There is no bus service or other public transportation to or from the airport and cruise-ship port. However, visitors booked on package tours through a travel agent, hotel, or the Bahamas Reservation Service (which specifically include airport transfers) are transported free of charge to their hotel. Within Freeport/Lucaya, scheduled bus routes cover most of the area, including some outlying villages. Check with your hotel desk for bus schedules and sightseeing tour schedules. Motor scooters and bicycles are available for rent at several resorts on the island. Rates for bicycles average $10 per day with a $10 deposit required; average rate for motor scooters is $18–$25 per day and required deposit $30–$50. Full day is 9 A.M.–5 P.M., and crash helmets are mandatory. Rates are subject to change.

Car rentals are offered by the following agencies: *Avis,* with locations at the International Airport, 352–7666; the International Bazaar, 352–7675; and in Lucaya opposite the Atlantik Beach Hotel, 373–1102. *Budget* is located at the International Airport, 352–8844; and at the Atlantik Beach Hotel, 373–4938. *Dollar,* at the International Airport, 352–3714. *Eddie's Auto Rentals,* at the International Airport, 352–3165. *Holiday,* at the International Airport, 352–8821. *National* has two locations, at the International Airport, 352–9308; and in Lucaya on Royal Palm Way, 373–4957. Average daily rates range from $40 to $75, depending on the season and the type of car. Insurance is recommended, and is available through all agencies. A significant deposit is required on all rental vehicles, unless payment is made with a major credit card.

TOURIST INFORMATION SERVICES. The *Bahamas Ministry of Tourism* operates information booths at the Freeport International Airport and the Freeport Harbour Cruiseship Port, and an office in the International Bazaar, Box F251, Freeport, Grand Bahama; tel. 352–8044. The *Grand Bahama Promotion Board* operates an office at the Sir Charles Hayward Library, East Mall, Freeport; tel. 352–7848 or 352–8356. Both tourism organizations offer a full range of colorful brochures, maps, rate sheets covering all hotels on the island for both winter and summer seasons, and information on what to do and sights to see on Grand Bahama Island.

SPECIAL EVENTS. Grand Bahama is internationally famous as the "Country Club Island," and year-round there are scheduled golf tournaments that attract amateurs and professionals alike. For dates, entry fees, and regulations, contact the organizations listed in "Tourist Information Services" above, or call the Bahamas Sports Hotline in the U.S. 800–32SPORT.

In December, between Christmas and New Year's, Grand Bahama offers a week-long celebration of *Junkanoo.* (For a complete description of Bahamian Junkanoo and its historic African roots, see Junkanoo under "Seasonal Events" in the *Facts at Your Fingertips* section.)

Vintage Car Grand Prix made its debut on Grand Bahama in 1986 and was a "roaring" success. It is held annually in early December. Headquarters is the Bahamas Princess Resort & Casino in Freeport, and about 200 vintage cars, representing half a dozen different countries participate. Grand Prix planners schedule 15 races, gala parties, golf, tennis, and fishing tournaments, and a native Bahamian music festival as part of the celebrations. All events are open to the public. Contact the Sports Hotline (800–32 SPORT), BRS, or your travel agent for details and package information.

Student Breakaway Programs. Every spring from March through April, the island attracts thousands of vacationing students with a series of fun-filled free (or inexpensive) events such as beach picnics, barbecues, moonlight cruises, sailing and fishing trips, and golf and tennis tournaments.

Conch-Cracking Contest. A real out-island-style native celebration held each Discovery Day, Oct. 12th (Columbus Day) at McLean's Town at the far eastern end of the island. Beach picnics, native food, and goombay music are all part of this free-for-all, fun-filled ritual. Locals sit cleaning mounds of fresh conch by hammering and cracking them. Current record is 25 conch in just over six minutes. Visitors are even invited to join in, but be sure you know how to pronounce the name correctly—"konk"—or you are automatically disqualified.

Princess 10K Road Race. Sponsored annually in January by Bahamas Princess Resort and Casino on their 10K course. Attracts amateurs and professionals from many countries.

Goombay Summer. Jun.–Sept. festival features bargain-rate packages at hotels and a full seven-day-a-week program of special events in the Freeport/Lucaya area. Among the special activities offered free or at drastically discounted prices from winter season are tours at the Rand Memorial Nature Center; tea parties in the Garden of the Groves; "Beer Fest" at Tides Inn with snorkeling lessons at UNEXSO; sports tournaments; races; goombay music festival; beach picnics and barbecues; and a weekly Junkanoo festival with masquerade costumes and music. Details and brochures from the Bahamas Tourist Offices and Grand Bahama Promotion Board.

TOURS. A variety of guided bus tours is available on Grand Bahama Island. Hourly rates for a taxi/tour with driver range from $20–$25, and for long trips rates can generally be negotiated. Always settle in advance exactly what the charge will be. You can even hop aboard a sightseeing airplane to visit nearby islands or make a day-long expedition to Nassau. Most tours may be booked through the tour desk in your hotel lobby, through information booths at the airport or cruise-ship port, or directly by calling the following ground tour operators and airlines: *Bahamas Travel and Tours,* Box F–3778, Freeport, Grand Bahama; tel. 352–3141. *Executive Tours,* Box F-2509; tel. 352–8858. *Grand Bahama Tours Ltd.,* Box F-453; tel. 352–7234/7347. *Greenline Tours,* Box F-2631; tel. 352–3465. *International Travel Tours Ltd.,* Box F-850; tel. 352–9311. *Playasol Travel Service Ltd.,* Box F-2585; tel. 352–4811. *Reef Tours Ltd.,* Box 7-2609; tel. 373–5880.

Two airlines that provide sightseeing flights around Grand Bahama, to nearby Family Islands, and to Nassau are: *Helda Air Holdings Ltd.,* Box F-3335, Freeport; tel. 352–8832; and *LucayaAir,* Box 7-4006, Freeport; tel. 352–8885.

Glass-Bottom Boat Tours. *Reef Tours Ltd.,* next to the Lucayan Bay Hotel, Lucaya (tel. 373–5880/5891/5892) offers daily offshore tours to spectacular reefs and sea gardens aboard the *Mermaid Kitty* ("World's largest glass-bottom boat"), at 10 A.M., 12:30 P.M., and 2:30 P.M. for $10 for adults, $5 for children. Also offered are daily Tri-Wind Cruises (two hours) and Moonlight Cruises (two hours). Rates are approximately $16 for adults, $8 for children.

Sailing Cruises also offered by *Reef Tours* aboard a 52-foot Trimaran, as follows: "Snorkeling and sailing cruise" daily at 9:30 A.M., $10 per person; "Snorkeling/Sailing/Beach Party Cruises" 12 noon, $18 adults, $9 children, includes picnic lunch and rum punch; evening "Wine and Cheese Cruise" each Tues., Thurs., and Sat., at 9 P.M., $15 to $18.

Daily cruises depart from St. Tropez Marina aboard the 65-foot pleasure yacht *Shangri La.* "Snorkeling, Swim and Sail Cruise" at 11:30 A.M. "Wine and Cheese Cruise" at 3 P.M.; "Sunset Booze Cruise" at 6 P.M. For rates and reservations call 352–4222.

 PARKS AND GARDENS. *The Rand Memorial Nature Center.* Settler's Way East. One-hundred-acre park and preserve for more than four hundred varieties of native subtropical plants, trees, flowers, and foliage, plus sanctuary for thousands of native and migratory birds. Within the park are well-marked nature trails. Guided walks offered by resident naturalists. Open daily with a nominal charge for admission. Guided tours available at 1:30 P.M., 2 P.M., and 4 P.M., except Fri. and Sun. For information call 352–5438.

The Garden of the Groves. Prize-winning botanical gardens covering more than a dozen acres. Some five thousand varieties of rare and familiar subtropical and tropical trees, shrubs, plants, and flowers. Well-marked pathways with identifying markers for plant species; tiny native-stone chapel. Small museum, *Discovery House,* traces four centuries of Bahamian history. No admission, but a donation of a dollar or two is requested for the museum, open from 10 A.M. to 2 P.M. The gardens are open all day, seven days a week. For information call 373–2422.

 PARTICIPANT SPORTS. Grand Bahama offers five tournament-quality championship 18-hole golf courses, among the best in the Caribbean. The island is bordered by 60 miles of ocean beach and fringed by living reefs offering some of the most thrilling diving anywhere. UNEXSO, a world-class scuba school, is located here. There are 50 hard-surface and clay tennis courts, most lit for night play, and six full-service marinas for boat charters, fishing, snorkeling, and sightseeing adventures and many other sports facilities. A selection of sports offerings in Freeport/Lucaya, their locations, and sample rates follow:

Fishing and Boating. Small-boat rentals are available through your hotel or at beach concessions in oceanside resorts. Fishing is excellent around Grand Bahama. Snapper, yellowtail, hogfish, grunts, kingfish, and jacks may be caught on nearby reefs; in deep-water channels there are marlin, wahoo, and sailfish; bonefish are caught in the marshy flats. Boats can be chartered at several marinas, and rates average $25 an hour for self-drive runabouts; $20 per person for four hours of drift fishing; and $40 and up per person for half a day of deep-sea fishing (party of six). Recommended marinas are:

Lucayan Harbour Marina. Tel. 373–1639. Charter boats, fishing excursions, dockage and taxidermist agency.

Running Mon Marina. Tel. 352–6834/5. Complete marina service, dockage, taxidermist agency, six sport-fishing charter yachts, and fishing trips.

Xanadu Beach Hotel Marina. Tel. 352–6780. Bahamas Air Sea Rescue base, dockage, and 28- and 46-foot sport-fishing boats on charter for deep-sea fishing.

West End–Jack Tar Village. Tel. 346–6211. Full-service marina, with deep-sea fishing, drift fishing, and bonefishing expeditions arranged.

Golf. Green fees range from $14–20 for 18 holes to $9–11 for 9 holes.

Bahamas Princess Golf Courses. The Emerald and The Ruby, both 18-hole championship layouts, PGA rates at par 72. Each course has its own clubhouse, restaurant, and pro shop. Golf carts are mandatory on both courses. Golf packages available through the Bahamas Princess Resort & Casino. Both located in Freeport, tel. 352–6721.

Bahama Reef Golf & Country Club. Within easy walking distance of hotels in the Lucaya beach resort area; 18-hole championship course, par 72. Driving range, pro shop, lessons available on request. Tel. 373–1055.

Lucayan Golf & Country Club. Naturally hilly setting overlooking picturesque Bell Channel in Lucaya; 18-hole championship course, par 72. Practice range, putting green, pro shop, clubhouse serves lunch and dinner. Tel. 373–1066.

Golf-West End. Jack Tar Village offers three nine-hole courses, which can be played in various combinations for 9, 18, or 27 holes. All are championship rated, par 36. Tel. 346–6211.

Horseback Riding. *Pinetree Stables,* located on Beachway Drive, Freeport, offers guided riding trips three times daily through island trails and along the beach. Dressage and jumping lessons by appointment. Tel. 373–3600.

Parasailing. Soar high over the water harnessed to a parachute and towed by a speed boat. You don't even get wet—launch and landing is from a moored raft. Expensive, but enthusiasts say it is worth every penny. Available at the *Atlantik Beach Hotel, Holiday Inn, Lucayan Beach Hotel,* and *Xanadu Beach Hotel.* About $20 for a six-minute flight.

Scuba-Diving. One of the most famous scuba schools and NAUI centers in the world is UNEXSO, the Underwaters Explorers Society, headquartered at the Lucayan Beach Resort. Beginners can learn to dive on their vacation for $59, which includes all equipment, three hours of professional instruction in the club's training pools, and a shallow reef dive. For experienced divers, there are four dive trips daily, night dives, inland blue hole dives, and multi-dive discounts. Certification, instructor training, dive medicine courses for physicians, and cave-diving training are all available. The club has equipment for rent and for sale, nine professional instructors, four dive boats, a unique 18-foot training tank, and a decompression chamber. Additional amenities are a small Underwater Museum and Tides Inn snack bar and lounge serving liberal libations and super sandwiches, with good conversation and nonstop underwater films. Tel. 373–1244 or write UNEXSO, Box F-2433, Freeport, Grand Bahama. UNEXSO serves most hotels in Freeport/Lucaya.

Tennis. *Bahamas Princess Country Club* has six Laykold courts, two lighted. *Bahamas Princess Towers* has six courts, three Laykold, three clay, all lighted. Both hotels charge $5 per hour daytime, $10 per hour at night. *Holiday Inn* has four hard-surface courts, none lighted. $5 per half-hour, $10 per hour. *Lucayan Beach Hotel* has 4 hard-surface courts, guests free, visitors pay a fee, pro instruction available. *Discovery Bay* has 10 hard surface courts, free to guests. *Silver Sands Hotel* has two hard-surface courts, guests free, visitors $3 per hour. *Xanadu Beach Hotel* has four hard-surfaced courts, two lighted, $4 per hour. West End–*Jack Tar Village* has 16 courts, ten cushion, six clay, all lighted, guests only.

Windsurfing. Several hotels offer rentals at beach concessions, and the *Atlantik Beach Hotel* offers a complete windsurfing school, with instruction, simulation, variety of boards, and certification. For courses, rates and dates call 373–1444 or write Atlantik Beach Hotel, Box F-531, Freeport, Grand Bahama.

MUSIC, DANCE, AND STAGE. Freeport and Lucaya have a sophisticated population of Bahamian professionals and foreign entrepreneurs, as well as a growing community of American, Canadian, and European visitors who spend several months a year on the island. Many have become active in promoting the performing arts. One group, *Friends of the Arts,* sponsors plays, musical groups, and guest artists from abroad, with tickets available to the general public. A local amateur group, *The Grand Bahama Players,* presents several Bahamian dialect comedies each year, and the *Freeport Players Guild* puts on ambitious productions of popular Broadway dramas, musicals, and comedies at the four-hundred-seat *Regency Theatre* in Freeport (tel. 352–5533). Performances by local groups and guest artists are well-publicized in the daily newspaper, on local radio and TV; posters and flyers are generally available at tourism information centers and at most hotel desks.

SHOPPING. There are hundreds of stores, shops, and boutiques throughout Freeport/Lucaya area, in hotels and resorts, shopping centers, and in the downtown center. However, the best bargains on fine imported goods such as perfumes, cameras, crystal, china, watches, cashmeres, linens, and European fashions are to be found in the International Bazaar where savings can be as much as 20 to 40 percent over U.S. and Canadian prices. (And remember prices is no sales tax anywhere in The Bahamas.) Shop carefully and compare prices before making any major purchase—and "know before you go." Take a tip from experienced travelers—if you are in the market for an expensive foreign camera, watch, china, crystal, or silver patterns, check prices before you leave home by phoning your local department and discount stores—then you'll be sure that you are getting a real Bahamian bargain. The shops listed below are open 10 A.M. to 6 P.M. and are located in the *International Bazaar,* Freeport. A new shopping and entertainment complex, *Port Lucaya,* in the Lucayan Beach area, is scheduled to open in late 1987.

Anata-O. Large collection of Italian gold and silver jewelry and precious stones in interesting settings. Chains, bracelets, and money clips.

Beachcomber. One-stop for an excellent variety of Bahamian handicrafts and souvenirs, including shark's teeth mounted and unmounted; coconut-shell jewelry; driftwood and shell items and souvenirs.

Bahama Mama. Delightful "Bahamas Hand Print," silk-screened patterns on fine cotton and washable blends sold by the yard or made into fashions. Designs are handcrafted with delightful Bahamian patterns. Large selection of souvenirs and T-shirts.

Bahama Coins & Stamps. Excellent selection of collectable international stamps and coins. Coin jewelry and Bahamas Coin Collections.

Bombay Bazaar. Exotic Indian brassware; jewelry in coral, jade, and tigereye; colorful clothing for men, women, and children.

Casablanca. Wide selection of imported French perfumes and a variety of Lancôme cosmetics and skin-care products.

Casa Miro. An excellent collection of fine Spanish porcelain including Nao and Lladró, along with small gift items from Spain such as tooled leather purses and wallets, colorful fans, Majorca pearls, 14- and 18-carat gold jewelry.

Charm Chest. This haven for charm collectors sells unique Bahamian designs and zodiac signs fashioned in 14- and 18-carat gold and sterling silver. Also offers fine fashion jewelry, and watches.

Colombian Emeralds Ltd. Largest and finest jewelry store in The Bahamas, offering substantial savings as well as certified appraisals, unconditional guarantees, and a U.S.-based service office. Magnificent collection of set and unset emeralds; outstanding diamond, sapphire, ruby, pearl, gold, and silver jewelry. You can watch exquisite jewelry being made by local craftsmen. Note: No U.S. duty is charged on unmounted emeralds.

Discount Bazaar. Specializing in brand-name watches and gold and silver jewelry at discount prices. Check this shop and compare prices before making a major watch purchase elsewhere in the Bazaar.

El Galleon. Attractive Spanish antiques and gift items, a large selection of watches, imported jewelry.

Evelyn of Lucaya. A very attractive women's boutique featuring original resort wear, European resort and evening wear, Italian sandals and jewelry.

Glass Blower Shop. Watch the glass-blowers make ships and figurines.

Ginza. Full line of imported cameras. Fine gold and silver jewelry, including Mikimoto pearls.

Hong Kong Tailors. Custom-made, Hong Kong-tailored suits from a wide selection of wool and lightweight fabrics. Ten days to two weeks delivery time.

India House. Exotic brassware, laquerware, wood carvings, and jewelry.

Kon Tiki. Exquisite shells from Bahamas and Philippines. Jewelry and souvenirs.

La Sandale. European designer footwear; watches by Michel Herbelin and Courréges.

Leather & Things. Imported luggage, handbags, briefcases, and accessories.

London Pacesetter Boutique. British and European sportswear. Excellent selection of Gottex swimwear, Pringle and Braemar cashmeres.

Midnight Sun. Grand Bahama's finest collection of crystal and porcelain figurines. Two shops in the International Bazaar—second shop offers imported gourmet cookware, cutlery, dinnerware. Both feature unique Lapponia jewelry designed by Bjorn Weckstrom and fashioned from Lapland gold.

Perfume Bar. Outstanding collection of French perfumes at discount prices.

Pipe of Peace. Superb collection of pipes, tobaccos, cigars, lighters from around the world. Good selection of watches.

The Plaka. A good collection of Greek handicrafts, jewelry in gold and silver, and an interesting selection of Grecian clothing for men, women, and children.

Strawmarket. Just to the right of the International Bazaar—this is not to be missed. Thousands of souvenirs and practical gift items woven by hand from straw, raffia, and palm fronds. Other handcrafted items made from shell, wood, berries, etc. All prices are negotiable so be sure to bargain with the straw ladies.

 RESTAURANTS. There is a nearly endless list of restaurants, dining rooms, country clubs, bars, lounges, and oceanside or poolside snack shops in the Freeport/ Lucaya area and in the International Bazaar. The choice of cuisines and atmospheres is nearly as varied, with everything from gourmet dining Continental or American style to native specialties like cracked conch, boil fish, or peas 'n rice with grouper; from exotic Indian curries and Japanese Kobe steak to fast food such as McDonald's, Kentucky Fried Chicken, and Wendy's.

We call $36 and up *Deluxe;* $25–35 *Expensive;* $15–24 *Moderate;* and under $15 *Inexpensive* for a three-course meal for one, excluding tip and beverage. Be sure to call ahead for reservations, particularly at Expensive to Deluxe restaurants. It is also wise to call ahead if you plan to pay for a meal with a credit card.

Freeport

The Crown. *Deluxe.* Located at Princess Casino. Tel. 352–7811. An international gourmet dining room. Jackets required. AE, DC, V.

Escoffier. *Deluxe.* Newly re-opened in Xanadu Beach Hotel. Tel. 352–6782. Elegant decor. If it lives up to its former reputation for superb French cuisine and elaborate Sunday brunch, it will be one of the best on the island. Dinner only. Jackets required. AE, BA, DC, M, V.

Rib Room. *Deluxe.* Located at the Bahamas Princess Country Club hotel. Tel. 352–6721. English hunting-lodge motif. A gourmet steakhouse whose specialty is beef. Try the steak Diane or fine prime rib—both are outstanding. Dinner only, jackets required. AE, DC, V.

Ruby Swiss Restaurant. *Deluxe.* Gourmet dining room located at the Princess Ruby Golf Course. Tel. 352–8507. Grand Bahama's largest selection of true gourmet fare, overseen by a noted Swiss chef. Breakfast buffet and menu selection for early golfers; fine luncheon menu includes Swiss sausages, quiche Lorraine, smoked salmon, fresh seafood. Superb dinner offerings include veal Cordon Bleu, fondue Bourguignonne, beef Wellington. Escoffier desserts and fine Swiss pastries. Superb wines to $150, cognacs and liqueurs. Dancing and entertainment in the evenings. AE, MC, V.

La Trattoria. *Deluxe.* Located in the Princess Tower. Tel. 352–9611. Elegant restaurant, with the finest international Italian cuisine. Dinner only. Jackets required. AE, DC, V.

Guanahani's. *Expensive.* Tel. 356–6721. Very attractive Bahamian architecture and island decor, located poolside at the Princess Country Club hotel. Informal dining on such specialties as Chinese smoked ribs, pan-fried grouper, and lobster pot. Prix-fixe dinner menu includes everything from salad to the chocolate fondue specialty dessert. Dinner only. AE, MC, V.

Island Lobster House. *Expensive.* Located on The Mall in Freeport. Tel. 352–9429. Live music and dancing to calypso music, exotic tropical drinks. Menu includes a good salad bar, filet of grouper, steak, and the specialty: whole Bahamian lobster stuffed with crabmeat. AE, MC, V.

Sir Winston Churchill Pub. *Moderate.* Located on The Mall in Freeport. Tel. 352–8866. Serves lunch (moderate) and dinner (expensive) daily. The Chartwell Room for dinner features English roast beef with Yorkshire pudding. Lively pub atmosphere with dart games, British brews, and authentic pub decor. AE, V.

Mai Tai. *Moderate.* Located in Bahamia, overlooking the Princess Emerald Golf Course. Tel. 352–7637. A classic Chinese menu, graceful atmosphere, exotic tropical drinks. Try one of their famous Polynesian or Szechwan specialty entrees. Lunch, dinner, and late snacks. AE, MC, V.

Churchill Square Restaurant. *Inexpensive.* Downtown Freeport. Tel. 352–2296. Good native specialties such as Boil Fish, Stew Fish, Curry Mutton, Conch Omelette with Johnny Cake and Guava Duff. Indoor and outdoor seating, bar. Breakfast, lunch daily. Most major credit cards.

Mum's Coffee Shop & Bakery. *Inexpensive.* In Freeport's downtown shopping center. Tel. 352–3416. Super sandwiches on fresh Bahamas bread, hot soups including conch chowder, and a delicious selection of pastries. Daily for breakfast and lunch. No credit cards.

Pancake House. *Inexpensive.* In Freeport on Sunrise Highway. Tel. 373–3200. All sorts of pancakes served until 10 P.M.; a good selection of lunch and dinner specialties including steak and seafoods. No credit cards.

Freeport/International Bazaar

Café Valencia. *Expensive.* In the Spanish section. Tel. 352–9521. Matador Room indoors or patio outdoors serve lunch, dinner, and late-night menu, featuring succulent ribs, lamb, beef, seafood, and fine wines. AE, V.

Japanese Steak House. *Expensive.* In the Oriental section. Tel. 352–9521. Hibachi tables, kimono-clad staff, and Japanese decor. Experts prepare traditional Kobe steaks, shrimp, fish, and chicken. Dinner only. AE, MC, V.

Café Michel. *Moderate.* French section. Tel. 352–2191. Indoor/outdoor dining in a delightful French sidewalk-café setting. Excellent omelettes and crêpes, plus pizza. Breakfast, lunch, and dinner except Sun. AE, MC, V.

China Palace. *Moderate.* Located in the great Oriental Pagoda. Tel. 352–5610. Very good Chinese food at very reasonable prices. Cantonese cuisine and some Polynesian and American offerings served in an exotic setting. The Pagoda Bar offers a fine variety of tropical drinks. Lunch and dinner Mon.–Sat., Sun. dinner and late snacks only. AE, DC, MC, V.

The Pub on the Mall. *Moderate.* At Ranfurly Circus in Freeport, opposite International Bazaar. Tel. 352–5110. A splendid English pub with authentic decor and atmosphere. Two dining rooms: The Prince of Wales Lounge serves good pub fare during the day; Baron's Hall, with elegant banner-hung medieval splendor, serves superb dinners at night—try the coquille St. Jacques, Cornish game hen, or roast beef and Yorkshire pudding. English beer, ales. AE, MC, V.

Le Rendezvous. *Inexpensive.* French café with striped umbrellas on the terrace, in the French section. Tel. 352–9610. Open 24 hours, indoors and outdoors, serving all kinds of snacks—ice cream, sandwiches, pancakes—or full meals, including pizza. Calypso band plays frequently. MC, V.

Lucaya

Alfredo's. *Deluxe.* Tel. 373–1444. In the Atlantik Beach Hotel. Award-winning European chef does wonders with fresh native seafood and imported veal, lamb, and beef. Impeccable service, good wine selection. Accepts major credit cards.

Lucayan Country Club. *Deluxe.* Tel. 373–1066. A beautiful room with splendid views across the golf course. Lunch features chef's salad, eggs Benedict, omelettes, cold stone crab. For dinner: oysters Rockefeller and fine Continental cuisine including rack of lamb, scampi, chauteaubriand, and roast pheasant, flaming desserts. Good wine selection. AE, MC, V.

Les Oursins. *Deluxe.* Tel. 373–7777. Elegant gourmet dining room in the Lucayan Beach Hotel. Continental cuisine with a French accent. Outstanding veal dishes, rack of lamb, and a memorable Caesar Salad. Sophisticated atmosphere, attentive service, fine wines. Dinner only. Jackets required. All major credit cards.

Bahama Reef Club. *Expensive.* Tel. 373–1056. Fine dining room at Bahama Reef Country Club, overlooking the golf course. Specializes in seafood, rack of lamb, and steak. Open for dinner and late-night suppers. Major credit cards.

Captain's Charthouse. *Expensive.* On East Sunrise Highway at Beachway Drive, Lucaya. Tel. 373–3900. Treetop-level dining in an attractive setting. Menu features prime rib, steaks, Bahamian lobster, and a fine salad bar. Live calypso music and dancing. Happy hour nightly 5–7 P.M. AE, V.

Britannia Pub. *Moderate.* Located on the water, overlooking Lucaya Harbour. Tel. 373–5919. Authentic English Tudor pub serving British pub fare for lunch and dinner, plus Bahamian specialties and a delicious Greek shishkebab.

Informal, comfortable, with an open fireplace and Courage beer on tap. Darts and electronic games. Free happy hour fish n' chips. AE, MC, V.

Lucayan Lobster & Steak House. *Moderate.* Tel. 373–5101. Large, sprawling restaurant with attractive decor, located on Midshipman Road in Lucaya. Casual, informal atmosphere with good cracked conch, lobster tail, and New York strip steak entrees. Dinner only. AE, MC, V.

The Stoned Crab. *Moderate.* A delightful, romantic oceanfront restaurant on Grand Bahama's most beautiful public beach—Taino Beach in Lucaya. Tel. 373–1442. Informal atmosphere indoors and on a terrace overlooking the sea. Frosty island drinks and fresh seafood or char-broiled steaks. Specialty of the house is stone-crab claws and Bahamian lobster. Good wine selections. Dinner only; open 4 P.M.–to midnight. AE, MC, V.

Outside of Freeport

Buccaneer Club. *Expensive.* Located at Deadman's Reef, Eight Mile Rock. Tel. 348–3794. Lovely grounds, oceanside patio, indoor or outdoor dining in a rustic wooden chalet. Excellent native and continental meals featuring steak, lobster, veal, chicken, or seafood. A favorite stop for boat tours, with lunch or dinner on the terrace. Open Nov. through April. No credit cards.

Harry's American Bar. *Expensive.* Located at Deadman's Reef, near Eight Mile Rock on the road to West End. Tel. 348–2241. Casual, indoor/outdoor dining and drinking spot favored by Grand Bahamians and visitors alike. Good hearty seafood or charcoaled steaks, tall cold tropical drinks and a sunset view unmatched on the island. Lunch and dinner daily. No credit cards.

Pier I. *Expensive.* Tel. 352–6674. Attractive stilt-house restaurant overlooking the cruise-ship port. Good hearty Bahamian and seafood specialties; a lovely view. Calypso entertainment, lunch and dinner daily except Sunday. AE, MC, V.

Freddie's. *Inexpensive.* Tiny but terrific. At Hunters, just outside of Freeport. Tel. 352–3250. Hearty Bahamian cooking—souse pigfeet or boil fish, steamed conch, and curried mutton, all served up with peas 'n rice and johnnycake. Or choose steak and lobster. No credit cards.

New Peace & Plenty. *Inexpensive.* In Eight Mile Rock, on the road to West End. Tel. 348–2206. A big old house with a popular native restaurant serving such authentic Bahamian dishes as curried goat, mutton stew, and turtle steak. The bar serves up the usual blend of tropical drinks and cocktails, along with a few unique "bush-medicine brews" for the adventurous. No credit cards.

Scorpio's. *Inexpensive.* West Atlantic at Explorer's Way, Freeport. Tel. 352–6969. True Bahamian meals, including boil fish and stew fish at breakfast (a favorite throughout The Bahamas), and conch—served chowdered, fractured, steamed and scorched, or chopped up raw in a hot sauce and served as salad. Peas 'n rice, chicken, grouper and lobster along with steaks and burgers. Bar with TV, pool room, and video games. No credit cards.

Star Restaurant. *Inexpensive.* Tel. 346–6207. Open practically around the clock, in a weathered old hotel at West End, which claims to be the oldest hotel on the island, built by Austin Grant in the 1940s. The hotel hasn't let rooms for years, but Austin Jr. operates it as a bar and restaurant. Try the cracked conch or grouper fingers, with a cold beer. Rustic. No credit cards.

 NIGHTLIFE AND ENTERTAINMENT. Both are plentiful on Grand Bahama Island, particularly in the Freeport/Lucaya area. Top attractions on the island are the lively French revue at the Princess hotel's *Casino Royale Theatre;* native nightclub shows featuring calypso bands and steel drums, limbo dancers, fire-eaters and Bahamian balladeers; and half-a-dozen late-night discos that mix recorded music with live musicians. Also popular with visitors are the Caribbean luaus, Goombay and Junkanoo festivals regularly scheduled at poolside or oceanside by the major hotels. A sampling of nightlife offerings:

Atlantik Beach Hotel. Rum Runner's Lounge has dancing to a live band every night from 8 P.M. on. Tel. 373–1444.

Austin's Calypso Bar. Next to the Star Restaurant, near Jack Tar Village at the West End settlement. Local island combo, dancing and merriment most evenings attracts a good mix of locals and "change of pace" vacationers seeking a respite from the wholesome and predictable entertainment at the resort compound. Tel. 346–6207.

Bahamas Princess Country Club Hotel. In the Palm Pavilion, a large circular ballroom, it's showtime twice a week. Wed. from 6:30 P.M., it's the *International Festival,* featuring a buffet dinner and live Bahamian show. Sat. from 6:30 P.M., Goombay Festival, with live calypso band and buffet dinner. Tel. 352–6721.

Bahamas Princess Towers Hotel. Two festivals scheduled poolside each week. Mon. from 6:30 P.M., it's Caribbean Night, Thur. from 6:30 P.M., Junkanoo Luau. Both include live native shows with calypso band, limbo and fire dancers, and a Bahamian buffet. *Sultan's Tent Disco* has action under the lights nightly. Cover charge. Tel. 352–9661.

Casino Royale Theatre. Adjacent to the Princess Casino. *Soiree,* an elaborate, high-stepping French-style showgirl revue is on twice nightly except Mon. The extravaganza includes comedians, singers, adagio dancers, and a spectacular cancan finale. Show times 8:30 and 10:30 P.M., price around $20 with two drinks included. Tel. 352–7811. Reservations necessary, particularly when cruise ships are in port.

Electric City Disco. Freeport, at E. Atlantic Drive. Live band 10 P.M.–4 A.M., poolside dining and dancing. Bahamian dishes and seafood, take-out orders, too. Happy hour 5–7 P.M. daily. Tel. 352–6681.

Flamingo Showcase Theatre. Adjacent to the Monte Carlo Casino at the Lucayan Beach Hotel. An elaborate continental-style revue, with variety and comedy acts, which are changed often. Two shows nightly, dinner optional. Price for the show, 2 drinks, tax and gratuities is $23 per hour. Tel. 373–7777.

Freeport Inn. In Freeport, at the East Mall and Explorer's Way. A live native show every Wed. and Sun. evenings from 10 P.M.; featuring fire dancers, limbo artists, and steel drums. Live calypso band every evening, Tue.–Sun. Tel. 352–6648 or 352–2805.

Holiday Inn. On the beach in Lucaya. The hotel features special poolside "Theme Nights" four nights weekly. "Caribbean Luau" on Tue. night—Caribbean night buffet, live entertainment, and native show. "Steak & Rib Cookout" on Wed. night—live band. "Bahamian Festival" on Fri. night—live entertainment, native show, Bahamian buffet. "Steak & Lobster Festival" on Sun.—live entertainment. *Lobby Bar* features soft island music nightly 5 P.M.–1 A.M. *Panache Nightclub* offers dancing nightly 9 P.M.–3 A.M., to an excellent local reggae–calypso band. Cover charge. Tel. 373–1333.

Studio 69. In Lucaya. Newest and swingingest disco on the island attracts an enthusiastic crowd of locals and visitors. Disc jockey and recorded music. Throbs nightly to the wee hours. Cover charge. Tel. 373–2158.

Yellow Bird Show Club. At Castaways Resort in Freeport. One of the best native shows on the island, featuring top Bahamian artists in a colorful revue with calypso, limbo, fire dancers, balladeers, and steel drums. Nightly from 8 P.M. Cover charge. Tel. 352–6682.

CASINOS. The famed El Casino's name has been changed to *Princess Casino* and the establishment was completely updated, remodeled and refurbished in 1984. A second, called the *Monte Carlo Casino,* opened in February 1986, and is located at oceanside in the all-new Lucayan Beach Hotel and Casino.

Princess Casino. Located in Freeport at the Bahamas Princess Resort and Casino. A captivating, much-photographed Moorish-style extravangaza. The interior matches the exterior in opulence. The 20,000-square-foot casino is one of the largest in The Bahamas or Caribbean. Games include 450 slot machines (the latest models are computerized, with link-progressive jackpots paying off as high as $100,000—and they can be played on credit!) 40 blackjack tables, eight dice tables, eight roulette wheels, two money wheels, and 24 assorted video games. The casino also offers a fine gourmet restaurant, *The Crown Room,* a delightful coffee shop, *The Garden Cafe,* the elevated *King's Court* casino bar, where you can watch all the action below, plus the *Casino Royale Theatre.* (See "Nightlife and Entertainment" above.) Tel. 352–7811. For information call 653–3794 in Miami, 800–432–2294 in Florida, and 800–422–7466, in the U.S. or call Princess Casino Vacations, 800–545–1300 in the U.S.

Monte Carlo Casino. Located in Lucaya, at the new Genting Lucayan Beach Hotel & Casino. Attractive decor, continental gaming including blackjack, money wheels, dice tables, baccarat, and state-of-the-art slot machines with big money payouts. Includes *The Flamingo Showcase Theatre* and supper club, and several dining options from casual to gourmet. Tel. 373–1224. In the U.S. call 800–331–2538 or 800–772–1227 for Casino package tours.

THE FAMILY ISLANDS

Abacos, Andros, Bimini, Cat Island, Chub Cay,

Crooked Island, Eleuthera, Exumas, Inagua,

Long Island, Rum Cay, and San Salvador

There is a third world of vacation islands to be discovered in The Bahamas. These are the Family Islands, known to generations of visitors as the "Out Islands." "Out" from the glitter of Nassau and Freeport, these islands make up the rest of The Bahamas, and offer a vivid contrast in vacation styles and lifestyles. They are beautiful, peaceful, and secluded, with endless nearly empty beaches where water sports are a way of life. There are no all-night discos or plush casinos, no international bazaars, and few gourmet restaurants. Entertainment is low key and local—a village combo on Saturday night, a piano bar in the clubhouse, or a guitar strummer on a moonlit terrace. Betting on the size of the next fish, the depth of the next dive, or the length of the next drive replaces the roll of dice or the turn of a card. There are no cities and few settlements which can even be described as small towns. Sightseeing tends to be a quiet stroll through a picturesque village, island-hopping in a small boat between sheltered harbors, or a picnic excursion to a nearby cay.

Getting to the Family Islands can be slightly more complicated than getting to Nassau or Grand Bahama, although most have direct, scheduled service from Nassau by the national flag carrier Bahamasair. Some islands, such as the Abacos, Bimini, Eleuthera, and the Exumas, are also served directly by scheduled commuter airlines based on the Florida mainland. Others, particularly in the more remote regions, are served by licensed air charters operating from Florida gateways.

Although more than seven hundred islands make up the Bahamian archipelago, fewer than thirty of them are populated and less than twenty offer resort facilities. The listing below includes the following Family Islands: the Abacos, Andros, Bimini, Cat Island, Chub Cay, Crooked Island, Eleuthera, the Exumas, Inagua, Long Island, Rum Cay, and San Salvador. In addition, you will find listed some of the developed offshore cays that can be reached by ferry or water-taxi from the main islands, such as Eleuthera's Harbour Island and Spanish Wells and the Abacos' Elbow Cay, Great Guana Cay, and Green Turtle Cay.

The islands are listed in alphabetical order, with information on how to get there, carriers and airports serving each island, a listing of the resorts and sports on each island and other general information. A local address is provided for each resort and sport facility, as well as a local telephone number; a U.S. address and telephone contact has been listed whenever available. Mail to and from the Family Islands tends to be very slow. To expedite your reservation, telephone the resort directly, or through the Bahamas Reservation Service, 800–327–0787, U.S. and Canada.

Note: Many Family Island resorts and hotels close for a month or two in late summer or autumn for repairs and vacations. Be sure to check the closing dates when making your reservations.

Tourist Information Services

In the United States, the Family Islands Promotion Board has offices at 255 Alhambra Circle, Coral Gables, FL 33134, tel. 305–446–4111. The organization can provide you with brochures on individual hotels, booklets describing and detailing several of the islands, maps, and rate sheets for both summer and winter seasons of all Family Island hotels and resorts that are members of the Promotion Board.

Rental Homes, Apartments, and Town Houses

VHR Worldwide offers vacation home rentals throughout the Family Islands. Contact them at 235 Kensington Avenue, Norwood, NJ

07648. Tel. 201–767–9393. Other rental options are listed under each island.

THE ABACOS

The Abacos, in the northeastern Bahamas, are among the most beautiful of the out-island chains making up the Bahamian archipelago. The Abacos stretch in a great boomerang shape for 140 miles from tiny Walker's Cay in the north to Sandy Point at the southwestern tip. Near the center of the chain are two main islands, Great and Little Abaco, fringed on their windward shore by an emerald necklace of cays forming a living barrier reef against the broad Atlantic.

The main islands and the offshore cays were settled two centuries ago by New England loyalists who fought on the British side during the American Revolution. When the war was lost, they fled to The Bahamas. Other families arrived from Virginia and the Carolinas, bringing with them their plantation lifestyle and their slaves. But life was hard for the transplanted settlers. Thin soil and coral rock made it nearly impossible to wrest a living from the land. Many turned to the sea for sustenance, some to the dark art of "wrecking."

Charts of these waters had never been drawn, and there were no lighthouses in all of The Bahamas until 1836. The piratical wreckers worked by night, showing false lights to lure ships onto rocks and shoals to destruction—then harvesting the ship's cargo. Not all of the wrecks were caused by unscrupulous islanders, of course—many ships were lost in storms and foundered on hidden reefs as they passed through The Bahamas between the Atlantic Ocean and the Caribbean Sea. But by fair means or foul, "wrecking" was a thriving industry in Abaco until the middle of the 1800s.

The days of loyalist plantations and the dark deeds of the wreckers have long ago faded into history and legend. Today, some seven thousand descendants of the early settlers and their slaves live in harmony together on the Abaco islands. Friendly and hard working, many still are seafarers, and earn their living as boat builders and boat repairmen, fishermen or fishing guides. And increasing numbers earn their living in the thriving tourist industry, since the Abacos are linked to the rest of the world by modern airports at Marsh Harbour and Treasure Cay.

There is a broad variety of vacation lifestyles for visitors to the Abacos. Most of the tourist accommodations are near the busy little town of Marsh Harbour and the nearby offshore village of Hope Town on Elbow Cay. Others are located at the vast Treasure Cay complex fifty miles to the north, and in the small island villages of Green Turtle Cay, just off its shore.

The calm, turquoise waters that lie between the main islands and the offshore cays are known to Bahamians and international yachtsmen as

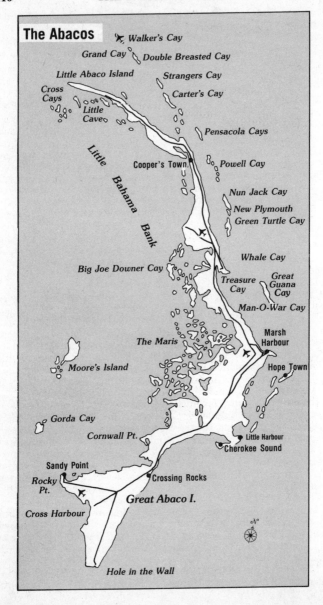

The Abacos

Walker's Cay
Grand Cay
Double Breasted Cay
Little Abaco Island
Strangers Cay
Cross Cays
Carter's Cay
Little Cave
Pensacola Cays
Little Bahama Bank
Cooper's Town
Powell Cay
Nun Jack Cay
New Plymouth
Green Turtle Cay
Whale Cay
Big Joe Downer Cay
Treasure Cay
Great Guana Cay
Man-O-War Cay
The Maris
Marsh Harbour
Hope Town
Moore's Island
Gorda Cay
Cornwall Pt.
Little Harbour
Cherokee Sound
Sandy Point
Rocky Pt.
Crossing Rocks
Great Abaco I.
Cross Harbour
Hole in the Wall

N

"The Sea of Abaco." The nearly one thousand square miles of sheltered cruising grounds are arguably the best in the entire Bahamas or Caribbean. Two major bareboat charter operators headquartered in the Abacos allow you to take advantage of this natural playground for sailors.

Exploring Marsh Harbour and Treasure Cay

Marsh Harbour, on Great Abaco Island, is an attractive, busy little town, the commercial center of the Abacos. The whole town and colorful harbor can easily be explored on foot or bicycle. A variety of stores and shops line the main road through town—which boasts the island's single traffic light. A favorite stop for tourists is The Loyalist Shoppe, which offers a good selection of imported gift items such as crystal, china, watches, and jewelry; a selection of newspapers, magazines, and books on The Bahamas; and handcrafted souvenirs. On a hilltop overlooking the town and the sea is an eccentric miniature "castle." It is the creation of Dr. Evans Cottman, an American scientist who lived on the island for many years, author of *Out Island Doctor,* a fascinating book on his Bahamian experiences.

In Marsh Harbour, there are several good inexpensive restaurants for lunch or dinner. Cynthia's Kitchen serves up native dishes such as curried goat in a friendly, frill-less atmosphere; Keys Bakery features the best baked goods on the island plus a range of meals from burgers to full-course Bahamian dinners. Just outside of Marsh Harbour, in the settlement of Dundas Town, is a "must stop" for locals and tourists alike: Mother Merle's Fishnet Restaurant, where Bahamian cookery reigns supreme. You'll find baked turtle pie and conch fritters, hot johnnycake, homemade coconut ice cream, and deep-dish pineapple and key-lime pies. Mother Merle herself presides over the rustic out-island setting. For more elegant dining, try the delightful Jib Room at Marsh Harbour Marina. An outdoor veranda and nautical dining room overlook the busy harbor, and the menu includes charbroiled steaks and fish, brandied seafood, and many island favorites. Atmosphere is casual but charming, and prices are moderate.

For a driving tour of the main island, a fair road winds northward to Treasure Cay, through vast Abaco pine forests where wild horses and boar are known to roam. Sights along the way include two colorful native villages, Dunda's Town and Murphy's Town; and a sprawling tropical nursery, Bahamas Plants Ltd., which ships one-hundred-thousand ornamental plants to the U.S. market each week.

At Treasure Cay, you'll find a beautiful residential-resort community, a multimillion-dollar complex set on fourteen hundred acres of tropical greenery, along a stunning four-mile-long strip of broad, white sand beach. Treasure Cay is not an island, but a large peninsula, connected to the mainland of Abaco by a narrow spit of land. There are a few small settlements in the area, clustered near the resort, and a good native eatery called A Touch of Class, where locals and tourists gather for fine Bahamian cooking and friendly service, music, and dancing. In the surrounding countryside, there is a huge three-thou-sand-acre truck farm, which grows winter vegetables, avocados, and citrus fruit for shipment to the Florida market.

But the main attraction in this part of Abaco is the Treasure Cay Beach Hotel and Villas, one of the most complete residential resorts in all of the islands. It offers dozens of gracious oceanside homes, privately owned by Americans, Canadians, and Europeans; several outstanding apartment-villa complexes overlooking the sea, the harbor, or the golf course and available for purchase or vacation rental; and an attractive small hotel. Amenities include a full-service marina for yachts to two hundred feet; an 18-hole championship golf course designed by Dick Wilson; ten tennis courts; five freshwater pools; and a full scuba train-ing facility. Just offshore is the charming island village of Green Turtle Cay, easily reached by regular ferry service—don't miss a day of ex-ploring this little gem. (See "Green Turtle Cay and the Village of New Plymouth," below.)

A rugged road winds south from Marsh Harbour for more than fifty miles to Sandy Point, a rustic fishing village at the southwestern tip of the Abacos. There are miles of beautiful ocean beach on the point, offering some of the finest shelling in The Bahamas. There is excellent fishing nearby, and boats can be rented for angling or shelling expedi-tions to Rocky Point and Gorda Cay offshore where, collectors claim, the shelling is even better. The dense woodlands in this area are a nature preserve set aside by The Bahamas National Trust as a sanctu-ary for the endangered Bahamian parrot. More than one hundred other species have been counted by avid bird watchers.

Exploring the Offshore Cays

No trip to the Abacos would be complete without at least a day or two to explore the quaint island villages on the offshore cays. They are easily accessible by modern motor-launch water-taxis, which cross the few miles of sheltered waters to the cays on a regular daily schedule.

Elbow Cay and the Village of Hope Town

The charming village overlooks a beautiful, sheltered harbour domi-nated by a great 120-foot-tall peppermint-striped lighthouse—perhaps the most photographed landmark in all The Bahamas. When the Im-perial Lighthouse Service put up the great light in 1838, the Hope Town villagers nearly sabotaged the entire project. They had counted on at least one wreck a month on their shores, and feared the light would change all that. But as late as 1860, the settlers were still living off of wrecks despite their new lighthouse. Today, the lighthouse keeper at Hope Town welcomes visitors hearty enough to climb the steep winding stairs to the top for an unsurpassed view of the turquoise waters and emerald cays that make up the great fringe reef off Abaco's shores.

Two narrow lanes circle the village and the harbor, one called Up Along, the other Down Along. Follow either for an interesting walking or biking tour of the delightful village, whose saltbox cottages, white picket fences, and flowering gardens will remind you of New England —but with the grays and browns of northern climes replaced by the pretty pastels of the tropics. The best example of loyalist architecture in the village is the Wyannie Malone Historical Museum, filled with memorabilia and artifacts of Hope Town and the Widow Malone, who settled on the island with her children in 1875. Many of her descendants still live in Hope Town. Look for the Ebb Tide Gift Shop on Up Along, which offers a variety of hand prints, coral and shell gifts; or Jeff's Native Touches with some unusual handcrafted souvenirs. Drop by Lorraine's Bakery for fresh, hot Abaco bread and donuts, or plan lunch at the Village Inn on Down Along, overlooking the harbor— inexpensive, with the accent on fresh seafood and conch chowder.

Great Guana Cay

A startlingly beautiful island, with a seven-mile-long beach on the ocean side fringed by sheltered waters within an unbroken line of offshore reefs. There's excellent snorkeling among colorful sea gardens and schools of tropical fish and fine shelling (especially after a "norther"). The tiny village has less than a hundred people and no roads. Flowered lanes and pathways wind amid tall coconut palms and island greenery. The spectacular reef attracts divers and underwater photographers, fishermen, and yachtsmen. Drop in to the Guana Beach Resort for a frosty "Guana Grabber" or hearty Bahamian lunch.

Little Harbor

Southernmost stop on the ferry line, this is the private island paradise of the Johnston family, artists and sculptors with an international following. Margot and Randolph and their three sons sailed to the island back in 1951 and decided to make it their home. They've told the story of their Swiss Family Robinson–style experiences in a book, *Artist on His Island*. The Johnstons have built a foundry for casting his superb bronze sculptures and a ceramic studio where she creates charming porcelain figurines of Bahamian fishermen, birds, fish, and boats. (Visitors are welcome at the studios from 10–11 A.M., 2–3 P.M., or by appointment.) Nearby, their son Peter and his wife Debbie, both noted sculptors, have a studio and bar called Pete's Pub and Gallery, offering cool drinks and good company along with an excellent variety of family art at a broad range of prices.

Man-O-War Cay

Known for generations as the "boat-building capital of The Bahamas," the Man-O-War Alburys still build sturdy handcrafted Bahamian workboats at their boatyard on the harbor, much as their forefathers did some two hundred years ago. Nearly everyone on the island is named Albury, and they are mostly descendants of the early loyalist settlers—proud of their heritage and their religion, (Bumper stickers are collector's items here—a favorite is "What do you miss by being a Christian? Hell!") There is no crime, no jail, no cars, few televisions, and even fewer telephones on Man-O-War Cay, and absolutely no liquor is sold or consumed. But the islanders are warm, friendly, and openly hospitable to visitors—willing to chat, direct you to some of their favorite fishing, crabbing, or picnicking spots, and show you where to rent a bicycle or golf cart (the only mechanized transport on the island) for exploring the tiny cay and its long, beautiful beachs. (No scanty bikinis or short-shorts please; the islanders disapprove.)

Some of the most delightful, creative craft shops in The Bahamas are on Man-O-War Cay. Look for Joe Albury's shop near the boatyard at harborside, where you will find hand-carved boat half-hulls, wooden furniture, and nautical accessories; or drop into Uncle Norman Albury's Sail Shop in the center of town, where the women of the family turn out handsome canvas or nylon duffle bags, sailing shirts and jackets, hats, and totes—each handmade, hand-signed and (optionally) emblazoned with a chic "Man-O-War Cay" embroidered patch. Nearby, you'll find Sally's Sea Side Shop, offering handmade shirts, blouses, sundresses, and skirts of fine denim or batiked and silk-screened island fabrics, as well as handcrafted straw hats and bags. All come at moderate to expensive prices. After your sightseeing stroll and shopping spree, drop by Albury's Dock 'N Dine restaurant (at the harborside dock, of course) for crispy conch fritters, hearty conch chowder, fresh fish, or perhaps just a tall frosty milk shake. And don't miss the devastatingly delicious homemade candy sold at the Bite Site, which is also a good spot for collectible bumper stickers, decals, banners, and posters with the unique Man-O-War Cay messages.

Green Turtle Cay and the Village of New Plymouth

A sprawling, two-mile-by-four-mile island with many deep bays, sounds, and a nearly continuous strip of fine ocean beach. Located just two miles off the shore of Treasure Cay, the cay boasts three main harbors: White Sound (dominated by Bluff House and the Green Turtle Cay Club on opposite shores), Black Sound, and Settlement Creek, location of picturesque New Plymouth village, whose roots go deep into Abaco's loyalist past. The Green Turtle Ferry Service from Treasure Cay makes stops at each of the harbors, and also calls at Coco Bay on the northern tip of the island. The easiest way to explore the whole island is by small outboard dinghy or Boston Whaler which can be rented by the hour or the day at most resorts and marinas.

The town pier is located at New Plymouth. The delightful village perches on a gentle hillside overlooking the busy harbor, and narrow flowered lanes wind between rows of neat little clapboard cottages painted in white and bright colorful gingerbread trim, or in pink, yellow, turquoise, aqua, and green. The most-visited attraction is the Albert Lowe Museum, housed in a lovely 150-year-old white clapboard two-story house. It overlooks a beautiful Sculpture Garden with fine bronze busts and a life-size sculpture of two island children—one black and one white—in a landing boat, representing the island's earliest settlers, the loyalists and their slaves. The museum and garden are the creation of internationally known artist Alton Roland Lowe, who named the museum for his father, a famous carver of wooden ship models. Both the father's and son's works are on display in the museum, along with a priceless collection of memorabilia of Green Turtle Cay, dating back to the loyalists' arrival in 1783–85. The opening of the Sculpture Garden in 1983 marked the beginning of a two-year Loyalist Bicentennial Celebration. To commemorate the event, The Bahamas government issued a series of beautiful postage stamps, replicas of artist Alton Roland Lowe's famous oil paintings depicting the loyalist era. Look for the old loyalist cemetery near the harbor where weathered headstones date back to the 1780s.

After your stroll through the village, you might stop for an informal lunch or snack at Miss Betty MacIntosh's Sea View Restaurant and Bar (inexpensive Bahamian specialties), or for a cool drink and local gossip at Miss Emily's Blue Bee Bar—both are favorites of locals and visitors. Or linger over an elegant luncheon at New Plymouth Inn, a historic 150-year-old house operated as a small inn and fine restaurant—try the turtle steak or lobster salad with a vintage wine or frosty stein.

PRACTICAL INFORMATION FOR THE ABACOS

HOW TO GET THERE. By air. Two international airports are located at Marsh Harbour and Treasure Cay. More than 50 miles and a rugged road separate the two, so visitors to the island must be certain they are routed to the proper airport. Both Marsh Harbour and Treasure Cay are served daily by *Bahamasair* from Nassau. They are served also by licensed, scheduled commuter airlines operating from Florida gateways, such as *Aero Coach, Caribbean Express, Gull Air, Eastern Express,* and *Piedmont Shuttle.* In addition, there are occasional charters which operate to the Abacos from U.S. cities in the northeast and from Toronto and Montreal (check with your travel agent for details). At Walker's Cay, northernmost island in the Abaco chain, there is a private airstrip served by *Walker's Cay Airlines* which offers daily scheduled service from Fort Lauderdale, Fla. and Chalk's International from West Palm Beach, Fla.

By mail boat. The mail boat *M/V Deborah K II* sails every Wed. from Potter's Cay Dock in Nassau and calls at Cherokee Sound, Cooper's Town,

Grand Cay, Green Turtle Cay, Great Guana Cay, Hope Town, Man-O-War Cay, and Marsh Harbour, returning to Nassau each Mon. The *M/V Captain Dean* departs Potter's Cay Dock each Tues., calling at Sandy Point, More's Island, Crossing Rock, and Bullock's Harbour, returning to Nassau each Sun. Call the Dock Master at Potter's Cay Dock in Nassau for details, tel. 323–1064.

TELEPHONES AND EMERGENCY NUMBERS. Area code for the Abacos is 809, although not all areas may be reached by (DDD) direct distance dialing. As most resorts in the Abacos offer telephone service only at the main desk, all emergencies should be reported immediately to the hotel management. There are clinics at the following settlements in the Abacos: Cooper's Town, Fox Town, Marsh Harbour (main clinic and health center, two resident nurses, and two private doctors), More's Island, Sandy Point, and Treasure Cay (private clinic with resident dentist and doctor).

HOTELS AND RESTAURANTS. Many of the hotels in the Abacos have restaurants. Other restaurants are mentioned earlier in the text and are not listed below. Hotels are listed according to the nearest airport. We have indicated whom to contact for reservations; in many cases you'll note that reservations may also be made through the Bahamas Reservation Service, tel. 800–327–0787, abbreviated below as BRS. We have also indicated which hotels do not accept any of the major credit cards. Generally speaking, hotel restaurants will accept the same credit cards that the hotel honors.

Hotel price categories, based on double occupancy in high season, are: $150 and up *Super Deluxe;* $125–149, *Deluxe;* $100–124, *Expensive;* $75–99, *Moderate;* under $75, *Inexpensive.*

Marsh Harbour Airport

MARSH HARBOUR. Abaco Towns-by-the-Sea. *Deluxe.* Reserve direct: Box 486, Marsh Harbour, Abaco; tel. 367–2221, or through BRS. 40 new, very modern, elegant townhouse villas, completely furnished with an island flair. Each features living room, kitchen, dining area, master bedroom, two baths, guest bedroom, and private patio. Well-landscaped gardens, a sparkling pool, and two tennis courts, all overlooking the sea. Available for purchase, timeshare or vacation rental. Each villa accommodates up to six.

Great Abaco Beach Hotel. *Moderate.* Box 419, Marsh Harbour, Abaco; tel. 367–2158; or through BRS. On a hillside overlooking the sea, thirty attractive, oversized, air-conditioned rooms (each with a telephone) and five housekeeping villas. Spacious grounds include a freshwater pool, two tennis courts, and a sheltered strip of beach. There's fine dining in the 200-seat restaurant, which attracts visitors and locals from around the island. The house specialty is fresh-caught seafood (moderate). Also popular is the attractive bar/lounge, which features native singers and combos. The resort arranges all types of fishing charters, scuba trips, boat rentals, and sightseeing tours. Bicycles, mopeds, and cars are available for rental; bus service is provided to Treasure Cay's 18-hole championship golf course. Four miles from the airport.

Conch Inn. *Inexpensive.* Box 434, Marsh Harbour, Abaco; tel. 367–2800/2233. A comfortably casual yachtsman's haven with 14 tasteful, air-conditioned rooms overlooking the harbor and 40-slip full-service marina. The inn is one of the most popular gathering spots on the island for cruising yachtsmen, private flyers, and guests of other resorts. They are drawn by excellent native food (like conch burgers) at the *Conch Crawl* snack shop at the marina, the congenial

Conch Out bar with island entertainment, and the delightfully tropical *Conch Inn Restaurant,* which serves some of the finest gourmet food in the Abacos (moderate to expensive). Other amenities include a large swimming pool, a well-stocked boutique, and a lovely ocean beach nearby. A two-bedroom housekeeping cottage and two efficiency apartments are also available. 6 percent service charge added. Located three miles from the airport.

HOPE TOWN, ELBOW CAY. Accessible by ferry from docks near Marsh Harbour Airport. Boats meet incoming and outgoing flights.

Abaco Inn. *Expensive.* Abaco Inn, Hope Town, Abaco; tel. 367–2666; or through BRS. A friendly, relaxing hideaway that sprawls along three lovely beaches at White Sound, Elbow Cay. There are three two-bedroom oceanfront cottages and six double rooms at harborside, all simple but nicely furnished and air-conditioned. Shelling is fine along the broad beaches; there is a nice swimming pool and a thatched solarium for au naturel sunbathing. All water sports and water-taxi tours are easily arranged at the resort; rental bicycles are available. An excellent restaurant offers dining indoors or outdoors and features creative cookery, including vegetarian fare and macrobiotic specialties (moderate to expensive). There is local entertainment in a congenial bar/lounge.

Elbow Cay Beach Inn. *Moderate.* Reserve direct: Elbow Cay Club, Hope Town, Abaco; tel. 367–2748; or through BRS. Set on a horseshoe-shaped lagoon on the Atlantic side. Thirty rooms and three housekeeping cottages, all neat and well maintained. Danish owners feature many European dishes in the popular restaurant, which draws crowds for special smorgasbord feasts. An informal bar and lounge is a favorite gathering spot for islanders and visitors, with local entertainment on weekends. There is an attractive pool and terrace set amid gardens and palms. Sailing, waterskiing, windsurfing, and dive trips are available at the resort's dock, and there is a 38-foot yacht for sightseeing trips and picnic cruises.

Hope Town Harbour Lodge. *Moderate.* Hope Town, Abaco; tel. 367–2277; toll free in the U.S., 800–626–5690; or through BRS. A charming old inn on a hilltop overlooking both the harbor and the Atlantic. There are 13 clean and cozy rooms in the main lodge and eight comfortable cottage rooms on the ocean side, clustered around a nice pool. Two attractive dining rooms serve a good international and Bahamian menu, and the traditional Sunday Champagne Brunch draws enthusiasts from all over the island and the mainland. Scuba, boating, water-skiing, fishing, and windsurfing are available at the resort's harborside marina.

GREAT GUANA CAY. Guana Beach Resort. *Inexpensive.* Box 474, Marsh Harbour, Abaco; tel. 367–2207, or through BRS. A small, cozy resort with 19 rooms on one of the most strikingly beautiful islands in the Abaco chain. Rooms are neat and simply furnished; some are air-conditioned. There is a dining room serving good, hearty Bahamian dishes, and a congenial bar where cruising yachtsmen gather. At harborside, there's a small marina and dock, and at oceanside a spectacular seven-mile-long beach.

Treasure Cay Airport

TREASURE CAY. Treasure Cay Beach Hotel and Villas. *Expensive to Deluxe.* Reserve direct: Treasure Cay Beach Hotel and Villas, 2301 S. Federal Hwy. Ft. Lauderdale, Fla. 33316; tel. 305–525–7711; 800–327–1584, U.S.; 800–432–8257, in Florida. All of the sophistication of a major international resort with the charm and style of an island village. There is an intimate hotel of 35 rooms, centered amid fourteen-hundred lushly green tropical acres overlooking four miles of broad white-sand beach. Through the gardens and along the seashore are nearly 200 additional accommodations located in beautiful villas and townhouses, rustic cottages and double-deck apartments overlooking the harbor and the sea (available for time-share or purchase). All are fully air-conditioned, attractively furnished, and offer full kitchens, large living rooms, terraces, or patios. Units have one, two, or three bedrooms. Sporting amenities include an 18-hole championship, Dick Wilson-designed golf course with club-house and pro shop; ten hard-surface tennis courts (four lighted for night play); five freshwater pools; a 150-slip, full-service marina; and a complete scuba-dive operation, plus sightseeing boat trips to offshore islands of Guana Cay and Green Turtle Cay and drift fishing expeditions. Golf, tennis, Sunfish sailboats, and snorkel gear are all free for guests. Bicycle, scooter, and car rental may be arranged through the hotel; fishing boats, Hobie Cats, and windsurfers can be rented at the marina. There are two good restaurants, the *Abaco Room* in the hotel and the lovely *Spinnaker Restaurant,* with entertainment every evening (expensive), and quiet drinks with a great view at the *Tipsy Seagull Bar* over-looking the marina. The resort also offers a complete shopping center, including doctor's and dentist's offices, bank, and post office. Located 7½ miles from the airport.

   GREEN TURTLE CAY. Accessible by water taxi from the docks near Treasure Cay Airport. Boats meet all incoming and outgoing flights.

   Green Turtle Club. *Expensive.* Green Turtle Cay, Abaco; tel. 367–2572; in the U.S., 305–833–9580; or through BRS. An elegant but informal yachtsman's rendezvous, this private-membership yacht club has ties to the British Royal Yachting Association and the Palm Beach Yacht Club in Florida. Guests are welcomed, however. Thirty-one luxurious, beautifully appointed rooms are available as doubles or in villas and cottages tucked amid tropical greenery on a hillside overlooking the harbor. They contain one to three bedrooms and one to three bathrooms, full kitchens, dining and living rooms, and private terraces. The harborside clubhouse houses a unique nautical bar. The attractive dining room here serves excellent food ranging from gourmet to traditional American fare, and authentic Bahamian cuisine, with the accent on fresh seafood. The service is impeccable, and guests enjoy dressing with casual elegance for dinner and dancing on the terrace (expensive). Amenities include a small private beach, a pool, one tennis court, a 22-slip full service marina, boating, and fishing and scuba expeditions.

   Bluff House. *Moderate.* Green Turtle Cay, Abaco; contact 2969 N. Dixie Hwy., Ste. 618, Ft. Lauderdale, FL 33334. Tel. 305–941–6987; ask operator for Green Turtle Cay 5211; or through BRS. A cozy, comfortable, well-run resort set on a high bluff overlooking a sheltered harbor and a small ocean beach. Superb views from the efficiency apartments in the main lodge, and from the two-story "tree-house" villas tucked here and there on the woodsy hillside acres. All units are air-conditioned and tastefully decorated, with kitchen facilities, spacious living areas, one or two bedrooms, and baths. In the main lodge, there is a candlelit dining room where complimentary wine is poured freely and excellent meals feature American, Continental, and Bahamian cuisine. It is a favorite dining-out experience for cruising yachtsmen and guests of nearby resorts (moderate to expensive). The resort has a pool, tennis court, and beach-side snack shop/bar. Arrangements are easily made at the resort's harborside marina for boating, water-skiing, deep-sea and bonefishing expeditions, and water-taxi tours around the island and to the village of New Plymouth.

   New Plymouth Inn. *Moderate.* Reserve direct: New Plymouth Inn, Green Turtle Cay, Abaco; tel. 367–5211; in the U.S., 305–665–5309. An elegant little historic inn overlooking a tropical garden and sparkling pool. There are just eight carefully restored rooms in the charming antique two-story house. The inn

THE ABACOS
is a fine example of Bahamian colonial architecture. All rooms have private bath
and shower. The inn's attractive dining room dishes up notable Bahamian
specialties such as turtle steaks, fresh native lobster, and conch, as well as roasts,
steaks, and chops—all served with vintage wines or imported beers (moderate
to expensive). The *Galleon* lounge/bar is a favorite stop of island sightseers.
Nearby ocean beach. 15 percent service charged. No credit cards.

Rental Apartments and Cottages: There are many rental units available on
Green Turtle Cay. Rates at the following recommended establishments range
from inexpensive to moderate:

Bougainvillea Apartments. Two two-bedroom apartments in an attractively
refurbished 150-year-old island home. Both are well equipped with full kitchens
and baths. Box 541, Green Turtle Cay; tel. 5277.

Coco Bay Club. Box 836, Green Turtle Cay; tel. 5933; or through Beacon
Tours, Largo, FL 813–536–1911. Seven attractive cottages set along two beautiful winding beaches. All offer full kitchens, spacious living areas and private
baths, two or three bedrooms.

Linton's Beach Cottages. Green Turtle Cay, Abaco; ask operator for Green
Turtle Cay. Four two-bedroom cottages along a lovely private beach, each with
living/dining room, full kitchen, and private bath.

Sea Star Beach Cottages. Box 282, Gilam Bay, Green Turtle Cay, Abaco; tel.
Green Turtle Cay 5444. Four attractive kitchenette cottages located on 19
oceanside acres along a lovely private beach.

Walker's Cay Airport

Walker's Cay Club. *Expensive to Deluxe.* Reserve direct: Walker's Cay Club,
700 S.W. 34th St., Ft. Lauderdale, FL 33315; tel. 305–523–4300; toll-free in the
U.S. 800–327–3714; toll-free in Florida 800–432–2092. Served by private scheduled air service from Ft. Lauderdale and Chalk's seaplanes from West Palm
Beach. A completely self-contained resort on the northernmost island in all of
The Bahamas. A favorite of private-plane flyers and international divers, the
island is best known for spectacular sport fishing. The club hosts several major
tournaments each year, including a leg of the prestigious Bahamas Billfish
Championship and the famed Bertram–Hatteras Shootout. There are 62 luxurious hotel rooms, attractively furnished and air-conditioned, and four exclusive
villas. The quaint dining room overlooks the sea and serves up Bahamian and
American specialties—especially fresh-caught fish—complimented by a superb
wine list. The patio bar and lounge are favorite gathering spots for swapping fish
tales and watching the weigh-ins at the dock. Sports amenities include a 75-slip
full-service marina with a fleet of charter boats and rental skiffs available for
both deep-sea and light-tackle fishing expeditions; two hard-surface tennis
courts; two swimming pools (one saltwater, one freshwater); and a full scuba
program.

 HOW TO GET AROUND. There is direct **taxi** service
to all resorts on Great Abaco Island served by Marsh
Harbour airport, or to the docks for water-taxi service
to resorts at Hope Town on Elbow Cay, Man-O-War
Cay, and Great Guana Cay. From Treasure Cay Airport there is direct taxi
service to Treasure Cay Beach Hotel and Villas and to the docks for ferry service
to Green Turtle Cay resorts.

Taxi tours of Great Abaco island may be negotiated at the airports or
arranged through your resort. Rental cars are available in Marsh Harbour
through the following agents: *H & L Rentals,* Box 490, Marsh Harbour, Abaco,

tel. 367–2854; *Shell Gas Station,* Box 438, Marsh Harbour, Abaco, tel. 367–2854.

For **sightseeing** expeditions to the offshore cays from main island resorts, water-taxi or ferry service is available from the docks serving both Marsh Harbour and Treasure Cay airports. Services generally coincide with incoming and outgoing flights. Visitors should check at their resorts for exact schedules or contact the following: Marsh Harbour—*Albury's Ferry Service,* at the dock near the Great Abaco Beach Hotel, tel. 367–2306. The firm offers regular service to Hope Town, Elbow Cay, Man-O-War Cay, and Great Guana Cay; organizes charters on longer trips (for up to eight passengers) to Treasure Cay and Green Turtle Cay. From docks near the Treasure Cay Airport, the *Green Turtle Cay Ferry Service* operates frequently to several points on Green Turtle Cay. There is no phone service, but the ferry stands by on CB channel 11 and may be contacted by radio from the Treasure Cay Beach Hotel and Villas or the airport. In the island villages of the offshore cays, there are few cars. Sightseeing is on foot or by rental bicycle, available at most of the resorts and through small shops in the villages or at marinas along the harbors. Your ferryboat captain or water-taxi driver is a good source of information on where to rent bikes or scooters and how much they should cost.

 SPECIAL EVENTS. *Abaco Week.* a "roots" festival held each November attracts hundreds of visitors from The Bahamas, Key West, Nova Scotia, and the West Indies, where other loyalists found new homes during the great refugee migrations which began during the American Revolutionary War and peaked in 1783–85 after the British were defeated. There are arts-and-crafts fairs, choral groups, Junkanoo masqueraders, plus golf, tennis, and fishing tournaments throughout the Abacos. For details, write to The Abaco Chamber of Commerce, Box 509, Marsh Harbor, Abaco; tel. 367–2663.

Bahamas Billfish Championship Tournament. Two legs of the prestigious tournament series are held in the Abacos: *Walker's Cay Billfish Tournament* held in April, and the *Treasure Cay Billfish Tournament,* held in June. Both resorts host several other major fishing events.

Annual Green Turtle Cay Fishing Tournament. Held in May at the Green Turtle Yacht Club, a fun-filled week for less serious fishermen and families.

Regatta Time in Abaco is held in June and July with a fun-filled, three-week-long series of races and regattas throughout the Abacos. Most resorts, marinas, and yacht clubs participate—from Marsh Harbour to Treasure Cay on the main island and the offshore cays of Hope Town, Man-O-War Cay, and Green Turtle Cay. The parties and picnics ashore match the rivalry and revelry at sea, with something for everyone, visitors and locals alike. You don't even need a boat to join in the fun. Traditionally, the race weeks begin the last week of June and encompass both U.S. Independence Day on the 4th of July and Bahamas Independence Day on the 10th of July, with appropriate celebrations and fireworks marking both occasions. For details contact the Bahamas' toll-free sports hotline, 800–32SPORT.

 SPORTS. Bareboat Charters. Large fleets of modern sailboats and powerboats are headquartered at the marinas in Marsh Harbour and at Hope Town Harbor on Elbow Cay. The yachts may be chartered by the week or longer, with or without crew, and with or without full provisioning. Rates vary by season and size of yacht, and are subject to change:

Abaco Bahamas Charters. Weekly charter rates begin at $900, with full or partial provisions optional. Summer rates are lower, and two-for-one specials offered (two weeks for price of one) from mid-July to mid-Dec. Reserve direct: Abaco Bahamas Charters, Hope Town, Abaco. In the U.S., 800–626–5690.

Bahamas Yachting Services. Rates range from $1050 to $2295 per week, with full or partial provisions optional. Skippers available at extra charge. "Instructional Charters" offered in summer, and "two for one" (two weeks for the price of one) from mid-July to end Nov. Reserve direct: Bahamas Yachting Service, Marsh Harbour, Abaco. In the U.S., 800–327–2276.

Fishing and Boating. The Abacos are noted for fine fishing of all types: deep sea, reef, bonefishing, and spearfishing. Small boats for harbor-hopping and sightseeing or light-tackle fishing are available through most resorts. A sampling of the facilities and approximate rates on the mainland and offshore cays:

Great Guana Cay. Deep sea fishing in 25-foot Bertram, $275 full day; $175 half day. Sailboat rentals, 25- to 26-foot, $350 wk./, Reserve direct: Pinder's, tel. 367–2207.

Green Turtle Cay. Two 25-foot sport-fishing boats for deep-sea fishing, $200 full day; $100 half day. 14-foot Boston Whalers also available. Reserve direct: Green Turtle Cay Club, Green Turtle Cay, Abaco; tel. 367–2572.

Hope Town, Elbow Cay. Small boats available for reef fishing and bonefishing at $60 per half day. Reserve direct: Elbow Cay Club, Hope Town, Abaco; tel. 367–2748.

Treasure Cay. Bonefishing boats with guide, $140 full day; $100 half day. Reef fishing with guide, $35 per person. A 22-foot sport-fishing boat with captain, $250 full day; $200 half day. Reserve direct: Treasure Cay Beach Hotel and Villas, Box TC 4183, Treasure Cay, Abaco; tel. 367–2570.

Walker's Cay. Boston Whalers with guide, $115 full day; $70 half day; without guide, $70 full day, $40 half day. Reef fishing on 23-foot Mako, full day $160, half day $110; 26-foot Mako, full day $300, half day $175 (both with captain). Trolling on 23-foot Mako, full day $200, half day $135; 26-foot Mako, $325 full day, $200 half day. Reserve: Sea Lion Marina, 700 S.W. 34th St., Ft. Lauderdale, FL 33315; tel. 305–522–1469.

Golf. *Treasure Cay Golf Club.* 18-hole championship course par 72 designed by Dick Wilson. Clubhouse, resident pro, pro shop, and driving range. No greens fees for guests. Golf carts are mandatory. For advance reservations: Box TC-4183, Treasure Cay, Abaco; tel. 367–2570.

Scuba. Dive trips may be arranged through your resort, or directly through the following operators in the Abacos. Each offers instruction, a full line of equipment for rent or sale, and daily dive trips.

Brendal's Dive Shop. Green Turtle Cay, Abaco. Tel. 367–2572.

Dave Gale's Island Marine. In Hope Town at the Abaco Inn. Reserve direct: Dave Gale's Island Marine, Hope Town, Abaco; tel. 367–2822.

Dive Abaco. In Marsh Harbour, Box 555, Abaco, Bahamas. Tel. 367–2014.

Elbow Cay Beach Inn. Offers a scuba program. Contact the resort at 367–2748.

Great Abaco Dive and Photo Center. Boat Harbour Marina, Box 511, Marsh Harbour, Abaco. In the U.S., 305–763–5665.

Treasure Cay Dive Center. Located at Treasure Cay Marina. Reserve direct: Treasure Cay Dive Center, Treasure Cay, Abaco; tel. 367–2570.

Walker's Cay Dive Shop. At Walker's Cay Marina. Resort course and PADI certification available. Reserve direct: Walker's Cay Dive Shop, 700 S.W. 34th St., Ft. Lauderdale, FL 33315; tel. 305–522–1469, 800–327–3714.

ANDROS

Vast Andros, largest island in the Bahamian archipelago, lies just 35 miles southwest of Nassau, yet it remains mysterious, mostly unsettled, and virtually unexplored. Over one hundred miles long and forty miles wide, the sprawling island is intersected at its midpoint by meandering creeks known as "Bights," and its lush green interior is covered with dense forests of pine and mahogany, fringed along the western shore by miles of mangrove swamp. Most of the island's few small settlements and secluded resorts are found along the eastern shore—offering miles of unspoiled beach to roam, great harbor-hopping in small runabouts, and extraordinary bonefishing and reef fishing. However, the island is best known for its spectacular diving. Running the length of its eastern shore is the Andros Barrier Reef, second in size only to Australia's Great Barrier Reef. But unlike the massive reef Down Under, which lies up to two hundred miles offshore and is accessible only by oceangoing vessels, the Andros Reef is just minutes away from the beaches, less than a mile offshore. Sheltered waters within the reef average six to twelve feet deep, but "over the wall" lie the fathomless depths of TOTO, the Tongue of the Ocean. This vast canyon is used by the U.S. and British Navies operating under the acronym of AUTEC—Atlantic Underwater Test and Evaluation Center—for testing submarines and underwater weapons systems. The large base, with nearly one thousand personnel, is located near Andros Town.

Exploring Andros

The vast northern section of Andros can be explored by adventurous travelers with a taxi/tour guide or rental vehicle, which can be arranged through most resorts. However, roads are rugged, fuel and repair stops are infrequent, and settlements are few and far between. Villages near the airports are easily explored by bicycle or scooter from nearby resorts, or by hiking along the beaches as nearly all of the Andros settlements overlook the sea. Those sights and legends that should not be missed are described below.

Androsia is a delightful cottage industry, near Small Hope Bay Lodge at Andros Town, that produces attractive, original batik fabric and island fashions in brilliant tropical colors and bold tropical designs. Visitors are invited to see the entire batik process from painting the designs in hot wax, dying and drying, to cutting and sewing the final fashions—and are even invited to create their own designs, a truly unique Bahamian souvenir. The pride of Andros, Androsia fashions for men and women are shipped to hotel shops and boutiques on all the other Bahamian islands, down to the Caribbean, and into the United

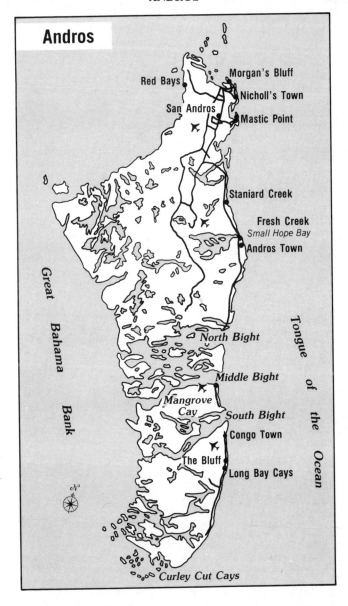

Andros

Red Bays

Morgan's Bluff

Nicholl's Town

San Andros

Mastic Point

Staniard Creek

Fresh Creek
Small Hope Bay

Andros Town

Great

Bahama

Bank

North Bight

Tongue

Middle Bight

Mangrove
Cay

South Bight

Congo Town

of

The Bluff

Long Bay Cays

the

Ocean

Curley Cut Cays

States and Europe—but nowhere are they found in more variety, color, and style (and at lower prices) than in the small shop where they are created. Androsia is operated by Rosi Birch, wife of the owner of Small Hope Bay Lodge, and employs over 75 local artisans.

The Blue Holes of Andros are vast inland ocean holes which rise up through the coral, and are often more than two hundred feet deep. They are found here and there throughout Andros, and were made famous by Jacques Cousteau. Ask your resort hosts or taxi/tour guide to direct you to local sites.

While you're visiting, you might hear about the *chickcharnies.* You may never actually see one, but according to Androsians they are everywhere in the pine forests and silk-cotton trees of Andros. Legendary, mischievous creatures, these Bahamian "elves" are supposed to have three fingers, three toes, fearsome red eyes, green feathers and beards, and hang upside down by their tails. They bring good luck to friendly visitors, and enjoy playing tricks—but Androsians will warn you that it's not wise to irritate a chickcharnie. Should a human not believe in them or scoff at them, he may just find that suddenly his head is turned backward on his shoulders.

Great headlands circle a crescent beach at *Morgan's Bluff,* and legend has it that the eighteenth-century pirate Sir Henry Morgan buried his treasure nearby. Located north of the settlement at San Andros and Nicholl's Town, the small village is relatively easy to reach from resort centers in the area.

Red Bays Village was settled in the 1840s by refugee Seminole Indians and blacks escaping Spanish slavery on the Florida mainland. Until very recently, their descendants have lived isolated and virtually unknown in a small island community off the northwestern shore of Andros. Today, Red Bays is connected to the main island by a short causeway, and visitors are welcomed, but the people maintain a tribal society unchanged for more than a century in which the leader is acknowledged as chief. Accessible by road from San Andros and Nicholl's Town in the north.

PRACTICAL INFORMATION FOR ANDROS

HOW TO GET THERE. By Air. There are three airports which are ports of entry on Andros: *San Andros* in the north; *Andros Town* in the central area; and *South Andros* at Congo Town in the south. There is an airstrip at *Mangrove Cay.* (Visitors should be certain that they are routed to the proper airport, because on Andros the old adage "you can't get there from here" is literal.) *Bahamasair* offers daily flights to the airports on Andros from Nassau, and *Small Hope Bay Lodge* and *Andros Beach Hotel* offer private charter flights from Ft. Lauderdale, Fla.

By mail boat. The following sail to Andros from Potter's Cay Dock in Nassau: *M/V Lisa J II* sails from Nassau Thur., calling at northern Andros villages of Mastic Point, Morgan's Bluff, and Nicholl's Town, returning to Nassau on Tues. The *M/V Central Andros Express* sails from Nassau Wed., calling at Fresh Creek near Andros Town and Behring Point, returning to Nassau on Sun. *M/V Big Yard Express* sails to Mangrove Cay from Nassau on Fri., returning to Nassau on Wed. Contact dock master at Potter's Cay in Nassau, tel. 323–1064.

TELEPHONES AND EMERGENCY NUMBERS. The area code for Andros is 809. As most Andros hotels offer telephone service only at the front desk, all emergencies should be reported directly to the hotel management. There is a resident doctor in San Andros and health clinics in Mastic Point, Nicholl's Town, and Lowe Sound in north Andros. In central Andros, there is a clinic at Fresh Creek and one at Mangrove Cay. In south Andros, there is a clinic at Kemps Bay.

HOTELS AND RESTAURANTS. Many of the hotels on Andros have restaurants. Other restaurants are mentioned earlier in the text and are not listed below. Hotels are listed according to the nearest airport. We have indicated whom to contact for reservations. In many cases you'll note that reservations may be also be made through the Bahamas Reservation Service, tel. 800–327–0787, abbreviated below as BRS. We have also indicated which hotels do not accept any of the major credit cards. Generally speaking, hotel restaurants will accept the same credit cards that the hotel honors.

Hotel price categories, based on double occupancy in high season are: over $100, *Expensive;* under $75, *Inexpensive.*

Andros Town Airport

Small Hope Bay Lodge. *Expensive.* Box N-1131, Nassau, Bahamas; tel. 368–2014; in the U.S. toll-free 800–223–6961; or through BRS. Sophisticated ambience and rustic comfort in a south-sea-island setting. Just 20 rooms in cottages strung along a white-sand beach amid a grove of coconut palms. All are colorfully decorated in original batiks, have showers and ceiling fans, and a few have waterbeds. A comfortable lodge houses the dining room with a great fireplace, game room, extensive library, and *The Panacea,* an old dory rigged out as a bar (honor system only). Some of the finest diving in all The Bahamas. The oldest dive resort in the islands, it was built by Canadian Dick Birch 25 years ago, and is still owned and managed by the Birch family. Nearly everyone samples the snorkeling, and even novices are trained in a few hours and don mask and scuba gear to explore the shallow reefs. For trained divers, there are twice-daily dive trips to the great Andros Barrier Reef just offshore, and for après dive there's a redwood hot tub on the beach. Other sports include "crabbing" expeditions, reef fishing, biking, small boat sailing, and windsurfing. All rates are AP (American Plan), and all-inclusive packages—with transportation via the resort's private plane from Ft. Lauderdale—are available. Located four miles from Andros Town Airport.

Chickcharnie Hotel. *Inexpensive.* Reserve direct: Chickcharnie Hotel, Fresh Creek, Andros; tel. 328–3025. Just eight neat, air-conditioned rooms (some with private bath) in a small inn at Fresh Creek. A favorite of avid fishermen. A popular bar and restaurant attract locals and anglers with good basic food and cool drinks on an attractive patio. Fishing boats and guides for hire; bicycles available. There is a grocery and dry-goods store on the premises.

San Andros Airport

Andros Beach Hotel and Villas. *Inexpensive.* Nicholl's Town, Andros; Tel. 329–2012; contact Neal Watson's Underseas Adventures, Box 21766, Ft. Lauderdale, FL 33335. Tel. 305–763–2188; 800–327–8150; or through BRS. Twenty-four neat, air-conditioned rooms, attractive grounds, overlooking three miles of pristine beach. Nearby are the Tradewind Villas, 16 cottages with kitchen facilities set in a pretty community, which are operated in conjunction with the hotel and share amenities. There is a main dining room with lounge and bar offering frequent local entertainment, an attractive swimming pool, and a tennis court. A complete diving program including instruction and rental equipment has recently been inaugurated by new management, Neal Watson's Underseas Adventures. Daily dive trips to the nearby Andros Barrier Reef are offered. Fishing and boating excursions can be arranged, and there are rental cars, scooters, and bicycles available. Located eight miles from San Andros Airport.

South Andros Airport

Las Palmas Beach Hotel. *Inexpensive.* The Bluff, South Andros; Tel. 329–4661. A charming, Bahamian-owned ranch-style resort, twenty attractively decorated, air-conditioned rooms cluster around a freshwater pool and palm-shaded patio overlooking five miles of unspoiled ocean beach. Guests are treated like family, and are met at the airport with the resort's car. Sunfish, windsurfers, and Boston Whalers are available, and there are fishing boats for deep-sea angling or bonefishing. Snorkeling in the shallows inside the great Andros Barrier Reef. The dining room serves fine local and American specialties, and the bar/lounge offers entertainment nightly. Located two miles from South Andros Airport at Congo Town.

HOW TO GET AROUND. Fair to poor roads link settlements on Andros, and rental autos, scooters, and bicycles may be booked through most resorts on the island.

SPORTS. Fishing and Boating. The following marinas offer fishing expeditions with boat, tackle and guides, listed by proximity to nearest airport on Andros. Rates are approximate and are subject to change.

Andros Town Airport Area: *Charlie's Haven,* South of Andros Town at Behring Point. Bonefishing boats with guides, $80 for full day; tarpon-fishing boats with guides, $120 full day. Deep-sea fishing charters can be arranged. Tel. 329–5261. *Chickcharnie Hotel,* at Fresh Creek near Andros Town. Fishing boats with tackle and guides available. Deep-sea fishing, $150 full day; $85 half day; bonefishing, $60 full day, $40 half day; Boston Whalers, $60 per day with guide; Abaco boat, $40 per day with guide. $12 fuel surcharge. Tel. 328–2025.

San Andros Airport Area: *Andros Beach Hotel & Villas.* Eighteen-foot Boston Whalers, Sunfish, sport-fishing and charter boats available. Rates on request. Tel. 329–2012 or Neal Watson Underwater Adventures. In the U.S. 800–327–8150 or 305–763–2188.

South Andros–Congo Town Airport Area: *Las Palmas Beach Hotel.* Small-boat rentals available: Sunfish, $4 per hour; Boston Whalers, $6 per hour; 20-foot ski boat, $20 per hour; 20-foot fishing boat, $200 per day, $100 half day. Tel. 325–5441.

Scuba: There's superb diving off Andros's eastern shore, along the Great Andros Barrier Reef. Approximate rates for a half-day reef trip with gear, boat, and guide are $23–25 per person.

Andros Town Airport Area: *Small Hope Bay Lodge.* Four certified NAUI instructors offer free lessons to beginners and twice-daily dive trips to underwater attractions such as the Barrier Reef, coral gardens and caverns, and a World War II landing-craft wreck, along with drift dives and night dives. Three dive boats and all rental equipment available. Offers a range of all-inclusive dive packages including airfare on licensed charter from Ft. Lauderdale. In the U.S., toll-free 800–223–6961; 305–463–9130, FL.; or direct 367–2014.

San Andros Airport Area: *Andros Beach Hotel and Villas.* Two dive instructors, daily dive excursions to the Barrier Reef, sea gardens, drop-offs, and blue holes. The dive program is operated by Neil Watson's Andros Undersea Adventures, which offers all-inclusive packages via charter from Ft. Lauderdale. In the U.S., toll-free 800–327–8150 or 305–763–2188; or Andros tel. 320–2012.

BIMINI

Bimini, known for half a century as the "Big Game Fishing Capital of the World," lives up to its reputation. Anglers fishing these waters have rewritten the record books nearly every year since the 1930s when big-name fishermen such as Ernest Hemingway, Zane Grey, and Howard Hughes discovered the big game lurking just off Bimini's shores. Little has changed on the island since those halcyon days. Fishing is still Bimini's biggest draw, but divers are discovering the island, and there are several notable underwater attractions just offshore.

The nearest Bahamian island to the U.S. mainland, Bimini lies just fifty miles due east of Miami, across the mighty Gulf Stream which sweeps along the island's western shores. Each year Bimini attracts thousands of avid fishermen, divers, cruising yachtsmen, and sporting vacationers from Florida's Gold Coast, the rest of the United States, Canada, Britain, and Europe. Many come to participate in the dozen major international fishing tournaments held on the island each year from March through the first week in August. Reservations for tournament weeks are very difficult to get, and should be booked up to six months in advance.

You won't need a car on Bimini, because most of the "action" sprawls along Queen's Highway (barely wide enough for two cars to pass) which runs through the center of Alice Town for a mile or two, with bars, "nightclubs," grocery stores, souvenir shops, bait-and-tackle emporiums, and brightly painted houses crowded together along both sides of the road. On the Gulf Stream side of the island are long winding beaches and on the harbor side are a few rustic resorts with busy, bustling docks and marinas.

PRACTICAL INFORMATION FOR BIMINI

HOW TO GET THERE. By air. Bimini is just a half-hour from downtown Miami via *Chalk's International* seaplanes, and about forty minutes from Ft. Lauderdale, West Palm Beach, or Nassau. The seaplanes operate daily, and land in the harbor at North Bimini, near the resort center. Tel. 800–327–2521, U.S.; 800–432–8807, FL. There is a paved airstrip on South Bimini, linked to the main island by a short ferry ride, which accommodates private planes.

By mail boat. The *M/V Bimini Mack* sails from Potter's Cay in Nassau every Thurs., calls at Cat Cay and Bimini, returns to Nassau Tues. Contact dock master at Potter's Cay, tel. 323–1064.

TELEPHONES AND EMERGENCY NUMBERS. The area code for Bimini is 809, and may be dialed direct from the U.S. or Canada. For Police and Fire, dial 919; for the medical clinic, dial 7–2210.

HOTELS AND RESTAURANTS. Most of the hotels in Bimini have restaurants. We have indicated which hotels do not accept at least one of the major credit cards. Generally speaking, hotel restaurants will accept the same credit cards that the hotel honors.

Hotel price categories, based on double occupancy in high season, are: $75–99, *Moderate;* under $75, *Inexpensive.*

Bimini Big Game Fishing Club. *Moderate.* Reserve direct: Bimini Big Game Fishing Club, 2857 S.W. 27th Ave., Miami, FL 33133; in Florida tel. 305–444–7480; in the rest of the U.S., 800–327–4149; in Bimini, tel. 347–2391. Owned and professionally managed by the Bacardi Company, the club offers the most luxurious accommodations on Bimini. There are 51 large, attractive rooms and six cottages, all air-conditioned. The dining room offers legendary island fare, specializing in the catch of the day, and there is casual dining and entertainment in the popular bar and on the terrace overlooking the pool and the harbor. Sports include tennis on a hard-surface, night-lit court; big-game fishing, water-skiing, boating, scuba offered at a nearby facility. The club operates a modern 60-slip marina, and there's a broad beach just a few minutes' walk away. For serious anglers, the club sponsors five major fishing tournaments each year, including a leg of the prestigious Bahamas Billfish Championship series in April.

Bimini's Blue Water Resort. *Moderate.* Box 627, Bimini, Bahamas; tel. 347–2291. Twelve neat, cozy, air-conditioned rooms and two cottages. One of the cottages is famous as "Marlin Cottage," Ernest Hemingway's Bimini hideaway back in the 1930s. The resort has a swimming pool, a good 42-slip marina with all water sports, and a beautiful private beach. The resort sponsors four major international fishing tournaments annually, including The Hemingway in April, a leg of the Bahamas Billfish Championship, and the Native Tournament in August—one of the most popular events in the Bahamas.

Brown's Hotel. *Inexpensive.* Box 601, Bimini; tel. 347–2227. A locally owned, rustic motel bordering the harbor, with 28 neat, air-conditioned rooms and two kitchenette apartments. The bar is a popular gathering spot for local fishermen, and the restaurant serves hearty Bahamian fare. 22-slip marina with fishing boats for charter, and dive operation is headquartered at the hotel. No credit cards.

The Compleat Angler. *Inexpensive.* Box 601, Bimini; tel. 347–2122. A small historic inn, the oldest on Bimini, and a hangout for Hemingway in the 1930s. The 12 rooms are cozy, comfortable, and air-conditioned. The popular bar offers entertainment and houses a priceless collection of Hemingway memorabilia and old photographs of early anglers. Boating, fishing, tennis, and diving can be arranged, and rental scooters and bicycles are available.

 SPECIAL EVENTS. A list of **major fishing tournaments** follows. For exact dates, entry fees, and tournament regulations, call The Bahamas Sports Hotline weekdays from 9 A.M. to 5 P.M., toll free 800–32SPORT; or contact the sponsoring resort directly.

February: *Bimini Benefit Billfish Tournament,* Bimini Blue Water Resort.

March: *Bacardi Rum Billfish Tournament,* Bimini Big Game Fishing Club. *Hemingway Billfish Tournament,* 1st leg of Bahamas Billfish Championship, Bimini Blue Water Resort.

April: *Championship Billfish Tournament,* 2d leg of Bahamas Billfish Championship, Bimini Big Game Fishing Club.

May: *Bimini Blue Water Tuna Tournament,* Bimini Blue Water Resort.

June: *Blue Marlin Tournament,* Bimini Big Game Fishing Club.

July: *Jimmy Albury Memorial Blue Marlin Tournament,* Bimini Blue Water Resort.

August: *Native Tournament* (all fish), Bimini Blue Water Resort. *Big Game Rodeo* (all fish), Bimini Big Game Fishing Club.

September: *Small B.O.A.T. Tournament,* boats under 22', Bimini Big Game Fishing Club.

November: *The Wahoo,* Bimini Big Game Fishing Club. *Adam Clayton Powell Memorial Wahoo Tournament,* Bimini Blue Water.

SPORTS. Fishing and Boating. The following marinas offer fishing boats for charter (rates are approximate): *Bimini Big Game Fishing Club,* deep-sea fishing charter with tackle and crew, $200 half day; $400 full day. Tel. 347–2391. *Bimini's Blue Water Resort,* 13-foot Boston Whalers, $70 full day; $40 half day. Deep-sea fishing charter with tackle and crew, $450 full day; $350 half day. Tel. 347–2166/2291. *Brown's Marina,* deep-sea fishing, reef and shark fishing with tackle and crew, $350 full day, $225 half day. Tel. 347–2227. *Weech's Bimini Dock,* deep-sea fishing charters with tackle and crew, $500 full day, $300 half day. Boston Whalers, $80 full day, $40 half day. Tel. 347–2391.

Scuba. *Neil Watson's Bimini Underwater Adventures* offers four certified dive masters, equipment rentals, and three dive boats with daily trips to offshore reefs, drop-offs, and blue holes. Dive packages, including air fare to Bimini and accommodations available. Air charter service offered daily from Ft. Lauderdale. Reserve direct: Bimini Underwater Adventures, Box 21766, Ft. Lauderdale, FL 33335; 305–763–2188, or 800–327–8150.

CAT ISLAND

A beautiful, hilly, windswept island lying across the Sound from the Exuma Cays, Cat Island boasts the highest elevation in all of The Bahamas—206-foot Mount Alvernia. Ideal for the sophisticated traveler seeking new islands to conquer, Cat Island is still relatively untouched by the twentieth century, and the small local population fishes and farms much as their ancestors did. But along its hundreds of miles of coastline with untrod beaches, there is a handful of get-away-from-it-all resorts attracting mostly fishermen and divers. One is located at Fernandez Bay on the western shore, another at Cutlass Bay on the southwestern tip of the island, and a third at Port Howe on the southeastern shore. All are served by private airstrips reasonably close by, and all are within close (but rugged) access to the island's prime sightseeing attraction, "The Hermitage" atop Mount Alvernia. It was the home of legendary Father Jerome, once an Anglican and later a Catholic missionary in the southern Bahamas, builder of the two great churches on Long Island. Father Jerome died in 1956 at the age of eighty, and is buried in a cave near the top of the high hill he loved.

PRACTICAL INFORMATION FOR CAT ISLAND

HOW TO GET THERE. By air. *Bahamasair* offers twice-weekly service to Arthur's Town Airport at the northern end of the island, and the resorts arrange licensed charter service to private airstrips from south Florida.

By mail boat. The *M/V Lady Eula* departs Nassau from Potter's Cay weekly on Fri., returning on Sun.; the *M/V Willaurie* departs Nassau on Tues., calling at Cat Island, Rum Cay, and San Salvador, returns to Nassau on Sun. Contact dock master at Potter's Cay in Nassau, tel. 323–1064.

HOTELS AND RESTAURANTS. All of the hotels on Cat Island have restaurants. None accept credit cards. All Cat Island hotels are *Moderate* to *Inexpensive*, based on double occupancy in high season 1985–86. Rates in the low season tend to be 10 to 20 percent lower.

Cutlass Bay Yacht Club. Reserve direct: Cutlass Bay Yacht Club, c/o Red Aircraft, Box 22640, Ft. Lauderdale, FL 33335; tel. 800–327–2514 in the U.S. A modern lodge with eight attractive double rooms, a dining room with notable local specialties, casual bar, swimming pool, and excellent private beach. Activities include tennis, boating, snorkeling, and fine diving. Deep-sea fishing can be arranged, and there are Boston Whalers for rent for harbor-hopping and bottom-fishing along the shore. All inclusive packages available, AP only.

Fernandez Bay Village. Reserve direct: Fernandez Bay Village, Box 2126, Ft. Lauderdale, FL 33303; 305–764–6945. Eight full housekeeping units, dining room and bar in the main lounge—all well maintained and tastefully decorated in a tropical style. All sports can be arranged, and there are rental vehicles available for exploring.

Greenwood Inn. Port Howe, Cat Island; telephone operator for Port Howe, Cat Island. Located at Port Howe, an informal resort with twenty rooms, a tennis court, swimming pool, and private beach. The dining room serves good local Bahamian food, and there's a bar with entertainment and a disco. Resort arranges transportation from the airport, and there are rental cars, bicycles, and scooters for hire.

CHUB CAY

A somewhat luxurious private island at the southern end of the Berry Island chain, across the Great Bahama Bank from Bimini. The island perches at the edge of a vast deep-water canyon called TOTO, the Tongue of the Ocean, and borders the shallow banks, providing top action for every sort of fisherman—those who troll the deep sea for big blue marlin and those who stalk the fiesty bonefish. The island is also known for spectacular diving, with easy access to beautiful reefs less than ten minutes offshore. Owned by members of the Chub Cay Club, it is one of the most exclusive private fishing clubs in The Bahamas. The club includes accommodations for visitors.

PRACTICAL INFORMATION FOR CHUB CAY

 HOW TO GET THERE. By air. Chub Cay has a private airstrip which is an official port of entry, and the Chub Cay Club offers licensed charter service from Ft. Lauderdale or Miami.

By mail boat. The mail boat *M/V Captain Dean* departs Potter's Cay Dock in Nassau each Tues. for Chub Cay, and returns to Nassau on Fri. Contact dock master at Potter's Cay, tel. 323–1064.

HOTEL AND RESTAURANT. The Chub Cay Club. *Moderate.* Reserve direct: Club Cay Club, Box 661067, Miami Springs, FL 33166; or call 305–445–7830 in Florida. A beautiful resort stretched along miles of pristine beach, overlooking a sheltered harbor. There are 15 comfortable, air-conditioned rooms at the Yacht Club on the harbor and villas along the beach, in the gardens, and aboard a moored houseboat. Amenities include a swimming pool, full-service marina with 75 slips, a custom-built 54-foot sportfisherman for charter, two all-weather tennis courts lighted for night play, a 250-yard driving range for golf buffs, and a full scuba program. To reserve, contact *Neil Watson's Underwater Adventures,* Box 21766, Ft. Lauderdale, FL 33335; 305–763–2188. For divers, the club provides a PADI instructor, a line of rental equipment, and three dive boats with daily excursions to offshore reefs. For anglers, the club sponsors three major international fishing tournaments annually, including the Chub Cay Blue Marlin Tournament in early July, the last leg of the Bahamas Billfish Championship series. (Major credit cards accepted).

CROOKED ISLAND

A remote, friendly, but as yet untamed island in the southern Bahamas. The island overlooks the famed Windward Passage dividing The

Bahamas from the Caribbean Sea, which was a stopover point for sixteenth- and seventeenth-century galleons and men-of-war sailing the Spanish Main. Today, the island hosts just one small "barefoot" resort, catering to private plane flyers harbour-hopping through The Bahamas, and offers superb diving off the virtually unexplored virgin reefs. Among the island's worthwhile sights are Bird Rock Lighthouse, dating from 1872, which guards the Crooked Island Passage; and Castle Island Lighthouse, which marks the southern entrance to the islands.

PRACTICAL INFORMATION FOR

CROOKED ISLAND

HOW TO GET THERE. By air. *Bahamasair* offers twice-weekly service to Colonel Hill airport on Crooked Island. The resort also offers licensed charter flights from Florida to Crooked Island. For private plane flyers, there's a good airstrip just minutes from the clubhouse.

By mail boat. The *M/V Commonwealth* mail boat sails each Sun. from Potter's Cay Dock in Nassau for Crooked Island and neighboring cays, returns to Nassau each Fri. Contact the dock master at Potter's Cay, tel. 323–1064.

HOTEL AND RESTAURANT. Pittstown Point Landings. *Expensive.* Reserve direct: Pittstown Point Landings, c/o Bahamas Caribbean International, Box 9831, Mobile, AL 36691; 205–666–4482. An attractive, totally self-sufficient little 16-room resort that is gaining a top reputation among divers and private-plane flyers. The resort sprawls along miles of white-sand beach, overlooking a turquoise bay. Informal conviviality marks the nautical bar, and good seafood is served in the comfortable dining room. The resort has its own private airstrip and transportation to and from the Colonel Hill Airport 16 miles away. For divers, there is rental equipment, three dive boats, and certified instruction. AE.

ELEUTHERA

Eleuthera means freedom. The name is derived from the ancient Greek, and it symbolized hope for religious dissenters in the mid-seventeenth century, who fled as storms of religious controversy raged over England. Most famous of the refugee bands were the Pilgrims who founded Massachusetts Colony. But there were others—some fled to Bermuda and a small hearty band of adventurers found their way to "Cigatoo" (the Arawak name) in The Bahamas. They renamed the island Eleuthera and set up the first democracy in the New World.

More than a century later, in the 1780s, Eleuthera received a new and even larger band of refugees. They were loyalists fleeing the American Revolution, with their families and their slaves. Most settled on the offshore islands of Spanish Wells and Harbour Island, where many of their blonde, blue-eyed descendants still live today. When Bahamaian slaves were emancipated, most settled on the main island where their descendants also live today in small, attractive seaside settlements along the length of Eleuthera.

The island is startlingly beautiful, a long, narrow ribbon of green surrounded by pink-sand beaches and a turquoise sea. Eleuthera is one hundred miles long and barely two miles wide, and a fair road runs the length of the island, making it possible for the adventurous to explore Eleuthera's picturesque villages and beaches by automobile.

The variety of resorts on Eleuthera and its offshore cays is the most extensive on any of the Family Islands. Vacationers may stay in a cluster of cottages along the beach, an elegant old home overlooking the sea, a posh country-club resort, or small family-owned hotels.

Three international airports currently serve the island. North Eleuthera Airport serves the northern third of the island and the off-shore cays of Harbour Island and Spanish Wells. The center third of the island is served by Governor's Harbour Airport. The southern third of the island is served by Rock Sound Airport. (Visitors should be certain that they are routed to the proper airport, as transportation between them can be extremely expensive and difficult to arrange.)

North Eleuthera Area

A driving tour of the northern section of the island, either by rental car or a taxi driver–tour guide (easily arranged at the airport or through your hotel) is an interesting—but slightly bumpy—experience. One of the most famous sites on the island is Preacher's Cave, which lies northeast of the airport, toward the Harbour Island ferry dock. The cave sheltered the early band of Eleutheran Adventurers in 1647 after their ship foundered on a nearby reef. They managed to salvage a small boat and sent it to Massachusetts for supplies to start their colony. Later, the Eleutherans repaid their benefactors by sending a shipload of Braziletto wood to Boston, with instructions that the cargo be sold and the proceeds donated to Harvard College, "to avoid the foul sin of ingratitude."

Traveling south from the airport, you'll pass through tiny villages like The Bluff, and vast acres of small farm plots known as "The Commonage." These lands were a legacy to the loyalists from King George III, and are still handed down from generation to generation. Stop for lunch or a snack at Arlie's Place in the village. Continuing south, pass through the villages of Upper and Lower Bogue to reach the Glass Window, where the island narrows to the width of the road and a bridge spans two great limestone cliffs. From the Atlantic side a giant surf pounds through the narrow cut, meeting the tranquil, turquoise waters of the island's western shores. The views are spectacular. The road winds southward through rolling hills and valleys.

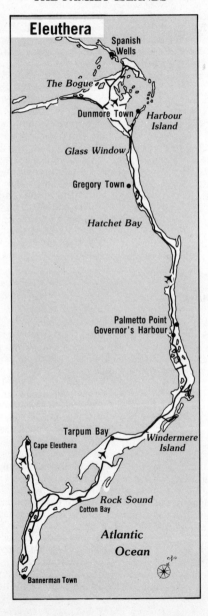

Twenty miles from your starting point at the airport, you'll reach the picturesque village of Gregory Town, situated at the head of a narrow, deep cleft in the island's cliffs, with a commanding view. Here you'll find a beach famed among surfers as "the second-best wave in the world." At the least, it's the best surfing beach this side of Hawaii. If the surf does not quite beat Hawaii's—the pineapples do! They grow in profusion in the area and one bite of the tiny, sweet, and delicately flavored fruit will convince you. A wonderful tasting Pineapple Rum is made from the local fruit and is sold everywhere in the Bahamas. Try a sample from a local liquor store. If the rum samples have sparked your spirit of adventure, ask in the village about a local guide (usually an experienced teenager) to show you The Caves, which lie just a few miles south of Gregory Town. The entrance is marked by a great, gnarled ficus tree that legend claims was planted by pirates in the 1600s to screen the entrance to their favorite hideout and cache of ill-gotten gains. The cave system is formidable, with massive caverns filled with harmless bats, stalactites and stalagmites, and winding, sloping tunnels that end at an eighty-foot cliff overlooking a pounding sea.

Harbour Island

Harbour Island is a centuries-old island village lying just off the windward shore of north Eleuthera, known to generations of visitors as one of the most beautiful towns in all of The Bahamas. Even if you are vacationing on the main island take a day to explore this gem— ferry boat/water taxis depart regularly from the North Eleuthera docks, and it's just a 20 minute ride.

Just two square miles in area, Harbour Island boasts a three-mile-long strand of perfect pink-sand beach on its oceanside. (Yes, the powdery sands are actually pink—they're made up of eons-worth of crushed conch shells and coral.) At harborside is the delightful colonial village of Dunmore Town, named for Lord Dunmore who served as Governor of The Bahamas after being driven from the U.S. by American revolutionaries.

Today, Dunmore Town lies sleepy under a tropical sun, its flowered lanes and pastel-tinted saltbox cottages edged by white picket fences—a reminder of old New England in The Bahamas. Ask anyone to point out Loyalist Cottage, the oldest house on the island, overlooking the harbor. Drop by the two distinguished old churches, St. John's Anglican, built in 1768, and Wesley Methodist, built in 1848. You won't need an auto to explore Harbour Island, although they are available. You'll see and enjoy more by walking or biking from the harbor side to the ocean side of "Briland," as generations of "Brilanders" have affectionately called the island. Nestled here and there amid the sea-grape-, palm-, and pine-shaded dunes overlooking the broad ocean beach, are half a dozen resorts, whose styles range from elegant to rustic.

Spanish Wells

This old island village off Eleuthera's northern shores gained its name when sixteenth-century Spanish galleons filled their casks here before heading back across the broad Atlantic to Spain. The blonde, blue-eyed people of Spanish Wells trace their heritage back more than three centuries to the original Eleutheran Adventurers, and still earn their living from the sea much as their forefathers did. Today, the island is the most prosperous in all of The Bahamas, with a modern commercial fishing fleet specializing in Bahamian lobster, in great demand for export to the Florida mainland as well as Nassau and Freeport. The island is delightfully picturesque, with neat rows of pastel-colored homes, flowered lanes, and tidy farm plots producing fine crops. You can bike around the entire island in an afternoon, with time for browsing in quaint shops, perhaps bargaining for one of the distinctive broad-brimmed fisherman's hats of hand-woven straw or a colorful quilt, a specialty of the island women. There are just two small locally owned resorts on the island, reachable by ferry from the Eleuthera mainland and by taxi from North Eleuthera Airport. Don't miss an opportunity to explore this charming island—one of the oldest settlements in all of The Bahamas.

Eleuthera's Central and Southern Areas

From Governor's Harbour Airport, the center of the long narrow island, the government road continues south through tiny settlements, over rolling hills, past harborside beaches and Atlantic side cliffs. To the north of the airport is Hatchet Bay, headquarters of a large American-owned plantation specializing in milk, eggs, chicken, and ice cream. Traveling south from the airport you'll hit the village of Governor's Harbour, nestled in a crescent cove called Cupid's Bay, settled centuries ago by the Adventurers and Loyalists. After continuing south for several miles, you'll see a road branching eastward which leads to the small bridge linking Eleuthera to Windermere Island. If you've planned ahead, made reservations, and are dressed properly (designer casuals are the norm), you can stop for a gourmet buffet luncheon at the most elegant resort in The Bahamas, the Windermere Island Club. Down the road is one of the most picturesque villages on the island, Tarpum Bay, site of a small, but growing, artists' colony. Look for local studios where you might find a bargain in watercolors or pastels.

At the southern end of the island is Rock Sound, the largest settlement on Eleuthera, with a modern airport nearby. In the village there is a small shopping center with shops for food, liquor, gifts, souvenirs. Neat, quaint homes with flowering shrubs and picket fences line the narrow lanes, and the old church and cemetery are worth a visit. For good, hearty native cooking at modest prices, try Edwina's Place, a favorite of cruising yachtsmen who drop anchor off her beach. Avid golfers may want to continue driving southwest to Davis Harbour, home of the posh Cotton Bay Club and its world-class 18-hole Robert Trent Jones course. Visitors are welcome, but guests are given preference and green fees are high.

PRACTICAL INFORMATION FOR ELEUTHERA

HOW TO GET THERE. By air. *Bahamasair* offers daily service from Nassau to North Eleuthera, Governor's Harbour, and Rock Sound. Several licensed, scheduled commuter airlines offer nonstop or one-stop daily service to one or more of Eleuthera's airports from south Florida gateways: Miami, Fort Lauderdale, and West Palm Beach. Among these are *Aero Coach, Caribbean Express, Gull Air,* and *Piedmont Airlines.* Check with your travel agent for the most convenient carrier and schedule.

To Harbour Island and Spanish Wells. Flights serving Harbour Island and Spanish Wells from Florida or Nassau land at North Eleuthera airport. From the airport, taxis will take you to the Harbour Island ferry dock or the Spanish Wells dock. There small, modern multi-seat power boats take you across to the offshore cays at reasonable rates. Dockside on the island, taxis will be waiting to whisk you to your resort.

By mail boat. The following mail boats sail from Potter's Cay Dock in Nassau to Eleuthera weekly: *M/V Current Pride* departs Nassau Thurs. for Current Island, Lower and Upper Bogue, returning to Nassau on Tues. *M/V Bahamas Daybreak II* departs Nassau Thurs. for North Eleuthera, Spanish Wells, and Harbour Island, returning to Nassau on Mon. *Charley and Charley* departs Nassau Mon. for Central Eleuthera, Hatchet Bay, Governor's Harbour, South Palmetto Point, and Tarpum Bay, returning to Nassau on Tues. *M/V Miss Juanita* departs Nassau on Mon. for South Eleuthera, Davis Harbour, Rock Sound, Weymss Bight, Deep Creek, and Bannerman Town, returning to Nassau on Thurs. Contact the dock master at Potter's Cay, Nassau, tel. 323–1064.

TELEPHONES AND EMERGENCY NUMBERS. Area Code for Eleuthera, Harbour Island, and Spanish Wells is 809, although not all areas have direct distance dialing yet. Emergency numbers on Eleuthera include: Governor's Harbour Police, 2–2111; doctor, 2–2001. Harbour Island police, 3–2111; doctor, 3–2225; clinic, 3–2227. Rock Sound Police, 4–2244; clinic, 4–2226.

HOTELS AND RESTAURANTS. Most of the hotels on Eleuthera have restaurants. Other restaurants are mentioned earlier in the text and are not listed below. Hotels are listed according to the nearest airport. We have indicated whom to contact for reservations; in many cases you'll note that reservations may also be made through the Bahamas Reservation Service, tel. 800–327–0787, abbreviated below as BRS. We have also indicated which hotels do not accept at least one of the major credit cards. Generally speaking, hotel restaurants will accept the same credit cards that the hotel honors. Hotel price categories, based on double occupancy in high season, are $150 and up, *Super*

Deluxe; $125–149, *Deluxe;* $100–124, *Expensive;* $75–99, *Moderate;* under $75, *Inexpensive.*

North Eleuthera Airport/Gregory Town

Cambridge Villas. *Inexpensive.* Box 1548, Gregory Town, Eleuthera; Gregory Town, tel. 332–2690; or through BRS. Twenty one neat, attractive rooms and apartments (some with air-conditioning and kitchens) owned and operated by a friendly, local Bahamian family. The complex surrounds a shady terrace and saltwater pool. The dining room serves excellent native food, and there's tea every afternoon at 4. The cheerful bar is popular with locals as well as visitors. A bus shuttles guests to a magnificent oceanside beach a mile and a half away, famed for fine surfing and shelling. Boating, fishing, and diving excursions can be arranged. Located 20 miles from the airport.

Carefree Cottages. *Inexpensive.* Box 5206, Gregory Town, Eleuthera; tel. 332–2269. A dozen neat, roomy cottages with single, double, and a few three-bedroom units, gift shop on the premises. Nearby beach privileges with boating, snorkeling, fishing, and tennis in the area. Strictly self-catering. Restaurant and grocery stores nearby. Located in Gregory Town, 18 miles from the airport. No credit cards.

Oleander Gardens Villas. *Inexpensive.* Box 5165, Gregory Town, Eleuthera, tel. 333–2058. Sixteen casual, modern one- and two-bedroom apartments with a central dining room and bar, along a nice private beach. Boating, snorkeling, and fishing trips can be arranged. Located in Gregory Town, 19 miles from the airport.

Sea Raider Cottages. *Inexpensive.* Reserve direct: Sea Raider Cottages, 922 N. Broadway, Rochester, MN; tel. 507–288–7472. Nine efficiency and studio apartments by the seaside near the village of Current, all large and airy and equipped with kitchens and patios. No dining room, but there are nearby grocery stores and daily maid service. There's a tennis court nearby and all water sports can be arranged.

North Eleuthera Airport/Harbour Island

Dunmore Beach Club. *Super Deluxe.* Box 122, Harbour Island, Eleuthera; tel. 333–2200. An elegant, intimate, beautifully decorated resort with 16 rooms in charming cottages tucked among trees and flowering shrubs. A clubhouse overlooks the sea, and the dining room offers gourmet meals—reputed to be the best on the island. Sports include tennis, deep-sea and bonefishing, and sailing; a beautiful private beach. No credit cards.

Coral Sands Hotel. *Deluxe.* Harbour Island, Eleuthera; tel. 333–2350/2320; or through BRS. On 14 hilly acres overlooking the sea stands this comfortable resort with 33 rooms and cottages along the pink-sand ocean beach. Fine Bahamanian and American food in the dining room, and a relaxed lounge, library, and game room. There are three bars—one in the main lounge, one on the beach, and another at the *Nightclub in the Park,* an outdoor pavilion for dancing under the stars, where a local combo entertains on weekends. Sport facilities include a night-lit tennis court, surf riders, snorkeling gear, and small sailboats. Rental golf carts and bicycles.

Pink Sands. *Expensive.* Box 87, Harbour Island, Eleuthera; tel. 333–2030/2060; or through BRS. Complete charm with dignified informality is the hallmark of this famous resort, where the third generation of family hoteliers greet the third generation of club guests. First and foremost is a private club, with the public invited when accommodations are available. There are 49 cottage suites dotted here and there amid 40 acres of forest glen, paved pathways, and tropical greenery—the site has been designated a bird sanctuary by the Audubon Society. The cottage suites offer huge living rooms and bedrooms, dressing rooms, private baths, kitchens, and spacious patios. Sports include tennis on three fine courts, bird-watching, shelling, sailing or motor-boating. All types of fishing and other water sports are available. The clubhouse offers a lovely dining room (ties or ascots at dinner and long skirts for the ladies), fine Bahamian and American cuisine, a comfortable lounge and well-stocked library. No credit cards.

Romora Bay Club. *Deluxe.* Box 146, Harbour Island, Eleuthera; tel. 333–2325; P.O. Box 7026, Boca Raton, FL 33431, tel. 800–327–8286 in FL and Canada or 305–997–9699; or through BRS. A comfortable family-run resort offering 28 air-conditioned rooms and several housekeeping cottages, each with private balconies or terraces overlooking the harbor and tropical gardens which stretch across the island to the oceanside. The main house on a hillside serves as the clubhouse, with a cheerful dining room, rustic bar with local entertainment weekly, comfortable lounge, and library. Jacuzzi, masseur, and hammocks. Three dive masters give lessons, and lead daily dive trips; dive packages are offered. 15 percent service charge added ($111–146).

Runaway Hill Club. *Expensive.* Box 31, Harbour Island, Eleuthera; tel. 333–2150. "Small but elegant" describes this charming old island home with lush tropical gardens, and a broad veranda overlooking a sparkling pool and the sea. Just eight over-sized, beautifully decorated rooms upstairs or in an adjacent wing, most with patios or balconies. The ground floor of the main house is a superb dining room where "houseguests" dine free (most room rates include MAP), and visitors from all over the island reserve days in advance to enjoy the gourmet cuisine and impeccable service (expensive, full-course, fixed-price menu). All island sports and activities can easily be arranged, and the ocean is just a stroll away.

Valentine's Yacht Club. *Expensive.* Box 1, Harbour Island, Eleuthera; tel. 333–2142; or through BRS. Twenty-one comfortable rooms in a friendly, home-like atmosphere. There's a tranquil harborside beach, a refreshing freshwater pool, and the resort's private *Dunes Club* on the ocean side of the island. All water sports are available, from jet-skiing to windsurfing, but the resort is best known for an excellent dive program featuring free scuba lessons for beginners; advanced instruction, and full certification, with a range of dive packages and daily trips to offshore reefs. Dining room and nautical bar—a gathering spot for cruising yachtsmen who dock at the resort's harborside marina.

North Eleuthera Airport/Spanish Wells

Spanish Wells Beach Resort. *Moderate.* (See below for reservations.) Twenty-one attractive, completely renovated oceanfront rooms and six beach cottages with kitchenettes, comfortable for up to four people. All overlook a broad, beautiful, unspoiled beach. There's a cozy dining room with good Bahamian cooking, and a relaxing bar and lounge with entertainment on weekends. Sports include free bicycles, windsurfing, water-skiing, Sunfish sailing, boat trips to nearby cays for picnics, and half-day trips to Harbour Island for sightseeing. But the resort's prime attraction is an excellent dive program for beginners through experts, including certification. Two dive masters conduct daily dive trips to the legendary reefs which fringe Eleuthera's northern shores, and the sister resort on the harbor has a complete dive shop.

Spanish Wells Harbour Club. *Inexpensive.* Reservations for either resort: Spanish Wells Beach Resort, Box 31, Spanish Wells, Eleuthera; tel. 332–2645; In the U.S. 4316 W. Broward Blvd., Suite 5, Plantation, FL 33317; tel. 800–327–5118; 800–432–1362 in FL. Twenty crisply clean, simply furnished, airy rooms in the village overlooking the harbor and marina. The Club has its own dining room, bar, and entertainment and shares other amenities with the Beach Resort. Boating and fishing expeditions are easily arranged at the marina, and the dive boats leave from here.

Governor's Harbour Airport

Club Med Eleuthera. *Moderate.* Box 80, Governor's Harbour, Eleuthera; tel. 332–2270; or (800) CLUBMED. Continental Club Med ambience—with a distinctive Bahamian flair. Three hundred air-conditioned rooms, large free-form pool, dining room, disco, boutique, library, and café/bar with dance floor and stage for nightly entertainment. The club offers a full scuba program including underwater photography, deep-sea fishing, water-skiing, and sailing. There are eight tennis courts and areas for basketball and volleyball. An Atari Computer Workshop is an added bonus, and the Mini-Club for youngsters operates from 9 A.M. to 6 P.M. daily. Accommodations are neat, modestly furnished rooms with twin beds and showers. Rates are all-inclusive, and may be booked through travel agents or any Club Med office in the U.S., Canada, U.K., and Europe. No service charge. Eight miles from the airport.

Cigatoo Inn. *Inexpensive.* Box 86, Governor's Harbour, Eleuthera; tel. 332–2343; or through BRS. The inn sits on a hilltop amid flowering shrubs and gardens and overlooks an attractive pool. There are 24 nicely decorated, air-conditioned rooms and a popular dining room and bar featuring native specialties. Cigatoo offers beach privileges, a tennis court, and all water sports—from deep-sea fishing to scuba trips—are easily arranged. Weekly entertainment by an island combo makes the inn one of the liveliest spots in town. Located eight miles from the airport ($55).

Palmetto Beach Inn. *Inexpensive.* Box 102. Governor's Harbour, Eleuthera; tel. 332–2533. Eight attractive, air-conditioned rooms, apartments, and villas, each with private bath, TV, and telephone, set along a lovely private beach. There's a nearby marina and dock, with boating, fishing, and dive trips readily accessible. Located 13 miles from the airport at South Palmetto Point. No credit cards.

Palmetto Shores Vacation Villas. *Inexpensive.* Box 131, Governor's Harbour, Eleuthera; tel. 332–2305/2307; or through BRS. Fourteen air-conditioned villas. Private beach with marina and dock. Snorkel gear and windsurfers available. Casual and friendly atmosphere. Located 12 miles from the airport at South Palmetto Point. No credit cards.

Rainbow Inn. *Inexpensive.* Box 53, Governor's Harbour, Eleuthera; tel. 332–2290; or through BRS. A cluster of charming oceanfront studios, one- and two-bedroom apartments, and a three-bedroom villa—a total of 15 units. All are air-conditioned, with full kitchens and baths, attractively furnished, with terraces overlooking the sea. There's a delightful dining room with superb food, nautical bar, a seaside tennis court, and a saltwater pool. All water sports are easily arranged, with a major dock and marina just a few miles away featuring a colorful produce exchange market. A casual, friendly, family-owned resort. Located in the village of Hatchet Bay, six miles from the airport.

Rock Sound Airport

Cotton Bay Club. *Super Deluxe.* Box 28, Rock Sound, Eleuthera; tel. 334–2101/2156; In New York, 212–696–4566; U.S., 800–225–4255; or through BRS. "Where Who's Who in America goes barefoot in The Bahamas," is an apt description of the atmosphere at Cotton Bay, which has recently been purchased by a Bahamian group, with plans to completely renovate and expand the resort. The 77 attractively furnished rooms are in the main lodge or scattered in cottages and villas set amid acres of gardens and manicured lawns, overlooking a pool and miles of beautiful beach. The resort offers four fine tennis courts and one of the top 18-hole championship golf courses in The Bahamas. Trips for deep-sea fishing and bonefishing with local guides, sailboats, and power runabouts are available at the resort's private full-service Davis Harbour Marina, where ocean-going yachts find shelter and services. Located at Powell Point, 12 miles from the airport. Packages available, MAP only.

Windermere Island Club. *Super Deluxe.* Direct reservations (preference given to members): Box 25, Rock Sound, Eleuthera; tel. 332–2538; or in the U.S., 34 East Putnam Ave., Greenwich, CT, 203–661–3171, or 213–839–0222. Ultra-elegant private club where royalty mingles with business tycoons, heads of state, and international stars. It has recently been purchased by SEACO, owners of the Simplon Orient Express, and many luxury properties in Europe. Offers pricey visitor accommodations with temporary membership fees added. There's a rustically beautiful clubhouse; six tennis courts with a resident pro; stunning pool, bar, library, game rooms, and gourmet dining on the terrace or formal dining room—all this overlooking five miles of magnificent pink-sand beaches. Accommodations inside 22 air-conditioned, elegant, tropical rooms, apartments, and villas. Located 18 miles from the airport. Packages available, AP only.

Winding Bay Beach Resort. *Deluxe.* Box 93, Rock Sound, Eleuthera; tel. 334–2020; or through BRS. Located on the Atlantic shore near Windermere Island and the village of Tarpum Bay. Once the estate of Arthur Vining Davis of Alcoa, recently purchased by the Hotels of Distinction. The lovely landscaped grounds shelter 36 attractively decorated rooms in lodges overlooking a five-mile strip of perfect pink-sand beach. Casual atmosphere by day, elegant formality in the evenings. A tropical clubhouse with dining room, bar, and lounge; a lovely pool; marina and dock offering a broad range of water sports plus paddle boats, glass-bottom rowboats, and deep-sea fishing vessels; a well-equipped dive shop and instruction for beginners with daily dive trips. Located 7½ miles from the airport. Closed for renovation and expansion in 1987, expected to reopen in 1988 as Eden II-Eleuthera, under management of the Savoy Corp., which operates the Eden II in Ocho Rios, Jamaica, an all-inclusive resort.

Edwina's Place. *Inexpensive.* Box 30, Rock Sound, Eleuthera; tel. 334–2094; or through BRS. This is a tidy, relaxed colony of small cottages and ten air-conditioned motel-type rooms set amid flowering hibiscus and overlooking a swimming pool. There's a central dining room and a nearby private beach. Fishing, boating, and diving are easily arranged. Atmosphere is friendly and informal, owner-operated care and attention. Located one mile from the airport. No credit cards.

Hilton's Haven. *Inexpensive.* Hilton's Haven, Tarpum Bay, Eleuthera; tel. 334–2094; or through BRS. Neat, comfortable, folksy ten-room inn operated for a decade by nurse Mary Hilton, formerly Public Health Officer for the island. Located across from a lovely ocean beach in the village of Tarpum Bay, the genteel resort offers rest and relaxation and is a favorite hideaway for convalescent visitors. Fishing trips and other water sports are arranged, and there are bikes and car rentals available. There is a cozy dining room with down-home cooking and a small, friendly bar. Six miles from the airport. No credit cards.

HOW TO GET AROUND. Auto rentals and motor scooter rentals are available through most resorts. The following car-rental agents are located in settlements near resorts. At **Palmetto Point:** *Bethel Maitland,* tel. 332–2504. At **Harbour Island:** *Johnson's Rental,* tel. 3–2376. *Ross Garage,* tel.

3–2122. At **Governor's Harbour:** *ASA Rent-A-Car,* 332–2305. At **Rock Sound:** *Dingle Motor* Service, tel. 4–2031.

SPORTS. North Eleuthera: *Fishing and Boating.* Harbour Island and Spanish Wells are noted for fine bone-fishing in the shallows on the leeward side of the islands, and excellent reef and drift fishing along the miles of reef which line the windward shores. Charter boats with guides and gear are available on Harbour Island at the following rates: deep-sea fishing, $250 per day; bottom and bonefishing, $60 per half day. Tel. 333–2350. On Spanish Wells at *Spanish Wells Beach Resort* at the following rates: deep-sea fishing at $400 per full day, $250 half day; reef and bonefishing at $120 full day; $70 half day. Tel. 332–2645. All rates are approximate and subject to change.

Scuba. Some of the finest diving in The Bahamas is located off North Eleuthera's shores, near Harbour Island and Spanish Wells. Noted dive sites are Devil's Backbone, a treacherous barrier reef which has claimed a number of wrecks, and Current Cut, a narrow tidal channel separating Eleuthera Sound and the open sea—divers experience the thrill of a lifetime as they soar through the cut on an incoming tide. Scuba-dive operators in the area are: on Harbour Island at *Romora Bay Club,* tel. 333–2324. *Valentine's Yacht Club,* tel. 333–2309. On Spanish Wells at the *Spanish Wells Beach Resort,* tel. 332–2645.

Central and South Eleuthera: *Fishing and Boating.* Boats may be chartered and fishing excursions arranged at the following locations (rates listed are approximate): *Cotton Bay Club.* Located at Davis Harbour. Reef-fishing excursions, $15 per person per half day; deep-sea fishing for a party of four, $175 per half day including gear and guide. Tel. 334–2156. *Winding Bay Club.* Located south of Rock Sound. Reef-fishing excursions in a 14-foot Boston Whaler at $75 per half day; deep-sea fishing at $175 per half day with guide and gear. Small sailboats for rent at $6 per hour. Tel. 334–2020 (closed during 1987 to mid 1988).

Golf. The *Cotton Bay Club* course, designed by Robert Trent Jones, par 72. Lessons and all equipment available for rental. Greens fees year-round are $20 for 18 holes; caddy or carts at additional charge. Located at Davis Harbour. Tel. 334–2101.

THE EXUMAS

Little has changed in the two centuries since fleeing loyalists sought these islands in the sun. The long, languid, and lovely chain of islets and cays, which stretches from Nassau in the north, 140 miles down to Little Exuma in the south, still offers miles of beautiful crescent-shaped beaches, turquoise waters, and swaying palms. They are still unspoiled, unsophisticated, and mostly untrod.

No one has ever counted the Exuma cays. Some say there are 365 of them, one for every day of the year. Fliers, yachtsmen, anglers, and divers especially love these islands. A flight over the Exuma chain offers one breathtaking view after another. For sailors they are the ultimate cruising grounds, with hidden coves, quiet harbors, and sheltered anchorages throughout the length of the chain. For divers, the emerald, turquoise, and aquamarine waters are as clear as liquid sunshine and the islands and cays are fringed by living reefs, sea gardens, colorful coral, and schools of brilliant tropical fish. For anglers, there's everything from deep-sea big-game fishing and reef trolling to light-tackle angling from a skiff or handcasting from shore.

There are fewer than four thousand Bahamians living in the Exumas, most in tiny, widely scattered island settlements, where they earn their living in small-scale farming or from the sea. Over half of them are named Rolle—a legacy from the loyalists who settled the islands two centuries ago. Lord John Rolle, Baron of Steventon, was the largest of the landholders in the Exumas, with hundreds of slaves. When Britain passed the emancipation laws abolishing slavery in her colonies, Lord Rolle deeded his name and his land to his slaves. The land may never be sold, but is passed from generation to generation of Rolles.

There are just two resort centers in the Exuma cays. About midway down the island chain is Staniel Cay, some eighty miles southeast of Nassau; and at the southern end of the chain is George Town on Great Exuma Island, about 130 miles southeast of Nassau.

Staniel Cay and Surrounding Isles

Staniel Cay, just about a square mile in size, is surrounded by white beaches and crystalline seas. There is a Bahamian village with fewer than one hundred inhabitants, and several vacation homes owned by wealthy Americans and Europeans dot the island and surrounding cays. A favorite port of call for cruising yachtsmen and island-hopping private-plane flyers, and the center of social activity on the island is the Staniel Cay Yacht Club and the nearby Happy People Marina.

The village of Staniel Cay has just one paved road, which runs through Town from the Yacht Club to the airstrip. Drop into the rustic, red-roofed church, exchange pleasantries with the postmaster, and bargain with the straw ladies who weave their magic on hats and bags and souvenirs under a shady tree. The village boasts two stores for groceries and supplies and the only telephone station on the island. Or you can go down to the docks and swap tales with the guides and fishermen or the cruising yachtsmen around the marinas. Wander the beach on the ocean side of the cay, search for shells, or just lie in the sun. The waters are sheltered and calm for swimming, and there's good snorkeling just offshore. The only "nightclub" on the island is the Royal Entertainer Lounge. This is where Bahamians and visitors mix and mingle with typical out-island music and style. The restaurant serves three meals a day and the lounge really jumps twice weekly when local musical talent takes over. Check with the folks at Happy People Marina to find out which nights the "action" takes place.

To explore the half-dozen isles and cays within a few miles to the north or south, rent a Boston Whaler or a small sailboat for the day and bring along a picnic lunch. Or join a dive group heading for one of the spectacular underwater sites just a few miles offshore.

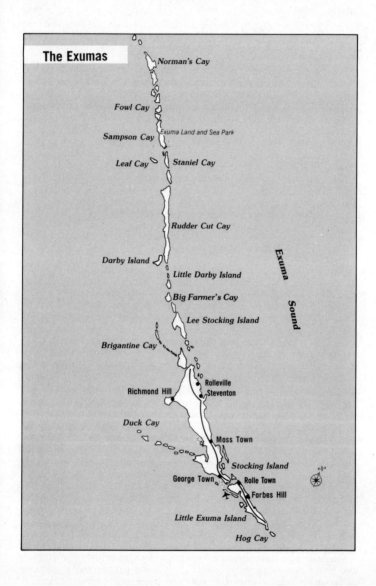

The Exumas

Norman's Cay

Fowl Cay

Sampson Cay — Exuma Land and Sea Park

Leaf Cay — Staniel Cay

Rudder Cut Cay

Darby Island

Little Darby Island

Big Farmer's Cay

Lee Stocking Island

Brigantine Cay

Rolleville
Steventon

Richmond Hill

Exuma Sound

Duck Cay

Moss Town

Stocking Island

George Town — Rolle Town

Forbes Hill

Little Exuma Island

Hog Cay

Exuma Cays Land and Sea Park is accessible only by boat and offers miles of protected cays, islands, reefs, and sheltered waters set aside for bird-watching, beachcombing, skin diving, and the preservation of natural beauty for future generations. Founded by The Bahamas National Trust, the park begins just north of Staniel Cay at Conch Cut and extends twenty-two miles north to Wax Cay Cut. Visitors may not remove any plant life or coral specimens from the park, but fishermen and divers are permitted a limited "day's catch" by hand, Hawaiian sling, or hook and line. There is a resident warden who lives aboard a houseboat in the park. He offers assistance and information to park visitors, and enforces The Trust's regulations and wildlife laws.

You may also want to visit Thunderball Grotto, a massive cliff, underwater cave, and grotto formations, a few miles offshore of Staniel Cay, said to rival the famed Blue Grotto of Capri. The site was made famous in the James Bond movies, *Thunderball* and *Never Say Never Again.* There is no souvenir hunting in this area, which is protected by The Bahamas National Trust.

George Town, Great Exuma, and Nearby Settlements

A timeless village by the sea, George Town is the undisputed "capital" of the Exuma chain. The picturesque community overlooks beautiful Elizabeth Harbour, one of the largest and finest in all The Bahamas. Running through the middle of the village is the Tropic of Cancer, that imaginary dividing line which marks the beginning of the tropics.

George Town is steeped in history. During the pirate days of the seventeenth century, its deepwater harbor sheltered buccaneers from the seven seas. In the eighteenth century it was populated by a plantation aristocracy from the Carolinas who sought refuge under the British flag. In the nineteenth century, the island served as a refitting base for British Man-of-War ships, and in this century it became an important U.S. naval base during World War II. Today, George Town boasts the largest population in the Exumas, with some eight hundred Bahamians living on Great Exuma Island and the surrounding cays. There are accommodations for around four hundred tourists on the island, with a broad choice of lifestyles—from crisply clean apartments above a general store in the village to elegant villas on a private beach.

There are a dozen small shops with groceries, supplies, and souvenirs in George Town. An absolutely charming strawmarket in the center of town sprawls under an ancient ficus tree. By the harbor there's a miniature town square with a white picket fence, surrounded by a quaint little library on stilts and the imposing pink government building which houses the Commissioner's office, police, courts, and jail. Atop a hill is St. Andrew's Anglican Church, dating from 1802, and an interesting old graveyard. There are beautiful views of sparkling Elizabeth Harbour everywhere, and of tiny Lake Victoria, which fringes the other side of the village. Stroll down to Government Wharf, where the mail boat calls and out-island farmers and fishermen gather to load their wares for the Nassau market. You can buy nearly every variety of fresh tropical fruits and vegetables, and bargain with the fishermen for a fresh catch.

To explore the settlements and cays to the north and south of George Town, you'll need a motor scooter, taxi/tour guide, or rental car. The Queen's Highway runs the full length of Great Exuma Island, and is in reasonable repair. To the north, you'll travel through "generation land" estates—Ramsey, Mount Thompson, Steventon, and Rolleville with such interesting villages and sights as Moss Town, The Forest, and Roker's Point. All along the route, you'll see the ruins of old plantation houses and meet the "descendants" of Lord Rolle. At Rolleville, stop for lunch or a snack at Kermit's Hilltop Restaurant and Tavern, where there's always fresh seafood on the menu, friendly villagers to meet, and a superb view seaward. On weekends, there's a local combo.

Heading southward from George Town, you'll reach Flamingo Bay and Pirate's Point. Nearby is Kidd Cove, a favorite anchorage for the notorious pirate Captain Kidd in the early years of the 1700s; and Rolle Town, another large "generation land" estate with plantation ruins and friendly Rolles. At a small settlement called The Ferry, there is a concrete bridge linking Great Exuma Island to Little Exuma. There you'll find rolling farmland, stunning views, and Pretty Molly Bay. Traveling south almost to the tip of the island, you'll find "The Hermitage." Built by loyalists and their slaves, it is the Exumas' only remaining intact plantation house from the era, now a privately owned dwelling.

Stocking Island is acknowledged by many to be the most beautiful island in all of The Bahamas. Just a mile offshore of George Town, it is accessible only by boat from several hotels and the government dock. The hilly, seven-mile long island shelters Elizabeth Harbour, and almost its entire coastline is fringed by exquisite beaches and swaying coconut palms. Atop a rocky cliff a two-hundred-foot-high beacon offers breathtaking views over the turquoise water of the harbor, and the intricate line of tropical cays that form the reef. There's fine swimming and sunning on the sheltered harborside, with Peace and Plenty's rustic beach club offering drinks and snacks. On the ocean side, there's a superb mile-long beach with excellent shelling.

PRACTICAL INFORMATION FOR THE EXUMAS

HOW TO GET THERE: By air. To *Staniel Cay:* There is a 3,000-foot paved airstrip serving the island, although it is not an official port of entry. *Airways Reservation Center,* headquartered in Ft. Lauderdale, Fla. offers U.S. carrier-licensed and Bahamas-certified charter flights on a regular basis to Staniel Cay with a stopover at a port of entry for customs clearance. The firm also handles reservations for resorts, scuba programs, and yacht cruises, offering a variety of moderate to expensive all-inclusive packages. Contact *Airways*

Reservation Center, 4250 S.W. 11th Terrace, Ft. Lauderdale, FL 33315. In Florida tel. 305–467–6850. U.S. toll-free, 800–327–3011.

To George Town, Great Exuma: Daily flights from Nassau on *Bahamasair;* daily flights from Miami on *Caribbean Express;* and daily flights from Ft. Lauderdale on *Aero Coach.* George Town International Airport, an official port of entry, offers a paved 5,000-foot landing strip, located approximately five miles from the village. There are plans underway to expand and upgrade the airport facilities.

By mail boat. To make arrangements for all mailboats sailing to the Exumas out of Nassau, contact the dock master at Potter's Cay (tel. 323–1064).

To Staniel Cay: The *M/V Lady Blanche* departs every Wed. from Potter's Cay in Nassau, calling at Staniel Cay, Farmers Cay, Black Point and Barreterre, Exuma, returning to Nassau every Sun.

To George Town, Great Exuma: The *M/V Nay Dean* departs every Tues. from Potter's Cay in Nassau, calling at George Town, Salt Pond, Simms, and Stella Maris, returning to Nassau every Fri. The *M/V Grand Master* departs every Tues. from Potter's Cay in Nassau, calling at George Town, Rolleville, Forest, Farmers Cay, and Black Point, returning to Nassau every Thurs.

TELEPHONES AND EMERGENCY NUMBERS.
Staniel Cay: There is just one telephone on the island, located at the telephone station in the village of Staniel Cay, with an operator on duty a few hours each day, seven days a week. Hours may vary, but are generally in the morning from 9–10:30, and in the afternoon from 12–1:30 and 4–5:30. Service is unreliable, but worth a try if you must reach someone in an emergency. The telephone number is 334–2217.

George Town, Great Exuma: Area Code for George Town is 809, and may be reached by direct distance dialing. Emergency numbers on the island include: Police, 6–2152; Ministry of Health Clinic, 6–2088; the resident doctor 6–2606.

HOTELS AND RESTAURANTS. Most of the hotels in the Exumas have restaurants. Other restaurants are mentioned earlier in the text and are not listed below. We have indicated whom to contact for reservations. In many cases you'll note that reservations may also be made through the Bahamas Reservation Service, tel. 800–327–0787, abbreviated below as BRS. We have also indicated which hotels do not accept any of the major credit cards. Generally speaking, hotel restaurants will accept the same credit cards that the hotel honors. Hotel price categories, based on double occupancy in high season, are: $100–and up, *Expensive;* $75–99 *Moderate;* under $75, *Inexpensive.*

Staniel Cay

Staniel Cay Yacht Club. *Expensive.* Reserve through BRS; or Airways Reservation Center, tel. 800–327–3011. The clubhouse with its nautical decor is the gathering spot for vacationers, cruising yachtsmen and private pilots. It offers hearty dining, a genial bar and a barefoot, relaxed ambience. Just steps away, tucked amid pines at the water's edge, are four guest cottages (each ideal for two), a permanently moored houseboat (accommodating up to four) and a two-bedroom guest house with full kitchen (comfortable for up to six). All have private baths and hot-water showers. A well-equipped marina accommodates 15 yachts and offers fuel, metered electricity, water, ice and shower facilities. Boston Whalers, small sailboats, windsurfers, and scuba gear available for rent.

Rates include all meals, and guests staying three nights or longer have complimentary use of sailing skiffs and runabouts.

Sampson Cay Club. *Moderate.* Reserve through Airways Reservation Center, tel. 800–327–3011. A small cottage colony on Sampson Cay just a few miles north of Staniel Cay. The club has accommodations for only ten guests in private villas overlooking the sea and a sheltered harbor, each with housekeeping facilities and bath. The clubhouse has a bar, lounge, dining room, and video movies for entertainment. For yachtsmen, there is protected dockage, a commissary, fuel, ice, and water. Boat rentals and guided dive trips to nearby reefs are available. No credit cards.

Happy People Marina. *Inexpensive.* Reserve through Airways Reservation Center, tel. 800–327–3011. A friendly, informal Bahamian-owned resort, offering 11 comfortable motel-style rooms along a sandy beach near the village of Staniel Cay. The small hotel has a popular restaurant for visitors and natives alike, a congenial bar and "nightclub" called the *Royal Entertainer Lounge,* where a local band plays a few nights a week. The dock and marina will accommodate nine yachts, and offers fresh water and electricity. No charge for children under 12 sharing a room with parents. No credit cards.

George Town, Great Exuma

Out Island Inn. *Expensive.* Box 49, George Town, Exuma, tel. 336–2171/2; or through BRS. The largest resort center in the Exumas, the inn has just been turned into an all-inclusive vacation resort. Its eighty rooms are spread through low, one- and two-story native stone buildings. Rooms are air-conditioned, neat, and comfortably furnished. The inn sprawls along a lovely palm-shaded white-sand beach, with thatched-roof sun shelters. The dining room is located oceanside, and offers hearty Bahamian and American fare. The *Reef Bar* overlooks the sea and is a popular gathering spot for guests, locals, and private pilots harbor-hopping the island chain. Amenities include a freshwater pool, two tennis courts, volleyball and shuffleboard courts, and a game room with darts, checkers, and backgammon boards. Rental cars, boats, scooters, bicycles, windsurfers, and water skis are available. From the thirty-slip marina, there's a twice-daily service to nearby Stocking Island beaches. Cost includes three meals, all drinks including wine with lunch and dinner, all sports, tax and gratuities. Five miles from airport, AP only.

Hotel Peace and Plenty. *Moderate.* Box 55, George Town, Exuma; tel. 336–2551/2; P.O. Box 21584, Ft. Lauderdale, FL 33335; or through BRS. A historic inn overlooking Elizabeth Harbour. Thirty-two charming, air-conditioned rooms, each with a balcony overlooking the sea and a freshwater pool on the terrace. The nautical bar is a favorite hangout for cruising yachtsmen, divers, and the angling set, both local and international. There's entertainment on weekends, and the attractive dining room serves good Bahamian and American dishes. The inn offers a private beach club on exquisite Stocking Island, just a mile across the harbor, with regular ferry service back and forth. Car rentals, scuba trips and equipment, fishing boats and guides, and island tours can be arranged at the front desk. No children under six. Located 3½ miles from the airport.

Pieces of Eight. *Moderate.* Box 49, George Town, Exuma; tel. 336–2600/1, or through BRS. A sister resort of the Out Island Inn, the two-story stone hilltop lodge lies just across Queen's Highway from the larger hotel and shares its beach and all amenities. There are 32 nicely furnished, air-conditioned rooms with balconies overlooking the sea and a patio with freshwater pool. There are superb views from the dining room, which serves good, down-home dishes, and from the yacht-y *Pirate's Den Bar,* which features occasional evening music. Exchange dining privileges with the Out Island Inn. Excellent dive program, offering lessons and daily reef trips. Located five miles from the airport.

Sand Dollar Beach Club. *Moderate.* Box 87, Forbes Hill, George Town, Exuma; tel. 336–2182 or 2522; or through BRS. A get-away-from-it-all resort on Little Exuma Island (linked by a brief concrete span to Great Exuma). The delightful hideaway offers 22 modern, air-conditioned rooms overlooking twin crescent beaches fringing Pretty Molly Bay. There's excellent food in a cozy dining room, and a relaxing bar. Superb snorkeling. Free bikes for exploring the island. Scuba gear and Sunfish are available for rental. Motorboat excursions to adjoining cays for picnics and shelling, and a van for trips into George Town. Located 11 miles from the airport.

Marshall's Guest House. *Inexpensive.* Box 27, George Town, Exuma; tel. 336–2571/2081. Adjoining Marshall's Grocery Store; 12 tidy, air-conditioned rooms and an inexpensive restaurant. Nearby beach privileges. In town, three miles from the airport. No credit cards.

Two Turtles Inn. *Inexpensive.* Box 51, George Town, Exuma; tel. 336–2545; or through BRS. Attractive wood-and-stone resort with just 12 cozy, comfortable rooms (some air-conditioned). Good local food served in a small dining room or in the cool green surroundings of the courtyard. There's a very nice gift shop and guests have beach privileges nearby. Located four miles from the airport.

APARTMENT AND VILLA RENTAL. *In Georgetown, Great Exuma.* **Flamingo Bay Club.** *Moderate.* Box 23, George Town, Exuma; tel. 336–2554; or Box N-8727, Nassau; tel. 327–8471. Four elegant two-bedroom villas, amid palm trees and tropical flowers, beautifully furnished and fully equipped for self-catering holidays. Amenities include a lively private beach, marina, and a tennis court. Rental vehicles and sports excursions arranged. An additional 33 villas are under construction, and will soon be available for vacation rental, time-sharing, or purchase. The Flamingo Bay Club is part of a major land development just half a mile from the airport, with thirteen hundred acres stretching from oceanside to harborside, 17 miles of paved roads, and more than 30 beautiful private vacation homes. No credit cards.

Exuma Supplies Apartments. *Inexpensive.* Box 50, George Town, Exuma; tel. 336–2506. Located in town, above the general store, are four neat, well-kept modern apartments with full kitchens. Children under 12 stay free with parents. Nearby beach privileges, rental vehicles, and sports can be arranged. No credit cards.

Regatta Point. *Inexpensive.* Box 6, George Town, Exuma; tel. 336–2206. Just five roomy, attractive, one- and two-bedroom apartments with full kitchens and ceiling fans. Located on lovely Kidd Cay in Elizabeth Harbour, linked to George Town by a causeway. No restaurant, but daily maid service is provided. A private beach, lawns, and gardens. No credit cards. Located three miles from airport.

HOW TO GET AROUND. In George Town, Great Exuma: Local taxis are available at the airport for transportation to all hotels in the area. Taxi drivers also serve as tour guides for the island. You may negotiate rates directly with them or book through your hotel. Motor scooters and bicycles are available through most of the resorts, and cars may be rented from the following agencies: *Exuma Transport,* Box 19, George Town; tel. 336–2101; *Peace and Plenty Hotel,* Box 55, George Town; tel. 336–2551/2; *R & M Tours,* Box 68, George Town; tel. 336–2112.

SPECIAL EVENTS. Staniel Cay: *New Year's Cup Race.* International yachts compete in a fun-filled racing series over the New Year holiday each year, with hundreds of boats from all over the islands making up the spectator fleet and their crews joining the revelry ashore. Headquarters for the race and center of the partying ashore is the Staniel Cay Yacht Club, with the Happy People Marina helping to absorb the overflow crowds.

Emancipation Day Regatta. Native workboats and their crews compete in a series of races off the settlement of Black Point, just a few miles from Staniel Cay by boat. The annual regatta celebrates the freeing of slaves in The Bahamas on August 1, 1834, and is accompanied by barbecue picnics, singing, dancing, and merriment ashore. Emancipation Day is a legal holiday in The Bahamas, and is celebrated on the first Monday of August each year.

George Town, Great Exuma: *Bonefish Bonanza.* Held annually in early November, sponsored by Hotel Peace and Plenty. Teams of international anglers stalk the feisty, elusive Bahamas bonefish in the reefy shallows off George Town. Good-natured fun and parties; prizes awarded. For details and dates, call the Bahamas sports hotline at 800–32SPORT or write to Hotel Peace and Plenty.

Family Island Regatta. The most important annual event in the Bahamian sporting calendar. Each year in mid-April, the usually tranquil village of George Town comes alive with rivalry and revelry during an unique out-island race week. The native workboat regatta, held for more than 30 years, pits handcrafted wooden sailing sloops from islands through The Bahamas against each other in a series of hotly contested races for trophies and cash prizes. Ashore, there are Junkanoo masquerades, goombay music, and the Royal Bahamas Police Force Band in concert and on parade; arts and crafts for sale; and thatched-roof stands serving an endless variety of down-home dishes. The small hotels and inns of George Town overflow with celebrating locals and visiting revelers, and the harbor is just as crowded. Book very early if you plan to join in the fun.

SPORTS. Staniel Cay: *Scuba.* One of the most popular sports in the islands. Scuba gear is available for rent by qualified divers, and guided dive trips are available at Sampson Cay. One of the most famous dive sites in the area is Thunderball Grotto. Another popular dive trip goes to the Exuma Cays Land and Sea Park. The firm offers a variety of packages which include airfare and accommodations at moderate rates. They may be booked through *Airways Reservation Center,* 4250 S.W. 11th Terrace, Ft. Lauderdale, FL 33315; tel. 800–327–3011 in the U.S.; 305–467–6850 in FL.

Fishing. There is fine bonefishing in the turquoise shallows of the Great Bahama Banks to the west of the island, and good gamefishing in the dark blue depths of Exuma Sound, which borders the eastern shore. Skilled local guides are available, and rates are "negotiable" for fishing excursions complete with boat, bait, tackle, and crew. Arrangements can be made at the *Staniel Cay Yacht Club, Happy People Marina,* and the *Sampson Cay Club.*

Other Sports. Windsurfers, Boston Whalers, small sailboats, and snorkeling gear may be rented at each of the resorts at moderate rates.

George Town, Great Exuma: *Scuba and Snorkeling.* Shallow- to medium-depth coral reefs and sea gardens off George Town attract both snorkelers and divers, and a unique attraction is a series of ocean blue holes. Popular dive spots are Stingray Reef and Angelfish Blue Hole. Most famous dive site is Mystery Cave on Stocking Island, which tunnels for more than four hundred feet beneath the island. Dive trips may be arranged through most George Town hotels or

directly with *Exuma Divers,* Box 110, George Town, Exuma; tel. 336–2710/
2030. The firm offers an experienced PADI instructor and a 38-foot houseboat
which carries up to 18 divers, and operates two dive shops in the George Town
area with all equipment for rental. Or *Exuma Aquatics,* Pieces of Eight Hotel,
Box 49, George Town, Exuma; tel. 336–2600/1. They offer an Underwater
Photo Center, certified instruction, a range of programs from Basic Diving to
Dive Master and Instructor training, plus daily dive trips to offshore reefs.

   Fishing. Fine gamefishing may be found in the cobalt depths of Exuma Sound
and in the deepwater cut known as the Tongue of the Ocean beyond the shallow
banks to the west of the cays. But the George Town area is best known for
bonefishing along the banks and reefy shallows just offshore. Fishing boats may
be rented at *Minn's Watersports,* Box 20, George Town, Exuma; tel. 336–2604;
or may be arranged for at your hotel. Guided bonefishing and bottom-fishing
trips may also be arranged for at your hotel, or through *Exuma Docking
Services,* Box 19, George Town, Exuma; tel. 336–2578. Rates may be negotiated
with individual guides.

INAGUA

   One of the farthest "out" of the Family Islands, 325 miles southeast
of Nassau, Inagua is little developed for tourists, but is highly regarded
by nature lovers, wildlife enthusiasts, and serious bird watchers. The
island shelters a vast, 287-square-mile wilderness preserve for the once
nearly-extinct West Indian Flamingo, national bird of The Bahamas.
These magnificent, long-legged, long-necked, brilliantly pink birds are
year-round dwellers and constitute one of the largest remaining flocks
in the Western Hemisphere—an estimated fifty thousand. There are
also dozens of other species of birds, both migratory and resident,
enjoying the protected acreage which sprawls along the shores of Lake
Windsor near the center of the island. Tours of the park are arranged
by The Bahamas National Trust. (Contact the organization at Box
N-4105, Nassau; or call 322–8333 or 325–4715.)

   The island is also known for the Morton Salt Company complex, the
world's second-largest solar evaporation center for salt production; and
a green turtle hatchery where the endangered species is bred and
released to the wild, a joint project of The Bahamas Ministry of Agriculture and Fisheries and the Caribbean Conservation Corporation.
Most Inaguans work in the salt fields, or earn their living by small-scale
farming or fishing.

   The Matthew Town Settlement is the only village on the vast island.
It has friendly people, a few houses, churches, bars, a telephone station,
post office, government offices, and a medical clinic. A picturesque
1870 lighthouse at Southwest Point guides ships to the Windward
Passage between Inagua and Hispaniola (Haiti and the Dominican
Republic) and the entrance to the Caribbean Sea.

PRACTICAL INFORMATION FOR INAGUA

HOW TO GET THERE. By air. *Bahamasair* offers twice-weekly flights from Nassau to Great Inagua's Matthew Town airport which is also used by charters and private craft and has a nearby ramp for seaplanes. **By mail boat.** The *Estore* departs Potter's Cay, Nassau every Tues., calling at Acklins, Mayaguana, and Matthew Town, Inagua; returns to Nassau Sat. Contact dock master at Potter's Cay; tel. 323–1064.

EMERGENCY NUMBERS. The number for Police is 255; for the clinic, 249; and the doctor's residence, 226.

HOTELS AND RESTAURANTS. The hotels in Inagua have restaurants. Inagua hotels fall into the *Inexpensive* category (under $50), based on double occupancy in high season.
Ford's Inagua Inn. Matthew Town, Inagua; tel. Inagua 277. Five neat, airy rooms, some with shared bath facilities. Dining room and bar. A beach nearby and sports can be arranged. One mile from the airport. No credit cards.
Main House. Matthew Town, Inagua; tel. Inagua 267. Eight comfortable air-conditioned rooms and a neat, modern dining room. A beach nearby and sports can be arranged. 1½ miles from the airport. No credit cards.

HOW TO GET AROUND. There are no rental cars, but you can negotiate a tour of the island with taxi drivers at the airport or through the hotel desks.

LONG ISLAND

Long Island is a long, narrow ribbon of land in the southern Bahamas, about four miles wide at its broadest and just over a mile in its narrowest point. It was one of Christopher Columbus's stops during his voyage of discovery in 1492. He anchored near the northern tip and called it Cape Santa Maria, naming the rest of the island Fernandina after his patron, King Ferdinand of Spain. On the island's Atlantic shore towering cliffs plunge to a surging sea, but on the sheltered leeward side of the island there are long, quiet beaches, a gentle surf, and hidden coves. There is only one major resort center on Long Island, Stella Maris Inn and Estates, located on the northeastern shore near the village of Burnt Ground—very near the spot where Columbus landed.

There's a fair-to-good government highway running the 57-mile length of the island, which Long Islanders call "Rhythm Road." It passes through a dozen delightful settlements with names like "Dead-man's Cay" and "Hard Bargain." Deadman's Cay is a pleasant village near the island's main airport. Look for sponges strung on lines to dry before being packed and shipped to Nassau markets. Note the "pothole" farming which flourishes in the area—natural or manmade holes in the coral rock containing fertile soil, sprouting crops of bananas and corn. Nearby are fascinating caves with stalactites and stalagmites, some with ancient Indian drawings on the walls, and the ruins of Lord Dunmore's plantation overlooking the sea.

Be sure to stop at Clarence Town, one of the prettiest settlements in the Family Islands. Father Jerome's two huge twin-spired churches are famed landmarks. Father Jerome, once a devout Anglican architect named Hawes, built St. Paul's Church. After his conversion to Catholicism, Father Jerome was determined to top his previous achievement by building St. Peter's Church to celebrate his new religion. The near-Gothic architecture is startling in a tiny out-island village.

As you drive along the island, be sure to watch for the "hex" signs drawn on houses along the road. You can picnic on a remote beach and hunt for shells or drop by a village tavern for a snack, a cool drink, and a chat with the locals. Don't miss the strawmarkets—nearly every village has one. Long Island is famed throughout The Bahamas for its fine strawwork. In Nassau they say "you can tote water in a Long Island hat." Look for strawwork by Ivy Simms—it is exquisite and is sold in exclusive Nassau shops. Fisherman, farmers, salt-rakers, or straw weavers, you'll find the thirty-three hundred Long Islanders friendly, courteous, and helpful. They'll point out interesting sights, guide you to old caves and plantation ruins, or share island tales and folklore.

If you are here in May, the Long Island Regatta matches George Town's races for rivalry and revelry. The annual workboat series is held each May and attracts up to fifty entrants from all over The Bahamas. The best place for viewing the races is at Salt Pond, between Stella Maris and Deadman's Cay.

PRACTICAL INFORMATION FOR LONG ISLAND

HOW TO GET THERE. By air. *Bahamasair* provides four flights each week from Nassau to Stella Maris airport in the north and Deadman's Cay in the center of Long Island. The Stella Maris Inn also operates frequent licensed charter flights from Ft. Lauderdale, Fla. For details, call Stella Maris' U.S. booking office at 305–467–0466; BRS; or 800–327–0787 in the U.S. and Canada.

By mail boat. The *M/V Nay Dean* sails weekly from Potter's Cay in Nassau to Clarence Town, Simms, Salt Pond, and Stella Maris on Tues., and returns to Nassau on Fri. Contact the dock master at Potter's Cay, Nassau; tel. 323–1064. The *Estore* departs every Wed., calling at Clarence Town, Deadman's Cay, Roses, Mortimers, Salina Point, and Inagua.

EMERGENCY NUMBERS. Area Code for Stella Maris is 809, available through Direct Distance Dialing. For on-island emergencies, call the operator.

HOTEL AND RESTAURANT. Stella Maris Inn and Estates *Moderate.* P.O. Box 105, Long Island, Bahamas. Reserve direct by calling 305–467–0466; or through Bahamas Reservation Service, 800–327–0787. A truly international resort and land-development center, popular with Europeans, Canadians, and Americans. The attractive lodge is set amid broad lawns and flowering shrubs, overlooking the sea. Charming dining room with excellent Bahamian, Continental, and American fare, rustic bar for relaxing, and attractive patio for dancing. Accommodations are air-conditioned and scattered over the vast acreage, with hotel rooms adjacent to the lodge; villas, apartments, townhouses, or cottages in the landscaped grounds—a total of fifty rooms. The Inn offers three miles of protected beach, two tennis courts, three swimming pools, 12-slip marina, and delightful Yacht Club where there is frequent entertainment such as Sunday afternoon guitar concerts and an occasional goombay "rake 'n scrape" band. The resort also offers a full dive program. Rental cars, jeeps, bikes, small sail- and power boats, water skis, jet skis, and even small private aircraft are available through the Inn. Deep-sea fishing and cruising boats may be chartered at the Yacht Club, and overnight excursions can be arranged for diving, fishing, or exploring nearby islands such as Rum Cay and Conception. The resort operates the Stella Maris Charter Service, with frequent licensed air charter service and a good range of inclusive packages available. Major credit cards are accepted.

HOW TO GET AROUND. Cars may be rented at the Stella Maris Inn, tel. 336–2106. Sidney Burrows and Joseph B. Carroll at Deadman's Cay also offer one or more vehicles for hire; telephone the operator at Deadman's Cay to make arrangements. Bicycles and motor scooters may be rented at Stella Maris Inn for nearby exploration and day excursions.

RUM CAY

Rum Cay is one of the most remote of the Family Islands, primitive and appealing, with just one small resort, the Rum Cay Club. The island was discovered by Columbus in 1492. He named it Santa María de la Concepción, after the Virgin Mary. It received its modern name in the 1700s when a West Indiaman laden with rum was wrecked on the reef off its shores. Once a major salt-raking center, it was devastated by a hurricane in 1908. The sleepy little island today has a population of fewer than a hundred people, almost all of whom live at Port Nelson, a picturesque village in a coconut grove hugging the seashore on the island's southeast coast. There are historic ruins to explore, miles of deserted beaches, lovely scenery with rolling hills, and a necklace of coral reef encircling the island's shores. Offshore is one of The Bahamas' most unusual dive sites, the wreck of the *H.M.S. Conqueror,* Britain's 101-gun man-of-war, which sank in 1861. The wreck is the property of The Bahamas Government, and no contents of the ship may be removed, but snorkelers and divers may easily see and visit it, as it lies in just 25 feet of water.

PRACTICAL INFORMATION FOR RUM CAY

HOTEL AND RESTAURANT. The Rum Cay Club. *Moderate to Expensive.* A variety of packages available. Reserve direct: Rum Cay Diving Club, P.O. Box 22396, Ft. Lauderdale, FL 33335; tel. 305–467–8355; 800–334–6869 or through BRS, 800–327–0787. A very attractive, surprisingly luxurious, barefoot and casual get-away-from-it-all resort. There are 19 rooms ranging from standard to deluxe, including a dormitory for dive groups. The comfortable dining room serves excellent Bahamian and American cuisine and tall, cool drinks on the terrace; there's a video lounge with an extensive library of underwater films. The club offers a complete dive center with certified instructors; rental equipment; three 34-foot Flattop dive boats which carry 18 divers each; a photo-processing center; plus catamarans, windsurfers, and fishing boats for rent; a hot tub overlooks miles of beach. The Rum Cay Club has its own airstrip, and offers all-inclusive eight-day/seven-night packages with private, licensed air charter service from Ft. Lauderdale. Major credit cards are accepted.

SAN SALVADOR

It seems appropriate to end this book with San Salvador, where the story of The Bahamas and the whole "New World" began. On October 12, 1492, Christopher Columbus discovered this wild, remote, and beautiful island in the southeastern Bahamas, gateway to the Americas, his first stop on the voyage of discovery.

Little has changed in the nearly five hundred years since Columbus landed. The handful of native Arawak Indians he found have been replaced by a handful of native Bahamians, descendants of freed slaves. They live in much the same simple fashion as the Arawaks lived, cultivating small farm plots and fishing in the bountiful waters that fringe the island's shores. The primitive beauty of the island is virtually unchanged, with lush tropical greenery, forest-covered hills, pristine beaches, and unexplored reefs.

When Columbus arrived, the natives called their island Guanahani. He renamed it San Salvador in thanks to the Holy Savior. But in the seventeenth century, it became known as Watling's Island, after a resident buccaneer. It wasn't until this century that university expeditions and intensive research by archeologists and historians determined that the island was the actual site of Columbus's landfall in the new world. In 1926, The Bahamas Parliament officially renamed the island San Salvador. Although the exact spot where Columbus first stepped foot ashore is unknown, three different monuments claim the honor.

Today, the largest settlement on the island is Cockburn Town (pronounced Coburn Town), on the western shore of San Salvador. Tiny

wooden pink and yellow houses cluster around a giant flowering al-
mond tree—which the locals call the "lazy tree"—overlooking the
harbor. There's an Anglican church and a Catholic church, the Commissioner's office, police station, courthouse, library, telephone station,
and health clinic all around the "lazy tree," and a pair of old cemeteries
nearby. The most exciting day of the week is when the mailboat calls
from Nassau, and the whole town goes down to the dock to welcome
it.

A few miles south of the village are two of the three monuments to
Columbus, a simple white cross and an Olympic flame. The eternal
flame was lit in 1968 by Olympians carrying the torch to the Olympic
Games in Mexico City. Near the white cross, archeologists from the
College Center of the Finger Lakes in New York have recently discovered fifteenth-century European artifacts, making it likely that this was
the site of Columbus's landfall.

On the opposite side of the island, on the northeast shore, stands the
Dixon Hill Lighthouse, one of the oldest landmarks in the islands. It
stands 163 feet above the sea and was built in 1856. The picturesque
beacon is the last of the original hand-operated kerosene-burning lights
in all of The Bahamas. Also on the eastern shore is the third monument
to Columbus, atop a high bluff overlooking the reef. It was erected back
in 1892 by the *Chicago Herald* newspaper, marking the four-hundredth
anniversary of Columbus's landing on San Salvador.

PRACTICAL INFORMATION FOR

SAN SALVADOR

You can get to San Salvador via *Bahamasair,* which offers two weekly flights
from Nassau to the island. In addition, the Riding Rock Inn offers weekly
licensed air charter service from Ft. Lauderdale every Saturday.

San Salvador's only resort, the **Riding Rock Inn,** located just north of Cockburn Town, reopened in mid-1986. A divers' mecca, it attracts enthusiasts from
around the world to the island's magnificent reefs, just offshore. The moderately
priced inn offers 24 comfortable, newly renovated air-conditioned rooms, a
freshwater pool, restaurant and lounge, a conference center and classroom for
divers, and a darkroom with film processing for underwater photography. There
are two well-equipped dive boats and two daily reef trips. Book through Out
Island Service Co. 701 S.W. 48th St., Ft. Lauderdale, FL 33315, 800–272–1492,
U.S.; 305–761–1492, FL.

Recently, a great deal of interest has been aroused in San Salvador and a
remote, uninhabited, reef-fringed island some 65 miles away, called Samana
Cay. In November 1986, *National Geographic* published findings, based on
computer studies, stating that Columbus actually landed on Samana Cay, not
San Salvador. The argument is still raging among the experts, but they all agree
that The Bahamas was the site of Columbus' first landfall in the New World—
despite the 65-mile dispute.

By 1992, The Bahamas government hopes to have a major attraction on San Salvador, in celebration of the five-hundredth Anniversary of the landing of Columbus. Visitors from all over the world will be invited to rediscover the "gateway to the New World," and to the rest of The Bahamas.

Index

FODOR'S TRAVEL GUIDES

Here is a complete list of Fodor's Travel Guides, available in current editions; most are also available in a British edition published by Hodder & Stoughton.

U.S. GUIDES

Alaska
American Cities (Great Travel Values)
Arizona including the Grand Canyon
Atlantic City & the New Jersey Shore
Boston
California
Cape Cod & the Islands of Martha's Vineyard & Nantucket
Carolinas & the Georgia Coast
Chesapeake
Chicago
Colorado
Dallas/Fort Worth
Disney World & the Orlando Area (Fun in)
Far West
Florida
Fort Worth (see Dallas)
Galveston (see Houston)
Georgia (see Carolinas)
Grand Canyon (see Arizona)
Greater Miami & the Gold Coast
Hawaii
Hawaii (Great Travel Values)
Houston & Galveston
I-10: California to Florida
I-55: Chicago to New Orleans
I-75: Michigan to Florida
I-80: San Francisco to New York
I-95: Maine to Miami
Jamestown (see Williamsburg)
Las Vegas including Reno & Lake Tahoe (Fun in)
Los Angeles & Nearby Attractions
Martha's Vineyard (see Cape Cod)
Maui (Fun in)
Nantucket (see Cape Cod)
New England
New Jersey (see Atlantic City)
New Mexico
New Orleans
New Orleans (Fun in)
New York City
New York City (Fun in)
New York State
Orlando (see Disney World)
Pacific North Coast
Philadelphia
Reno (see Las Vegas)
Rockies
San Diego & Nearby Attractions
San Francisco (Fun in)
San Francisco plus Marin County & the Wine Country
The South
Texas
U.S.A.

Virgin Islands (U.S. & British)
Virginia
Waikiki (Fun in)
Washington, D.C.
Williamsburg, Jamestown & Yorktown

FOREIGN GUIDES

Acapulco (see Mexico City)
Acapulco (Fun in)
Amsterdam
Australia, New Zealand & the South Pacific
Austria
The Bahamas
The Bahamas (Fun in)
Barbados (Fun in)
Beijing, Guangzhou & Shanghai
Belgium & Luxembourg
Bermuda
Brazil
Britain (Great Travel Values)
Canada
Canada (Great Travel Values)
Canada's Maritime Provinces plus Newfoundland & Labrador
Cancún, Cozumel, Mérida & the Yucatán
Caribbean
Caribbean (Great Travel Values)
Central America
Copenhagen (see Stockholm)
Cozumel (see Cancún)
Eastern Europe
Egypt
Europe
Europe (Budget)
France
France (Great Travel Values)
Germany: East & West
Germany (Great Travel Values)
Great Britain
Greece
Guangzhou (see Beijing)
Helsinki (see Stockholm)
Holland
Hong Kong & Macau
Hungary
India, Nepal & Sri Lanka
Ireland
Israel
Italy
Italy (Great Travel Values)
Jamaica (Fun in)
Japan
Japan (Great Travel Values)
Jordan & the Holy Land
Kenya
Korea
Labrador (see Canada's Maritime Provinces)
Lisbon
Loire Valley

London
London (Fun in)
London (Great Travel Values)
Luxembourg (see Belgium)
Macau (see Hong Kong)
Madrid
Mazatlan (see Mexico's Baja)
Mexico
Mexico (Great Travel Values)
Mexico City & Acapulco
Mexico's Baja & Puerto Vallarta, Mazatlan, Manzanillo, Copper Canyon
Montreal (Fun in)
Munich
Nepal (see India)
New Zealand
Newfoundland (see Canada's Maritime Provinces)
1936 . . . on the Continent
North Africa
Oslo (see Stockholm)
Paris
Paris (Fun in)
People's Republic of China
Portugal
Province of Quebec
Puerto Vallarta (see Mexico's Baja)
Reykjavik (see Stockholm)
Rio (Fun in)
The Riviera (Fun on)
Rome
St. Martin/St. Maarten (Fun in)
Scandinavia
Scotland
Shanghai (see Beijing)
Singapore
South America
South Pacific
Southeast Asia
Soviet Union
Spain
Spain (Great Travel Values)
Sri Lanka (see India)
Stockholm, Copenhagen, Oslo, Helsinki & Reykjavik
Sweden
Switzerland
Sydney
Tokyo
Toronto
Turkey
Vienna
Yucatán (see Cancún)
Yugoslavia

SPECIAL-INTEREST GUIDES

Bed & Breakfast Guide: North America
Royalty Watching
Selected Hotels of Europe
Selected Resorts and Hotels of the U.S.
Ski Resorts of North America
Views to Dine by around the World

AVAILABLE AT YOUR LOCAL BOOKSTORE OR WRITE TO
FODOR'S TRAVEL PUBLICATIONS, INC., 201 EAST 50th STREET, NEW YORK, NY 10022.